CUET

(UG) & Integrated PG

2022

Economics

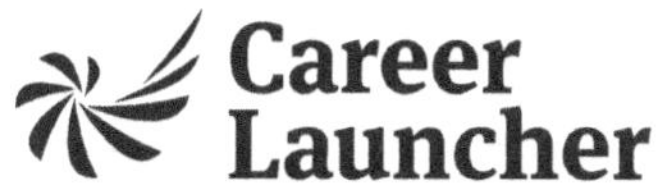

Career Launcher

Title   : CUET 2022 : Economics

Language   : English

Editor's Name : Anita Paul

Copyright ©   : 2022 CLIP

Typeset & Published by :

Career Launcher Infrastructure (P) Ltd.

A-45, Mohan Cooperative Industrial Area, Near Mohan Estate Metro Station, New Delhi - 110044

Marketed by :

G.K. Publications (P) Ltd.

Plot No. 9A, Sector-27A, Mathura Road, Faridabad, Haryana-121003

ISBN   **: 978-93-95101-20-2**

Printer's Details: Printed in India, New Delhi.

For product information :

Visit ***www.gkpublications.com*** or email to ***gkp@gkpublications.com***

CONTENTS

ECONOMICS

Part I : Introductory Microeconomics and Macroeconomics

Part II : Indian Economic Development

About CUET

A year ago, it would have been unimaginable that cut-offs in Delhi University would skyrocket to 100% for some of the undergraduate courses! While DU has always been known for its high cut-offs, there are several other universities where the story is no different.

However, the National Education Policy 2020 (NEP) aims to do away with the tyranny of the ever-rising cut-offs by introducing a Common Entrance Test for all the Central Universities in the country. NEP not only proposes a holistic approach in evaluating the students by giving them the option to select subjects based on their interest, but it also aims to simplify the process of admission to higher-education institutes.

To start with, there would be a Common Entrance Test for all the Central Universities, which would be conducted twice a year from 2022. While this might sound like a new concept to many, the fact is, there is already a CUET, which is conducted for the Central Universities established in or after 2009. As many as 14 of them already admit students based on their performance in the entrance test. The CUET scores are also accepted by four state universities of the country.

The proposed CUET aims to assess conceptual understanding and application of knowledge; and also, to lessen the burden of appearing in multiple tests.

CUET Eligibility

Getting into a premier University is every student's dream. The brand value of the University not only facilitates securing a seat in a master's program in a national/international institute, but also helps in getting job offers through campus placements.

Entry to a Central University, in most cases earlier, was based on merit, i.e., marks secured in Class XII Board exams. However, from the academic year 2021, all Central Universities will also consider the CUET score for admissions into their Undergraduate programs.

CUET 2022: Eligibility Criteria

While the official criteria will be learnt once the CUET 2021 notification is released, the stipulations are not expected to change much from those of previous years.

- A candidate must have passed Class XII (10+2) or equivalent from a recognized education Board.
- If the respective Board awards grades (or CGPA), the conversion factor given by the Board must be used to compute the percentage of marks.
- Candidates, who have completed their Class XII in 2021, and have passed the Board exams, will also be eligible to apply for CUET 2022.

Eligibility: Class XII Students

While CUET is for students who have passed the Class XII (or equivalent) Board exams, any student who is appearing for the Class XII Board exam in 2022 is also eligible to apply for CUET 2021. The candidate would be required to produce the marksheets and relevant certificates as mandated by the participating Central University, and follow the timelines provided for admissions.

Key Points

- Each participating Central University is free to decide its own eligibility criteria for admissions.

- The weightages for CUET and Class XII Board exam results(if, applicable) will be at the sole discretion of the Central University, to which admission is being sought.

- As of date, CUET does not have an age limit. However, Central Universities can fix minimum & maximum age limit for admissions to all (or any) of the programs on offer.

Reservation of Seats

As CUET is an entrance exam for admissions to Undergraduate courses at the Central Universities, which have been established under an Act of the Parliament, each Central University must follow the norms set by the Government of India, with respect to intake and reservation of seats.

Generally, the following break-up is followed:

Category	Reservation
Scheduled Castes	15%
Scheduled Tribes	7.5%
Other Backward Classes (Non-Creamy)	27%
Persons with Disability	5%

Some institutions might even have provisions for the Economically Weaker Sections, which can account for 10% of the total seats. These EWS seats are carved out from the Open Category.

To avail of the reservation benefit based on caste (or any other category as specified), a candidate must be able to produce valid documents/certificates to support such claims.

Conclusion

It is essential for every candidate to check the validity of their candidature for CUET, as well as the Central University he/she is applying to. The candidate should be aware of the documents that might be required while applying for the exam, or during the admissions.

CUET 2022 notification is expected in March 2022, and registration is also going to start then.

CUET: Exam Pattern

Examination Structure for CUET (UG) -2022:

CUET (UG) –2022 will consist of the following 4 Sections:

    Section IA –13 Languages

    Section IB –19 Languages

    Section II –27 Domain specific Subjects

    Section III –General Test

Choosing options from each Section is not mandatory. Choices should match the requirements of the desired University.

Broad features of CUET (UG) -2022 are as follows:

Section	Subjects/ Tests	Questions to be Attempted	Question Type	Duration
Section IA – Languages	There are 13* different languages. Any of these languages may be chosen.	40 questions to be attempted out of 50 in each language	Language to be tested through Reading Comprehension (based on different types of passages–Factual, Literary and Narrative, [Literary Aptitude and Vocabulary]	45 Minutes for each language
Section IB – Languages	There are 19** Languages. Any other language apart from those offered in Section I A may be chosen.			
Section II - Domain	There are 27*** Domains specific subjects being offered under this Section. A candidate may choose a maximum of Six (06) Domains as desired by the applicable University/Universities.	40 Questions to be attempted out of 50	• Input text can be used for MCQ Based Questions • MCQs based on NCERT Class XII syllabus only	
Section III- General Test	For any such undergraduate programme/ programmes being offered by Universities where a General Test is being used for admission.	60 Questions to be attempted out of 75	• Input text can be used for MCQ Based Questions • General Knowledge, Current Affairs, General Mental Ability, Numerical Ability, Quantitative Reasoning (Simple application of basic mathematical concepts arithmetic/algebra geometry/mensuration/s tat taught till Grade 8), Logical and Analytical Reasoning	

*** Languages (13):** Tamil, Telugu, Kannada, Malayalam, Marathi, Gujarati, Odiya, Bengali, Assamese, Punjabi, English, Hindi and Urdu

**** Languages (19):** *French, Spanish, German, Nepali, Persian, Italian, Arabic, Sindhi, Kashmiri, Konkani, Bodo, Dogri, Maithili, Manipuri, Santhali, Tibetan, Japanese, Russian, Chinese.*

***** Domain Specific Subjects (27):** 1. Accountancy/ Book Keeping 2. Biology/ Biological Studies/ Biotechnology/Biochemistry 3. Business Studies 4. Chemistry 5. Computer Science/ Informatics Practices 6. Economics/ Business Economics 7. Engineering Graphics 8.Entrepreneurship 9. Geography/Geology 10. History 11. Home Science 12.Knowledge Tradition and Practices of India 13. Legal Studies 14. Environmental Science 15. Mathematics 16. Physical Education/ NCC /Yoga 17.Physics 18.Political Science 19. Psychology 20. Sociology 21. Teaching Aptitude 22. Agriculture 23. Mass Media/ Mass Communication 24. Anthropology 25. Fine Arts/Visual Arts (Sculpture/ Painting)/Commercial Arts, 26. Performing Arts – (i) Dance (Kathak/ Bharatnatyam/Oddisi/ Kathakali/Kuchipudi/ Manipuri (ii) Drama- Theatre (iii) Music General (Hindustani/ Carnatic/ RabindraSangeet/ Percussion/ Non-Percussion), 27. Sanskrit *[For all Shastri (Shastri 3 years/ 4 years Honours) Equivalent to B.A./B.A. Honours courses i.e. Shastri in Veda, Paurohitya (Karmakand), Dharamshastra, Prachin Vyakarana, Navya Vyakarana, Phalit Jyotish, Siddhant Jyotish, Vastushastra, Sahitya,Puranetihas, Prakrit Bhasha,Prachin Nyaya Vaisheshik, Sankhya Yoga, Jain Darshan, Mimansa, AdvaitaVedanta, Vishihstadvaita Vedanta, Sarva Darshan, a candidate may choose Sanskrit as the Domain].*

- A Candidate can choose a maximum of **any 3 languages** from Section IA and Section IB taken together. (One of the languages chosen needs to be in lieu of Domain specific subjects)
- Section II offers 27 Subjects, out of which a candidate may choose a **maximum of 6 Subjects.**
- Section III comprises **General Test.**
- For choosing Languages (upto 3) from Section IA and IB and a maximum of 6 Subjects from Section II and General Test under Section III, the Candidate must refer to the requirements of his/her intended University.

Mode of the Test	Computer Based Test-CBT
Test Pattern	Objective type with Multiple Choice Questions
Medium	13 languages (*Tamil, Telugu, Kannada, Malayalam, Marathi, Gujarati, Odiya, Bengali, Assamese, Punjabi, English, Hindi and Urdu)*
Syllabus	**Section IA & IB:** Language to be tested through Reading Comprehension (based on different types of passages–Factual, Literary and Narrative [Literary Aptitude & Vocabulary]
	Section II : As per NCERT model syllabus as applicable to Class XII only
	Section III : General Knowledge, Current Affairs, General Mental Ability, Numerical Ability, Quantitative Reasoning (Simple application of basic mathematical concepts arithmetic/algebra geometry/mensuration/stat taught till Grade 8), Logical and Analytical Reasoning

Level of questions for CUET (UG) -2022:

All questions in various testing areas will be benchmarked at the level of Class XII only. Students having studied Class XII Board syllabus would be able to do well in CUET (UG) – 2022.

Number of attempts:

If any University permits students of previous years of class XII to take admission in the current year also, such students would also be eligible to appear in CUET (UG) – 2022.

Choice of Languages and Subjects:

Generally the languages/subjects chosen should be the ones that a student has opted in his latest Class XII Board examination. However, if any University permits any flexibility in this regards, the same can be exercised under CUET (UG) -2022 also. Candidates must carefully refer to the eligibility requirements of various Central Universities in this regard. Moreover, if the subject to be studied in the Undergraduate course is not available in the list of **27 Domain Specific Subject** being offered, the Candidate may choose the Subject closest to his choice for e.g. For Biochemistry the candidate may choose Biology.

Candidates are advised to visit the NTA CUET (UG)-2022 official website **https://cuet.samarth.ac.in/** for latest updates regarding the Examination.

CUET Syllabus

CUET Syllabus

Before you start your preparation for any entrance exam, it is important to understand the syllabus. Otherwise, your prep will be directionless, and you might be left wondering where things might have gone wrong!

With more than 1.68 lakh seats on offer for the undergraduate courses at the 54 Central Universities, CUET is one the most competitive examinations. For this very reason, while preparing for the exam, you will need to adopt a structured approach. And in doing that, understanding the syllabus is a critical step.

CUET 2022 Overview

CUET 2022 will be a Computer-Based Test (CBT), commonly referred to as an online exam. However, there is a difference between the two terms: CBT and online. In CBT, the questions are kept constant and simply presented in an online format; whereas in an Online Test, questions are stored as a bank, and the system decides which questions are to be presented to the candidate, based on a pre-defined logic.

CUET 2022 is likely to be a General Ability Test, with focus on English Language, Numerical Ability, Logical & Analytical Reasoning, along with General Awareness and Current Affairs.

CUET 2022 Syllabus

The CUET 2022 exam pattern gives a good idea about what is in store for the candidate and how one needs to prepare for the exam.

- **English Language:** The questions in this section will test one's proficiency in the language, based on comprehension passages, fundamentals of grammar, and vocabulary. In the Comprehension section, candidates will be evaluated on their understanding of a passage and its central theme, meanings of words used therein, etc. The Grammar section entails correcting grammatically incorrect sentences, filling of blanks in sentences with appropriate words, etc. Questions on synonyms & antonyms will check one's command over English vocabulary.
- **Numerical Ability:** Questions on Numerical Ability will test the candidate's knowledge of elementary mathematics. Areas like arithmetic, number system, basics of algebra, and modern maths will be central to these types of questions.
- **Logical & Analytical Reasoning:** This section tests the candidate's ability to identify patterns & logical links, and rectify illogical arguments. It can include a variety of Logical Reasoning questions, such as those on syllogisms, logical sequences, analogies, etc., along with Analytical Reasoning questions on series, directions, clocks & calendars, arrangements, and puzzles to name a few.
- **General Awareness and Current Affairs:** The General Awareness section includes static general knowledge, while questions on Current Affairs will gauge a candidate's knowledge of national & international current affairs.

CUET 2022 may or may not have a section on subject knowledge. Once the exam notification is out in March, there will be more clarity on this matter.

While there is no syllabus explicitly mentioned by CUET, the broad idea is always presented. One must look at the previous years' papers and solve the sample papers available to form a basic understanding.

About University of Delhi

University of Delhi (commonly known as DU) was established in 1922 and is one of the largest Universities in the country. With 16 faculties, 86 academic departments, 90 colleges and 540 programs on offer, Delhi University is no doubt one of the sought-after University in the country.

With 1, 96,000 students enrolled in UG programs, Delhi University is a valued university and constantly ranked among the top in the country. DU bagged 11th Rank in NIRF 2020 and ranked 6th in QS India Rankings 2020. The University has two Campuses: North and South.

DU UG Programs

Delhi University offers several programs at the undergraduate level. With more than 60 constituent colleges, the Delhi University offers many undergraduate courses.

Please refer to the table below for the important undergraduate courses offered by the DU and the intake across each program.

Program	Intake
B. A (Pass)	11249
B. A (Hons) Geography	788
B. A (Hons) Economics	2754
B. A (Hons) History	2791
B. A (Hons) Political Science	3657
B. A (Hons) Sociology	596
B. A (Hons) Psychology	670
B. A (Hons) Applied Psychology	252
B. A (Hons) Social Work	133
B. A (Hons) Philosophy	783
B. A (Hons) English	2886
B. A (Hons) Hindi	2829
B. A (Hons) Sanskrit	1407
B. A (Hons) Punjabi	214
B. A (Hons) Urdu	207
BA(Hons) French	49

Program	Intake
BA(Hons) German	49
BA(Hons) Spanish	49
BA(Hons) Italian	49
B. Com (Hons)	7953
B.Com (Pass)	7854
Program	Intake
B.Sc. (H) Biomedical Science	162
B.Sc. (H) Botany	937
B.Sc. (H) Chemistry	1487
B.Sc. (H) Computer Science	1265
B.Sc. (H) Electronics	624
B.Sc. (H) Mathematics	2428
B.Sc. (H) Physics	1659
B.Sc. (H) Zoology	944
B.Sc. Life Sciences	1515
B.Sc. Physical Science with Chemistry	703
B.Sc. Physical Science with Computer Science	553
B.Sc. Physical Science with Electronics	247
B. Sc (Hons.) Statistics	476
B. Sc. (Prog.) Applied Physical Science Industrial Chemistry	96
B.Sc. (Hons.) Home Science	900
B. Sc. (Hons.) Psychology	57
B.Sc. (H) Food Technology	179
B.Sc. (H)Instrumentation	99
B.Sc. (H) Microbiology	238
B.Sc. (H) Polymer Science	59
B.SC. Mathematical Science	224
B.SC. (Hons.) Biochemistry	146
B.SC. Industrial Chemistry	78
B.Sc. (Prog.) Physical Science	940
B.SC. (Hons.) Geology	98

DU UG Programs Eligibility:

As the University offers multiple programs and separate intake for male and female candidates, it is important to check the university official website regularly to keep oneself updated about the eligibility for each program, which can change.

DU UG Admissions:

Until 2021, Delhi University admitted students on the basis of class XII marks. From the academic year 2022, admissions to UG programs offered Delhi University will be based on CUET. CUET will be a common entrance for admissions to UG programs offered by all the Central Universities in the country.

Delhi University UG Programs Reservation:

DU being a Central University offers reservations in admissions according to central government rules.

Schedule Caste (SC): 15% of the total seats are reserved for students who belong to SC category.

Schedule Tribe (ST): 7.5% of the total seats are reserved for students belonging to ST Category.

Other Backward Classes (OBC): 27% of the total intake is reserved for students from Other Backward Classes (OBC), excluding those from creamy layer.

Economically Weaker Section (EWS): The University has reserved 10% seats for EWS category, in accordance with the directive of Ministry of Education.

Persons with Disability (PWD): 5% of the seats are reserved on horizontal basis for students from PWD category.

About BHU

Banaras Hindu University (BHU), situated in the holy city of Varanasi, was founded by Pandit Madan Mohan Malviya in cooperation with Dr. Annie Besant, in 1916 under the act of Parliament-B.H.U Act, 1915. BHU, which is a Central University, comprises of 6 Institutes, 14 Faculties, 144 academic departments, and 4 Inter-disciplinary centers, spread over 1300 acres. The University consists of 15,000 students, 1700 teachers and 8000 non-teaching staff.

BHU was ranked 3rd among the Universities in India in 2020. According to university submissions for NIRF 2021, BHU has 10, 585 students pursuing UG programs, of which 236 students are foreign nationals.

BHU UG Programs

BHU offers a host of undergraduate programs including medical and engineering. Through its various faculties, BHU offers a range of programs which caters to students learning abilities. The University along with its main campus, also offers the undergraduate courses from the following colleges: Mahila Mahavidyalaya (MMV); Arya Mahila Post Graduate College (AMPGC), Vasant Kanya Mahavidyalaya (VKM); Vasanta College for Women (VCW); DAV Post Graduate College (DAVPGC) and Rajiv Gandhi South Campus (RGSC).

Please refer to the table below for the important undergraduate courses offered by BHU and the intake across each program/campuses.

Faculty of Arts				
Course	Campus	Intake	Status	Duration
B.A (Hons) Arts	Faculty of Arts	765	Co-Ed	3 Years
	Mahila Mahavidyalaya	286	Women	3 Years
	Arya Mahila Post Graduate College	383	Women	3 Years
	Vasant Kanya Mahavidyalaya	286	Women	3 Years
	Vasanta College for Women	412	Women	3 Years
	DAV Post Graduate College	309	Co-Ed	3 Years
Faculty of Social Sciences				
Course	Campus	Intake	Status	Duration
B.A (Hons) Social Sciences [incl. B. A (Hons) Economics]	Faculty of Social Sciences	573	Co-Ed	3 Years
	Mahila Mahavidyalaya	193	Women	3 Years
	Arya Mahila Post Graduate College	383	Women	3 Years
	Vasant Kanya Mahavidyalaya	249	Women	3 Years
	Vasanta College for Women	210	Women	3 Years
	DAV Post Graduate College	326	Co-Ed	3 Years

Faculty of Commerce				
Course	Campus	Intake	Status	Duration
B. Com (Hons)	Faculty of Commerce	286	Co-Ed	3 Years
	Vasant Kanya Mahavidyalaya	96	Women	3 Years
	Arya Mahila Post Graduate College	96	Women	3 Years
	DAV Post Graduate College	227	Co-Ed	3 Years
	Rajiv Gandhi South Campus, Mirzapur	114	Co-Ed	3 Years
B. Com (Hons) Financial Markets Management	Faculty of Commerce	62	Co-Ed	3 Years
	Rajiv Gandhi South Campus, Mirzapur	62	Co-Ed	3 Years

Institute of Science				
Course	Campus	Intake	Status	Duration
B.Sc (Hons) Maths Group	Faculty of Science	573	Co-Ed	3 Years
	Mahila Mahavidyalaya	96	Women	3 Years
B.Sc (Hons) Bio Group	Faculty of Science	383	Co-Ed	3 Years
	Mahila Mahavidyalaya	193	Women	3 Years

Faculty of Visual Arts				
Course	Campus	Intake	Status	Duration
B.F.A (Bachelor of Fine Arts)	Faculty of Visual Arts	96	Co-Ed	4 Years
Faculty of Arts				
Bachelor of Vocation (Retail and Logistics Management)	Rajiv Gandhi South Campus	62	Co-Ed	3 Years
Bachelor of Vocation (Hospitality & Tourism Management)	Rajiv Gandhi South Campus	62	Co-Ed	3 Years
Bachelor of Vocation (Fashion Designing and Event Management)	Rajiv Gandhi South Campus	62	Co-Ed	3 Years
Bachelor of Vocation (Modern Office Management)	Rajiv Gandhi South Campus	62	Co-Ed	3 Years
Bachelor of Vocation (Food Processing & Management)	Rajiv Gandhi South Campus	62	Co-Ed	3 Years
Bachelor of Vocation (Medical Lab. & Technology)	Rajiv Gandhi South Campus	62	Co-Ed	3 Years

BHU UG Programs Eligibility:

Each of the courses have different eligibility for admissions. To be eligible for admissions, one must fulfil all the criteria as laid down by the respective faculties of the University.

B.A (Hons) Arts/ B.A (Hons) Social Sciences: Candidate must not be more than 22 years of age and must have passed class XII or equivalent with minimum 50% marks in aggregate.

B.A (Hons) Economics: Candidate must not be more than 22 years of age and must have passed class XII or equivalent with minimum 50% marks in aggregate along with mathematics as one of the papers.

B. Com (Hons)/B. Com (Hons) Financial Markets Management: Candidate must not be more than 22 years of age and must have passed class XII or equivalent with minimum 50% marks in aggregate with Commerce/ Economics/Maths/Computer Science/Finance/Financial Markets Management as one of the subjects.

B. Sc (Hons) Maths Group: Candidate must not be more than 22 years of age and must have passed class XII or equivalent with minimum 50% marks in aggregate in the subjects Physics, Maths plus any one of the following: Chemistry, Statistics, Geology, Computer Science, Information Technology and Geography and must have passed in each of the concerned three subjects.

B. Sc (Hons) Bio Group: Candidate must not be more than 22 years of age and must have passed class XII or equivalent with minimum 50% marks in aggregate in the subjects Physics, Chemistry plus any one of the following: Biology, Geology and Geography and must have passed in each of the concerned three subjects.

B. F. A (Bachelor of Fine Arts): Candidate must not be more than 22 years of age and must have passed class XII or equivalent with minimum 50% marks in aggregate.

Bachelor of Vocation: Candidate must have passed class XII or equivalent in any stream (Science for Food Processing and Medical Lab Technology) or level 4 NSQF certificate.

BHU UG Admissions:

Until 2021, admissions to BHU UG courses were based on Undergraduate Entrance Test (UET) conducted by the University. From the academic year 2022, admissions to UG programs offered by BHU will be based on CUET, which will replace the UET. CUET will be a common entrance for admissions to UG programs offered by all the Central Universities in the country.

BHU UG Programs Reservation:

BHU being a Central University offers reservations in admissions according to central government rules.

Schedule Caste (SC): 15% of the total seats are reserved for students who belong to SC category.

Schedule Tribe (ST): 7.5% of the total seats are reserved for students belonging to ST Category.

Other Backward Classes (OBC): 27% of the total intake is reserved for students from Other Backward Classes (OBC), excluding those from creamy layer.

Economically Weaker Section (EWS): The University has reserved 10% seats for EWS category, in accordance with the directive of Ministry of Education.

Persons with Disability (PWD): 5% of the seats are reserved on horizontal basis for students from PWD category.

About JNU

Ever wondered which University, the cadets from National Defence Academy (NDA) graduate from? Yes. It is Jawaharlal Nehru University (JNU). JNU started in the year 1969, three years after the act of Parliament in 1966. With several academic centres of JNU declared "Centres of Excellence" by the University Grants Commission, JNU has been ranked No. 1 by National Assessment and Accreditation Council (NAAC). JNU has been ranked No. 2 by National Institutional Ranking Framework (NIRF) 2020 and has been awarded the Best University Award by the President of India in 2017. The European Commission has awarded the Jean Monnet Centre of Excellence for European Union Studies in India (CEEUSI) to Jawaharlal Nehru University in 2018. This is one of the highest international recognition for any European Studies programme.

JNU was the first University to start integrated five-year Master of Arts in Language Courses. JNU actively collaborates with National and International Universities for student and faculty exchange programs.

According to university submissions for NIRF 2020, JNU has 1,048 students pursuing UG programs, of which 46 are foreign nationals.

JNU UG Programs

JNU offers a limited program at the undergraduate level, unlike other universities. The focus at undergraduate has been largely on language courses. In 2018, JNU started two programs in engineering and plans to add a few more specializations in future.

Please refer to the table below for the important undergraduate courses offered by JNU and the intake across each program.

School	Program	Intake	Duration
School of Language, Literature and Cultural Studies	B. A (Hons) Pashto	19	3 Years
	B. A (Hons) Persian	39	3 Years
	B. A (Hons) Arabic	39	3 Years
	B. A (Hons) Japanese	48	3 Years
	B. A (Hons) Korean	39	3 Years
	B. A (Hons) Chinese	44	3 Years
	B. A (Hons) French	48	3 Years
	B. A (Hons) German	48	3 Years
	B. A (Hons) Russian	68	3 Years
	B. A (Hons) Spanish	39	3 Years

School of Sanskrit and Indic Studies	B. Sc - M. Sc Integrated Program in Ayurveda Biology	20	5 Years
School of Engineering	B. Tech in Computer Science and Engineering & MS/M. Tech in Social Sciences/Humanities/Science/Technology	25	5 Years
	B. Tech in Electronics and Communication Engineering & MS/M. Tech in Social Sciences/Humanities/Science/Technology	25	5 Years

JNU UG Programs Eligibility:

Each of the courses have different eligibility for admissions. To be eligible for admissions, one must fulfil all the criteria as laid down by the respective faculties of the University.

B.A (Hons) Language Courses: Candidate must not be less than 17 years of age and must have passed Senior School Certificate (10+2) or equivalent examination with minimum of 45% marks.

B. Sc - M. Sc Integrated Program in Ayurveda Biology: Candidate must not be less than 17 years of age and must have passed Senior School Certificate (10+2) or equivalent examination with minimum of 45% marks.

B. Tech-M. Tech: Based on JEE Mains

JNU UG Admissions:

Until 2021, admissions to JNU UG courses were based on JNU Entrance Examination (JNUEE) conducted by the National Testing Agency (NTA). From the academic year 2022, admissions to UG programs offered by JNU will be based on CUET, which will replace the JNUEE. CUET will be a common entrance for admissions to UG programs offered by all the Central Universities in the country.

JNU UG Programs Reservation:

JNU being a Central University offers reservations in admissions according to central government rules.

Schedule Caste (SC): 15% of the total seats are reserved for students who belong to SC category.

Schedule Tribe (ST): 7.5% of the total seats are reserved for students belonging to ST Category.

Other Backward Classes (OBC): 27% of the total intake is reserved for students from Other Backward Classes (OBC), excluding those from creamy layer. Also, Central List of Caste to be followed.

Economically Weaker Section (EWS): The University has reserved 10% seats for EWS category, in accordance with the directive of Ministry of Education.

Persons with Disability (PWD): 5% of the seats are reserved on horizontal basis for students from PWD category.

About Jamia Milia Islamia

Jamia Milia Islamia (JMI) was founded in 1920 in Aligarh and became a Central University in 1988 by the act of Parliament. Jamia in Urdu stands for University and Milia means National, making Jamia Milia Islamia a National University. Jamia Milia Islamia moved to Delhi in 1925 and shifted to its present campus in Okhla in 1935.

Jamia Milia Islamia is a NAAC accredited University with grade "A" and was placed 10th in NIRF Rankings 2020. According to submissions made by University for NIRF 2021, Jamia Milia Islamia has a total of 5,911 students pursuing undergraduate courses at the University, of which 105 are foreign nationals. The University also manage to place a total of 681 UG students with an average salary ranging 4.2 Lacs-6.0 Lacs.

JMI UG Programs

Jamia Milia Islamia (JMI) offers a host of undergraduate programs for students. Through its various faculties, JMI offers a range of programs which caters to students learning abilities.

Please refer to the table below for the important undergraduate courses offered by Jamia Milia Islamia and the intake across each program.

Faculty	Course	Intake	Duration
Faculty of Humanities and Language	B. A (Hons) English	60	3 Years
	B. A (Hons) Hindi	40	3 Years
	B. A (Hons) Mass Media-Hindi	40	3 Years
	B. A (Hons) History	60	3 Years
	Bachelor of Hotel Management (BHM)	40	3 Years
	Bachelor of Tourism and Travel Management	40	3 Years
	B. Voc (Food Production)	40	3 Years
Faculty of Social Sciences	Bachelor of Arts (B. A)	68	3 Years
	B. Com (Hons)	55	3 Years
	BBA (Bachelor of Business Administration)	44	3 Years
	B. A (Hons) Economics	53	3 Years
	B. A (Hons) Sociology	42	3 Years
	B. A (Hons) Political Science	42	3 Years
	B. A (Hons) Psychology	42	3 Years
Faculty of Natural Sciences	B. Sc (Bachelor of Science)	50	3 Years
	B. Sc Biosciences	40	3 Years
	B. Sc Biotechnology	35	3 Years
	B. Sc (Hons) Chemistry	40	3 Years
	B. A/B. Sc (Hons) Geography	60	3 Years
	B. Sc (Hons) Mathematics	45	3 Years
	B. Sc (Hons) Applied Mathematics	45	3 Years
	B. Sc (Hons) Physics	45	3 Years
Faculty of Fine Arts	Bachelor of Fine Arts (Applied Art)	30	4 Years
	Bachelor of Fine Arts (Art Education)	20	4 Years
	Bachelor of Fine Arts (Painting)	20	4 Years
	Bachelor of Fine Arts (Sculpture)	10	4 Years

JMI UG Programs Eligibility:

Each of the courses have different eligibility for admissions. To be eligible for admissions, one must fulfil all the criteria as laid down by the respective faculties of the University.

B. Com (Hons) /BBA /B. A (Hons) Economics: Candidate must have passed class XII or equivalent with a minimum of 50% marks in five subjects.

BHM/BTTM/B. Voc (Food Production): Candidate must have passed class XII or equivalent with a minimum of 45% marks in five subjects.

B. A (Hons) Mass Media/B. A (Hons) Hindi: Candidate must have passed class XII or equivalent with a minimum of 45% marks in five subjects.

B. Sc/B. Sc (Hons): Candidate must have passed class XII or equivalent with minimum 50% marks in each of the science subjects i.e. Physics, Chemistry and Mathematics and 50% marks in aggregate of best 5-subjects.

JMI UG Admissions:

Until 2021, admissions to JMI UG courses were based on Entrance Test (JMI-ET) conducted by the University. From the academic year 2022, admissions to UG programs offered by JMI will be based on CUET, which will replace the JMI-ET. CUET will be a common entrance for admissions to UG programs offered by all the Central Universities in the country.

JMI UG Programs Reservation:

JMI is a minority reservation-based University and accordingly, seats are reserved for candidates as per the norms laid down by the University.

Muslim Minority: 30% of the total seats are reserved for Muslim applicants; 10% of the total seats are reserved for women applicants who are Muslim; 10% of the total intake is for OBC-NC candidates who are Muslims.

Persons with Disability (PWD): 5% of the seats are reserved for students from PWD category.

Jamia Students: 5% seats in all Undergraduate Programs shall be filled by internal students of Jamia who have passed their qualifying examination of the concerned programme (X or XII) from Jamia Schools as regular students.

In addition, Jamia Milia Islamia has supernumerary seats for Kashmiri Migrants and students from Jammu and Kashmir.

About Aligarh Muslim University

Aligarh Muslim University also referred as AMU was established by Sir Syed Ahmad Khan in 1875. The University started as Muhammadan Anglo-Oriental College and became a University (AMU) in 1920. The university has been ranked 801–1000 in the QS World University Rankings of 2021 and 17 in India by the National Institutional Ranking Framework in 2020.

Aligarh Muslim University is institution of national importance, under the seventh schedule of the Constitution of India.

AMU UG Programs

Aligarh Muslim University offers several programs at the undergraduate level. With 7 constituent colleges, the Aligarh Muslim University offers many undergraduate courses.

Please refer to the table below for the important undergraduate courses offered by the AMU and the intake across each program.

Course	Intake	Duration
B. Sc (Hons) Home Science	30*	3 Years
B.Sc (Hons) Agriculture	40	4 Years
B. A (Hons) Arabic	20+10*	3 Years
B. A (Hons) Communicative English	15+20*	3 Years
B. A (Hons) English	40+35*	3 Years
B. A (Hons) Hindi	40+25*	3 Years
B. A (Hons) Geography	50+20*	3 Years
B. A (Hons) Linguistics	20+25*	3 Years
B. A (Hons) Persian	15+25*	3 Years
B. A (Hons) Philosophy	20+10*	3 Years
B. A (Hons) Quaranic Studies	10+10*	3 Years
B. A (Hons) Sanskrit	15+10*	3 Years
B. A (Hons) Urdu	40+50*	3 Years
Bachelor of Fine Arts	15+15*	3 Years
B. Com (Hons)	180+100*	3 Years
B. Voc Production Technology	50	3 Years
B Voc Polymer and Coating Technology	50	3 Years
B. Voc Fashion Design and Garment Technology	50	3 Years
B. A (Hons) Chinese	20	3 Years
B. A (Hons) French	20	3 Years
B. A (Hons) German	20	3 Years

Program	Seats	Duration
B. A (Hons) Russian	20	3 Years
B. A (Hons) Spanish	20	3 Years
B. Sc (Hons) Biochemistry	30+30*	3 Years
B. Sc (Hons) Botany	60+40*	3 Years
B. Sc (Hons) Zoology	60+45*	3 Years
B. Sc (Hons) Physics	120+35*	3 Years
B. Sc (Hons) Chemistry	120+65*	3 Years
B. Sc (Hons) Mathematics	120+40*	3 Years
B. Sc (Hons) Geography	45+30*	3 Years
B. Sc (Hons) Geology	100+30*	3 Years
B. Sc (Hons) Statistics	60+30*	3 Years
B. Sc (Hons) Industrial Chemistry	20+10*	3 Years
B. Sc (Hons) Computer Applications	40+20*	3 Years

AMU UG Programs Eligibility:

As the University offers multiple programs and separate intake for male and female candidates, it is important to check the university official website regularly to keep oneself updated about the eligibility for each program, which can change.

AMU UG Admissions:

Until 2021, AMU conducted its own entrance test to admit students for the UG programs. From the academic year 2022, admissions to UG programs offered by Aligarh Muslim University will be based on CUET. CUET will be a common entrance for admissions to UG programs offered by all the Central Universities in the country.

University of Allahabad UG Programs Reservation:

Allahabad University being a Central University offers reservations in admissions according to central government rules. Kindly check the university website for further details.

ECONOMICS

PART – I

Introductory Microeconomics and Macroeconomics

CHAPTER 1

Introduction to Microeconomics and Macroeconomics

Chief concepts of this introductory chapter

- Microeconomics – Meaning of Microeconomics.
- Central Problems of an economy: what, how and for whom to produce; opportunity cost.

1. Meaning Of Microeconomics

Microeconomics is the social science that studies the implications of incentives and decisions, specifically about how those affect the utilization and distribution of resources. Microeconomics shows how and why different goods have different values, how individuals and businesses conduct and benefit from efficient production and exchange, and how individuals best coordinate and cooperate with one another.

- Microeconomics studies the decisions of individuals and firms to allocate resources of production, exchange, and consumption.

- Microeconomics deals with prices and production in single markets and the interaction between different markets but leaves the study of economy-wide aggregates to macroeconomics.

- Microeconomists formulate various types of models based on logic and observed human behaviour and test the models against real-world observations.

1.1 Basic Concepts of Microeconomics

The study of microeconomics involves several key concepts, including (but not limited to):

- Incentives and behaviours: How people, as individuals or in firms, react to the situations with which they are confronted.

- Utility theory: Consumers will choose to purchase and consume a combination of goods that will maximize their happiness or "utility," subject to the constraint of how much income they have available to spend.

- Production theory: This is the study of production—or the process of converting inputs into outputs. Producers seek to choose the combination of inputs and methods of combining them that will minimize cost in order to maximize their profits.

- Price theory: Utility and production theory interact to produce the theory of supply and demand, which determine prices in a competitive market. In a perfectly competitive market, it concludes that the price demanded by consumers is the same supplied by producers. That results in economic equilibrium.

1.2 Central Problems of an Economy

The problem of making a choice among alternative uses of resources is known as basic or central problem of an economy.

There are many central problems of an economy, one of them is the Problem of Allocation of Resources: Every economy has limited resources which can alternatively be used to produce different goods and services. Hence, it has to allocate its available resources in the production of different goods and services in such a manner that it ideally meets the needs of the society.

While allocating resources optimally, the following the decisions for three central problems of an economy are required to be taken:

(a) What to produce?

(b) How to produce?

(c) For whom to produce?

(a) What to produce?

What to produce refers to a problem in which decision regarding which goods and services should be produced is to be taken.

Since its resources are limited, every economy has to decide what commodities are to be produced and in what quantities will stop next line in view of limited resources when we produce more of a commodity, it means we will be able to produce less of another. Because more production of 1 commodity would force us to withdraw resources from the production of the other commodity.

Example: economy has to choose between capital goods (tools, machines, etc.), consumer goods (shoes, watch, etc.), military goods (guns, tanks, etc.), common necessities of life (food, clothing, housing, etc.)and luxury goods (car , refrigerator, etc).

(b) How to produce?

How to produce refers to a problem in which decision regarding which technique of production should be used is taken.

Goods and services can be produced in two ways: by using labour intensive techniques, and by using capital- intensive techniques.

Under labour intensive techniques, more of labour and less of capital per unit of output is used in producing goods and services, violent capital- intensive techniques more of capital and less of labour per unit of output is used.

Thus, the economy has to decide whether the chosen goods and services should be produced with the help of automatic machines or mobile handful stop every method of production has its own advantages and disadvantages.

For example automatic machines increases the quantity and improves the quality of production but it results in unemployment as it requires lesser number of labourers. On the other hand production by hand such as handicrafts generate more employment but produces smaller amounts of production.

The guiding principle for an economy in such a case is to decide about the techniques of production on the basis of cost of production. Those techniques of production should be used which lead to the least possible cost for unit of commodity or service.

(c) For whom to produce?

For whom to produce refers to a problem in which decision regarding which category of people are going to consume a good, that is, economically poor or rich.

As we know common goods and services are produced for those who can pursue them or have the capacity to buy them.

Capacity to buy depends upon how income is distributed among the factors of production. The higher the income, the higher will be the capacity to buy an vice versa. So, this is a problem of distribution

We know that the whole output is distributed among factors of production which have contributed to it.

Since production is the combined efforts of all the four factors of production, land, labour, capital and enterprise, it is distributed among them in the form of money income that is rent, wages, in Tristan profits. Who should get how much is, thus, the problem.

The guiding principle is that the economy must see here that the important an urgent ones of its citizens are being satisfied to the maximum possible extent.

1.3 Nature of the Basic Economic Problem

At any given point of time in an economy, output is limited by the resources and the technology available. There is therefore a basic condition of scarcity. On the other hand, the wants of the consumers are infinite or unlimited and the ability of the resources to satisfy those wants however are limited. There is therefore a need to make a choice as a result of this scarcity. This choice will be in terms of what to produce, how to produce and for whom to produce.

1. **Economic good:** An economic good has a benefit to the society. It is a consumable goods that is useful to people but at the same time scarce in relation to its demand. Also, economic goods have a price. Human effort is required to obtain economic goods. Economic goods come with an opportunity cost. Examples of economic goods include - piped gas, electricity, cars, mobiles etc.

2. **Free good:** it is a product that does not require any resources to make it and so does not have an opportunity cost. Example of free goods are - air, water, wind, etc.

The economic problem: It is due to scarcity that there exists a basic economic problem of not being able to satisfy the wants of all people.

The economic problem can never be solved because the economic problem is scarcity. As we know the wants are infinite, but resources are limited. The wants exceed resources as once grow faster than resources.

1.4 Factors of Production and their rewards

The economic resources of land, labour, capital, an enterprise are as a factors of production.

1. **Land:** it refers to all the natural resources used in the production such as oil, coal etc. In addition, the water, plants, animals et cetera are also included. Example: farmland, minerals, sea. Land resources are the raw materials in the production process. These resources can be renewable, such as forests or non-renewable such as oil or natural gas. Land also gives us rent.

2. **Labour:** labour stands for the human effort mental or physical that is used in producing goods and services. Example: A teacher, workers, in fact all people with their efforts, abilities and skills are termed as labour. Labour gets wages.

3. **Capital:** capital refers to all the man-made goods used in production. Example machinery and equipment, factories, conveyor belts, computers, delivery vans etc. Capital gives us interest.

4. **Enterprise:** it refers to the risk bearing and the key decision-making function in a business. This is needed as some events cannot be anticipated beforehand and might not qualify for being insured. Example: An entrepreneur. Enterprise gives us profit.

Entrepreneur is a factor that takes the risk in bearing the other factors together or combining the other factors in order to produce goods and services to make profits. Enterprise involves the taking of decisions in terms of what to produce? and how to produce? Enterprise operations are run by entrepreneurs who receive profits as rewards.

1.5 Meaning of Opportunity Cost:

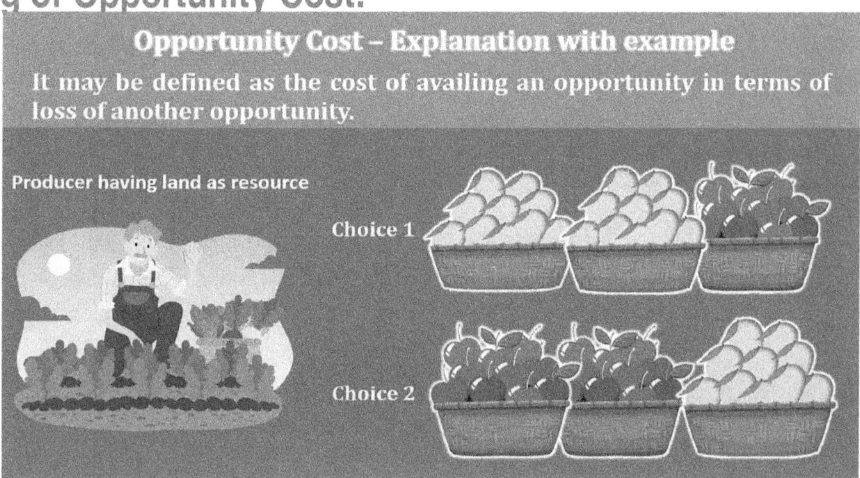

The opportunity cost concept is an important concept in economics. The resources we have, carry some alternative uses. When we use a resource in one use in place of others, we have to sacrifice the opportunity to use it in another use. Thus, the Opportunity cost is the value of the next best alternative use sacrificed.

It refers to the cost of shifting of resources from one use to another. In other words, it may be defined as the cost of availing an opportunity in terms of loss of another opportunity.

As we know that resources available for production and economic goods are limited and they have alternative uses. Thus, when we use an economic commodity or resources in one use, then we have to sacrifice the opportunity to use it in another use. Thus, it is the value of the factor in its best alternative use.

In the words of Samuelson,

"Opportunity cost is the value of the next best use (opportunity) for an economic good or resource or the value of the sacrificed alternative."

Example:

Suppose Mr Shubham has two job offers which include a job in a bank and another in school. The bank provides him with a salary of Rs. 15,000 per month whereas the school offers him a salary of Rs. 12,000 per month. Thus, he will go for the best alternative which is a bank job. As a result of choosing the bank job, he has to sacrifice the salary of Rs. 12000 which he can earn from school. Thus, the opportunity cost for choosing the bank job is the value of the best alternative i.e. Rs. 12,000 sacrificed from school.

1.5.1 Illustration of Opportunity Cost in Production:

Suppose a land of hectares is to be used by a producer for the production of apples. This is the one use of the land. If because of any reason, the producer has to use that land for the production of mangoes. This is another use of that same land. In economics, this use is known as an opportunity. Shifting from the production of apples to mangoes involves the same cost to the producer which is the loss of output of apples.

Types:

The opportunity cost can be classified as:

1. Total Opportunity Cost
2. Marginal Opportunity Cost

1. Total Opportunity Cost (TOC):

In production, this cost can be defined as the total loss of output when resources are shifted from one use to another.

For Instance, If the given 10 hectares of land is shifted to the production of apples worth Rs. 8,000 from mangoes worth Rs. 6,000. Thus, the total opportunity cost of shifting resources from one opportunity to another is equal to the loss of output of mangoes worth Rs. 6,000.

This concept can be explained with the help of Production Possibility Curve.

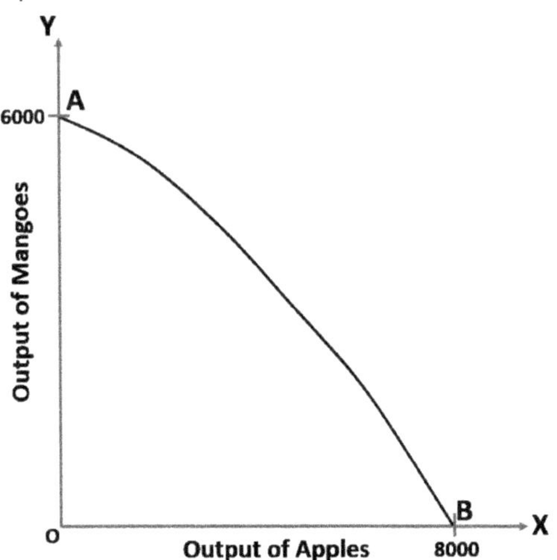

Total Opportunity Cost

In the above figure, X-axis shows the cost of mangoes and Y-axis shows the cost of apples produced. It is assumed that the production technique is constant, and the resources are fully utilized. In fig, it is shown that with the use of available resources, mangoes worth Rs. 6,000 and apples worth Rs. 8,000 are produced. If the resources are used for the

production of apples, then the opportunity cost will be Rs. 6,000 which is the cost of the best alternative use of land for the production of mangoes.

In short, the total opportunity cost of a resource for use in a given job is the amount it can earn in its next best alternative use.

2. Marginal Opportunity Cost (MOC):

It refers to the sacrificed cost per unit of additional output from another use when resources are shifted from one use to another. This Cost is based on two assumptions:

1. The factors of production are constant.
2. There is no change in production technology.

In other words, the marginal Opportunity cost of one commodity means the reduction in the production of another commodity, due to usage of constant resources for the production of both.

Therefore,

$$\text{Marginal Opportunity Cost} = \frac{\Delta \text{Loss of the output of Commodity-1}}{\Delta \text{Gain of the output of Commodity-2}}$$

Example:

Suppose a farmer has one acre of land. By changing its production techniques, he produces two commodities -Mangoes worth Rs. 4,400 and Apples worth Rs. 3,200. If he increases the production of apples to Worthing Rs. 6,400 on the same piece of land, then he will reduce the production of mangoes to worth Rs. 1,800. The worth of mangoes being sacrificed is called the marginal cost of apples.

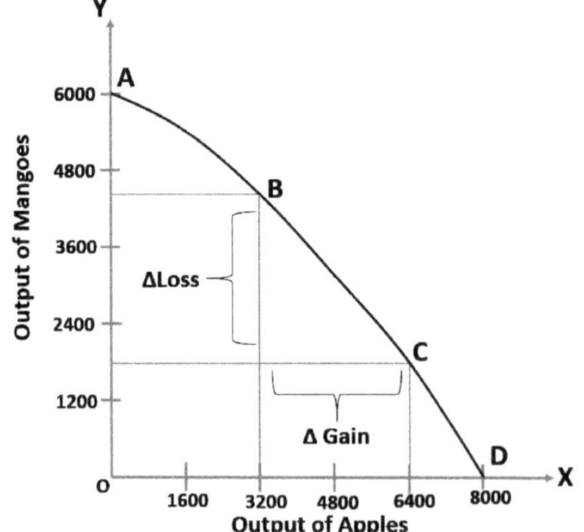

Marginal Opportunity Cost

In the above figure, X-axis shows the worth of output of apples and Y-axis shows the worth of mangoes. AD is the production possibility curve showing different combinations of apples and mangoes. When the resources are fully utilized, the apples worth Rs. 3,200 and mangoes worth Rs. 4,400 are produced. Here, point B shows the initial production of apples and mangoes on the same land whereas point C shows the increased production of apples and reduced production of mangoes. By increasing the production of apples, the producer is able to produce apples worth Rs. 6,400. As a result, the production of mangoes decreased to only worth Rs. 1,800 which would be sacrificed by him.

$$\frac{\Delta \text{Loss of the output of Mangoes}}{\Delta \text{Gain of the output of Apples}} = \frac{4400 - 1800}{6400 - 3200}$$

$$= \frac{2600}{3200} = 0.81$$

It means, the marginal cost of producing additional apples:

0.81 can be said as Slope of Production Possibility Curve. Hence, we can say that marginal opportunity cost is identical to the slope of PPC.

1.6 Production Possibility Frontier

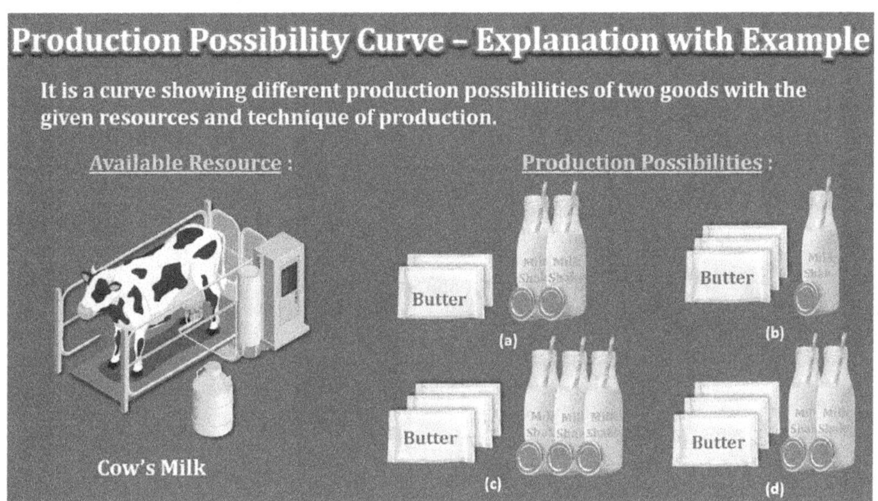

1.6.1 Meaning of Production Possibility Curve:

It is a curve showing different production possibilities of two goods with the given resources and technique of production. Also, this curve shows the limit of what it is possible to produce with available resources. Therefore, It is also known as Production Possibility Boundary or Production Possibility Frontier.

This curve is also called Transformation Line or Transformation Curve because it indicates that if more of a commodity is to be produced then factors of production will have to be withdrawn from the production of another commodity. In other words, one commodity is transformed into another.

In the words of Samuelson,

"Production Possibility Curve is that curve which represents the maximum amount of a pair of goods or services that can be produced with an economy's given resources and technique assuming that all resources are fully employed."

Assumptions:

1. The number of factors of production is given and assumed as fixed. They can be transferred from one use to another to some extent.

2. The given resources are utilized fully and efficiently.

3. There is neither any improvement nor innovation in technology.

4. It is assumed there are only two goods, or two sets of goods are produced in the economy. For example, apples and wheat or capital goods and consumer goods.

Explanation with Example:

Production Possibilities/Goods	Milk-Shake (in units)	Butter (in units)
A	500	0
B	450	50
C	360	100
D	270	150
E	150	200
F	0	250

Suppose a producer decides to produce only two goods namely, milkshake and butter with the available resource "cow's milk" and given technology. If all the resources are used for making milkshake alone, then 500 bottles of milkshake can be produced. On the other hand, if all the resources are used to produce butter only, then 250 units of butter can be produced. Moreover, If the producer produces both the goods, then within these limits, various combinations can be produced.

1.6.2 Production Possibility Schedule

The above schedule shows that if production is carried out under 'A' combination, then 500 units of Milkshake alone will be produced without any production off butter. On the other hand, if production is obtained under 'F' combination, then 250 units of butter will be produced without any production of milkshake. Besides these limits, there are many alternatives' possibilities of production of milkshake and butter. For instance, under 'B' combination, it is 450 units of milkshake and 50units of butter; under 'C' combination, it is 360 units of milkshake and 100 units of butter; under 'D' combination, it is 270 units of milkshake and 150 units of butter and under 'E' combination, it is 150 units of milkshake and 200 units of butter.

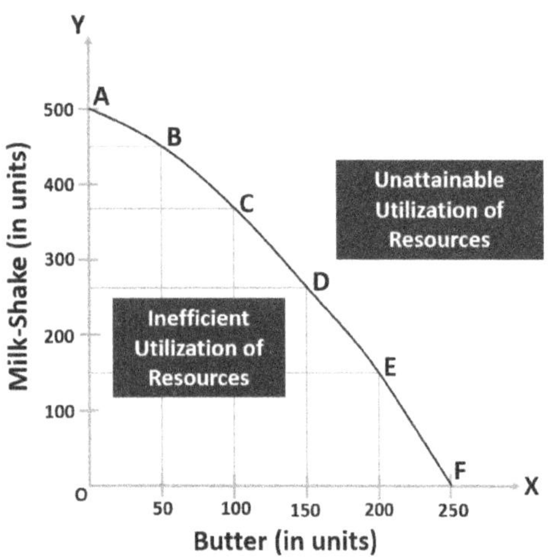

Production Possibility Curve

In the above figure, the quantity of butter is shown on X-axis and milkshake on Y-axis. Here, the first production possibility is 500 units of milkshake and no butter. In fig, this is marked as point A. Similarly, points B, C, D and E show different combinations of butter and milkshake. Lastly, Point F shows the production possibility of 250 units of butter and no milkshake. By combining these points, we get AF curve. This curve is known as the Production Possibility or Transformation curve. Furthermore, the area beyond this curve represents unattainable combinations and area inside the curve shows the inefficient utilization of resources.

1.6.3 Properties of PPC

Production Possibility Curve has the following basic properties:

1. **Production Possibility curve slopes Downward:** PPC curve slopes downward from left to right. Because, at the situation of full utilization of given resources, the production of both goods cannot be increased. It implies more of commodity-1 can be produced only with less of commodity-2.

2. **PPC is concave to the point of origin:** It is because, to produce every additional unit of commodity-1, more and more units of commodity-2 will have to be sacrificed. Consequently, the opportunity cost of producing each additional unit of commodity-1 tends to increase the loss of production of commodity-2. In other words, production will follow the law of increasing opportunity costs.

Key Statements

Economy: It is a system which provides people with the means to work and earn a living.

Economic Problem: It is a problem of choice involving satisfaction of unlimited ones out of limited resources having alternative uses.

Scarcity: Scarcity in economics is short supply in relation to the demand. Resources of the economy are scarce with the result that the economy can't produce all that the society needs.

Production: It is the process of transforming inputs ((raw materials) into output (finished goods). So, production means creation of goods and services.

Consumption: It is a process of using up of goods and services to satisfy human wants.

Consumption goods: Consumption goods are those goods which satisfy the wants of consumers directly.

Capital goods: Capital goods are defined as all goods produced for use in future productive processes.

Economics Agents: By economic units or economic agents, we mean those individuals or institutions which take economic decisions. They can be -

Consumers who decide what and how much to consume.

Producers of goods and services who decide what and how much to produce.

Few Facts about emergence of Microeconomics and Macroeconomics

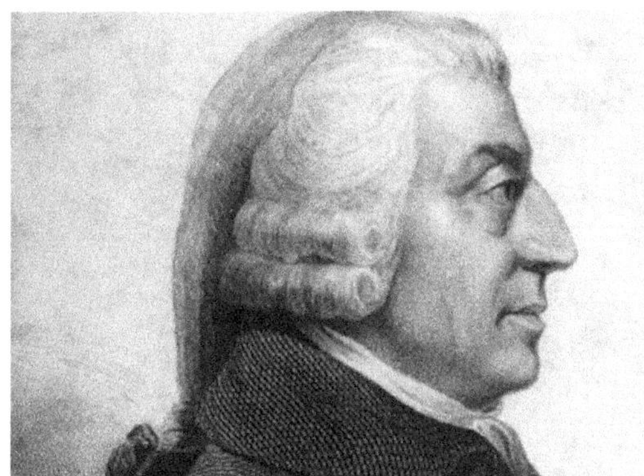

ADAM SMITH : 1723 – 17901

Adam Smith – Is regarded as the founding father of modern economics (it was known as political economy at that time). He was a Scotsman and a professor at the University of Glasgow. Philosopher by training, his well-known work *An Enquiry into the Nature and Cause of the Wealth of Nations* (1776) is regarded as the first major comprehensive book on the subject. The Physiocrats of France but prominent thinkers of political economy before Smith Adam Smith, had suggested that is the buyers and sellers in each market take the decisions following only their self-interest, economists will not need to think of the wealth and welfare of the country as a whole separately. But economists gradually discovered that they had to look further

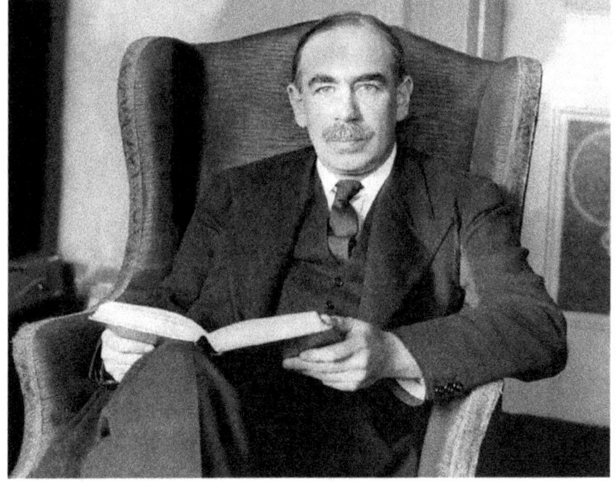

JOHN MAYNARD KEYNES : 1883 – 1946

John Maynard Keynes- macroeconomics, emerged as a separate branch of economics, after the British economist John Maynard Keynes published his celebrated book in 1936. The dominant thinking in economics before Keynes was that all the labourers who are ready to work will find employment and all the factories will be working at their full capacity. This school of thought is known as the classical tradition

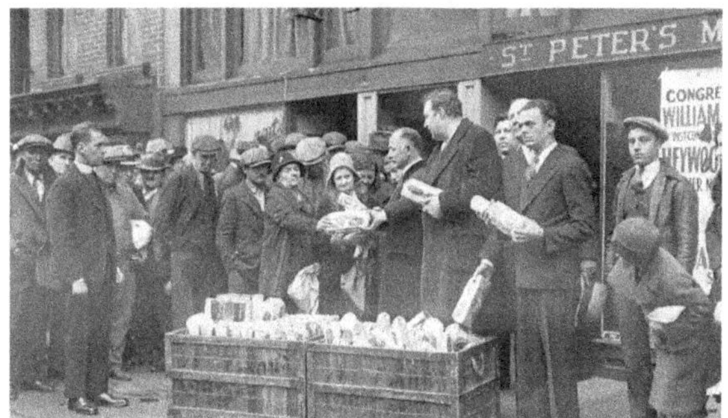

GREAT DEPRESSION: Started in 1929 and lasted until late 1930s

The Great Depression 1929- The Great Depression of 1929 was one of the worst economic depressions in the history of the world. It began when the U.S. stock market crashed in 1929 and lasted until the end of the 1930s. Several causes are considered to be responsible for this period of economic downturn. Raising debt levels, fall in profits and the gold standard system are some attributed causes.

The Great Depression led to a series of problems for the economy and the people. There was a drastic decrease in production and consumption in the economy. The rate of unemployment skyrocketed resulting in hardships across the population. A lot of prominent banks failed and ran out of business. Eventually, the great depression shaped the politics of the U.S. and laid the foundations for The New Deal.

Exercise

Frequently asked Questions (FAQ's)

1. What is the difference between microeconomics and macroeconomics?

2. Why does an economic problem arise?

3. What does the rightward shift of Production Possibility Curve indicate?

4. Why does the problem of what to produce arise? Explain.

5. What is Marginal Rate of Transformation? Explain With the help of an example.

Multiple Choice Questions (MCQ's)

1. The branches of the subject Economics is
   (*a*) Wealth and welfare
   (*b*) Production and consumption
   (*c*) Demand and supply
   (*d*) Micro and macro

2. In a centrally planned economy, the central problems are solved by:
   (*a*) Supply of goods
   (*b*) Demand for goods
   (*c*) Market mechanism
   (*d*) Planning authority

3. What is the other name for opportunity cost in economics?
   (*a*) Social cost   (*b*) Marginal cost next
   (*c*) Total cost   (*d*) Economic cost

4. The basic assumption regarding resources while drawing a PPC is:
   (*a*) Resources are unlimited
   (*b*) Resources depend on the kind of goods produced
   (*c*) Resources can be put to a particular use
   (*d*) Resources are constant and given

5. A growth of resources in an economy is shown on PPC by:
   (*a*) Leftward shift
   (*b*) Unchanged PPC
   (*c*) Rightward shift
   (*d*) None of the above

6. The problem of 'how to produce' relates to:
   (*a*) The choice of technique
   (*b*) Distribution of income
   (*c*) Market value of the goods and services
   (*d*) The choice of goods and services

7. Which of the following is not concerned with the problem of choice?
   (*a*) Excessive income
   (*b*) Alternative use of resources
   (*c*) Unlimited wants
   (*d*) Limited scarce resources

8. Example of microeconomic variable is:
   (*a*) Wholesale price index
   (*b*) National income
   (*c*) Market demand
   (*d*) Aggregate demand

9. Which of the following illustrates or decrease in the unemployment using the PPC?
   (*a*) A movement down along the PPC
   (*b*) A rightward shift of the PPC
   (*c*) A movement from a point on the PPC to a point inside the PPC
   (*d*) A movement from a point inside the PPC to a point towards the PPC

10. A PPC for butter and guns is drawn so that it is a straight line. It means:
    (*a*) Less and less units of butter are sacrificed to gain an additional unit of gun.
    (*b*) More and more units of butter are sacrificed to gain an additional unit of gun.
    (*c*) Same units of butter are sacrificed to gain an additional unit of gun.
    (*d*) None of the above

11. Which of the following is not a microeconomic study?
    (*a*) Determination of price of a commodity
    (*b*) Study of a manufacturing sector
    (*c*) Determination of wage- rate of computer engineers
    (*d*) Determination of cost of a product

12. If the marginal rate of transformation is constant, the PPC would be:
    (*a*) Convex to the origin
    (*b*) Straight line
    (*c*) Concave to the origin
    (*d*) None of the above

13. Which of the following statement is false?
    (*a*) A point above the PPC represents increase in resources.
    (*b*) Due to unemployment, production in the economy is below its potential.

(c) PPC shows what an economy can potentially produce, and not what it actually produces.

(d) Inflow of foreign capital will cause rise in production potential leading to economic growth

14. In the given figure $X_1 Y_1$ and $X_2 Y_2$ all Production Possibility Curves in two different time periods T_1 and T_2 respectively. A_1 and A_2 represent actual outputs in T_1 and T_2 Periods respectively. P_1 and P_2 are potential outputs in T_1 and T_1 Periods respectively.

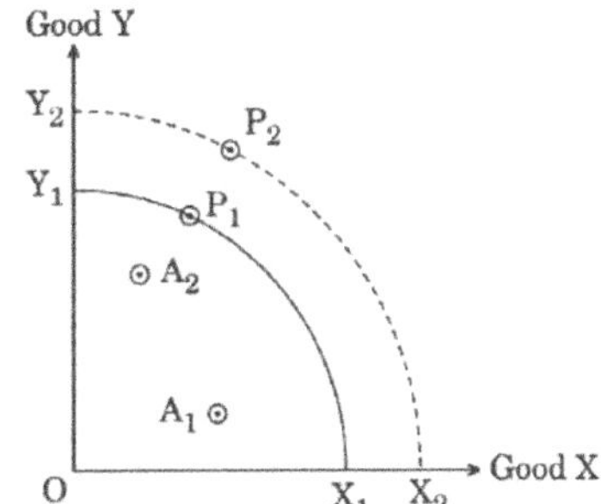

The change in potential production over the two periods would be represented by a shift from:

(a) P_2 to A_2 (b) A_1 to A_2

(c) A_2 to A_1 (d) P_1 to P_2

15. Identity The Founding Father of economics

(a) J M Keynes   (b) Karl Marx

(c) Adam smith   (d) Samuelson

16. The central problems arise in:

(a) Capitalist economies

(b) Socialist economies

(c) All economies

(d) Mixed economies

17. Which of the following will lead to a leftward shift of PPC?

(a) Growth of resources

(b) Efficient utilisation of resources

(c) Inefficient utilisation of resources

(d) Decrease in resources

18. Which of the following will not lead to a shift in the PPC?

(a) Upgradation of technology

(b) exploration of new oil results

(c) Massive unemployment

(d) Destruction of resources

19. What is known as the study of individual units?

(a) Macroeconomics

(b) Microeconomics

(c) Income and Employment Theory

(d) Development economics

20. What is the main cause of all economic problems?

(a) Abundance   (b) Convenience

(c) Scarcity   (d) None of the above

21. Study of aggregates is known as _________

(a) Macroeconomics

(b) Microeconomics

(c) Price theory

(d) Factor price determination

22. The basic factors of production are land, labour, capital, and _________.

(a) Enterprise   (b) Investment

(c) Machinery   (d) Resources

23. Which of the following is the salient feature of (factors or resources)?

(a) These are limited as compared to wants

(b) These have alternative uses

(c) Both (a) and (b)

(d) None of the above

24. The problem of 'what to produce' relates to:

(a) The choice of technique

(b) Distribution of income

(c) Market value of the goods and services

(d) The choice of goods and services

25. What is the name of the book written by J.M.Keynes?

(a) Well stop nation

(b) Political economy

(c) The General Theory of Employment, Interest and Money

(d) None of the above

🔑 Solutions

Frequently asked Questions (FAQ's)

1. **Microeconomics**
   - Deals with the behaviour, choices and incentives of individuals or individual companies.
   - Pioneered by economists such as Alfred Marshall
   - Can be used to explain consumer behaviour, the theory of price and marketing principles.

   Macroeconomics
   - Deals with the whole economy, including governments, corporations, and regulatory institutions.
   - Pioneered by economists such as John. Maynard. Keynes

2. An economic problem arises due to relative scarcity of resources having alternative use and unlimited human wants.

3. The rightward shift of Production Possibility Curve indicates the increase in the resources or improvement in the technology of production of the economy, which expands production of both the goods.

4. Problem of 'what to produce' arises as the economy has limited resources. Because of scarcity city of resources, producers are unable to produce everything in desired quantity, but they will have to make a choice as to which one is important as a whole, so that limited resources can be rationally managed.

   Problem of 'what to produce' involved two fold decisions; kinds of goods to be produced and quantity of goods to be produced.

5. It is the ratio of number of units of good 'Y' sacrificed to produce an additional unit of good 'X'. Marginal Rate of Transformation of a particular good along PPC is the amount of a particular good which is sacrificed to increase the production of the other good by one unit. It is also called marginal opportunity cost.

Multiple Choice Questions (MCQ's)

1. (d) Micro and macro
2. (d) Planning authority
3. (d) Economic cost
4. (d) Resources are constant and given
5. (c) Rightward shift
6. (a) The choice of technique
7. (a) Excessive income
8. (c) Market demand
9. (d) A movement from a point inside the PPC to a point towards the PPC
10. (c) Same units of butter are sacrificed to gain an additional unit of gun.
11. (b) Study of the manufacturing sector
12. (b) Straight line
13. (a) A point above the PPC represents increase in resources (False)
14. (d) P_1 to P_2
15. (b) Adam Smith
16. (c) All economies
17. (d) Decrease in resources
18. (c) Massive unemployment
19. (b) Microeconomics
20. (c) Scarcity
21. (a) Macroeconomics
22. (a) Enterprise
23. (c) Both (a) and (b)
24. (d) The choice of goods and services
25. (c) The General Theory of Employment, Interest and Money

CHAPTER 2

Consumer Behaviour and Demand

Chief concepts of this chapter –

- **Consumers equilibrium:** meaning and attainment of equilibrium through utility approach: One and two commodity cases.

- **Demand:** market demand, determinants of demand, demand schedule, demand curve, for movement along and shifts In the demand curve, price elasticity of demand, measurement of price elasticity of demand- percentage, total expenditure, and geometric methods.

Consumer: is an economic agent who consumes final goods or services for a consideration.

2.1 Utility

Utility is want satisfying power of a commodity.

Total Utility: It is the total satisfaction derived from consumption of given quantity of a commodity at a given time. In other words, It is the sum total of marginal utility.

Marginal Utility: It is the change in total utility resulting from the consumption of an additional unit of the commodity. In other words, It is the utility derived from each additional unit.

$$MU_n = TU_n - TU_{n-1}$$

Relation between total utility and marginal utility

UNITS	MU	TU
1	10	10
2	8	18
3	6	24
4	4	28
5	2	30
6	0	30
7	-2	28

1. When MU diminishes but positive TU increases at a diminishing rate.

2. When MU is zero, TU is maximum.

3. When MU is negative, TU diminishes.

Law of Diminishing Marginal Utility : As consumer consumes more and more units of commodity the Marginal utility derived from each successive units go on declining. This is the basis of law of demand.

Consumer's Bundle : It is a quantitative combination of two goods which can be purchased by a consumer from his given income.

Law of Equi-Marginal Utility- It states that when a consumer spends his income on different commodity he will attain equilibrium or maximize his satisfaction at that point where ratio between marginal utility and price of different commodities are equal and which in turn is equal to marginal utility of money.

Budget set : It is quantitative combination of those bundles which a consumer can purchase from his given income at prevailing market prices.

Consumer Budget : It states the real purchasing power of the consumer from which he can purchase the certain quantitative bundles of two goods at given price.

Budget Line : A graphical representation of all those bundles which cost the amount just equal to the consumers money income gives us the budget line.

Monotonic Preferences : Consumer's preferences are called monotonic when between any two bundles, one bundle has more of one good and no less of other good as it offers him a higher level of satisfaction.

Change in Budget Line : There can be parallel shift (leftwards or rightwards) due to change in income of the consumer and change in price of goods. A rise in income of the consumer shifts the budget line rightwards and vice-versa. In case of change in price of one good, there will be rotation in the budget line. Fall in price cause outward rotation due to rise in purchasing power and vice-versa.

Marginal Rate of Substitution (MRS) : It is the rate at which a consumer is willing to substitute $\left(\dfrac{\text{good Y}}{\text{good X}}\right)$ one good to obtain one more unit of the other good. Generally, It is the slope of indifference curve.

$$\text{MRS} = \dfrac{\text{Loss of Good Y}}{\text{Gain of Good X}} \text{ or } \dfrac{\Delta Y}{\Delta X}$$

2.2 Indifference Curve

Indifference Curve is a curve showing different combination of two goods, each combinations offering the same level of satisfaction to the consumer.

Characteristics of Indifference Curve

1. Indifference curves are negatively sloped(i.e. slopes downward from left to right).

2. Indifference curves are convex to the point of origin. It is due to diminishing marginal rate of substitution.

3. Indifference curves never touch or intersect each other. Two points on different IC cannot give equal level of satisfaction.

4. Higher indifference curve represents higher level of satisfaction.

2.3 Consumer's Equilibrium

A consumer is said to be in equilibrium when he maximizes his satisfaction, given his money income and prices of two commodity. He attains equilibrium at that point where the slope of IC is equal to the slope of budget line.

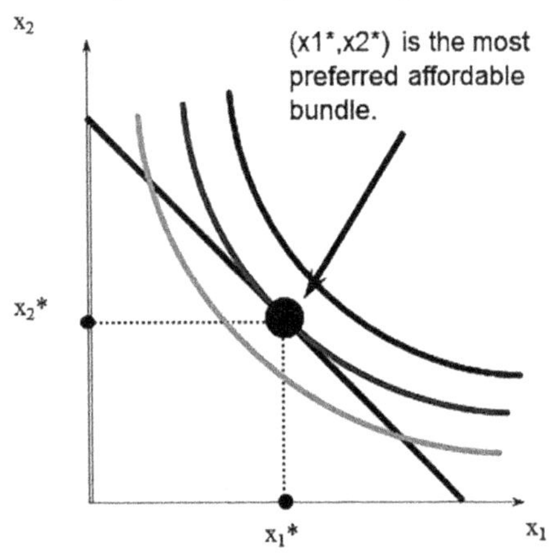

2.4 Condition of Consumer's Equilibrium

(a) **Cardinal approach (Utility Analysis):** According to this approach utility can be measured. "Utils" is the unit of utility.

Condition:

1. In case of one community

$$\text{MUm} = \dfrac{\text{Mux}}{\text{Px}} \quad [\text{ If MUm = 1, MUx= Px}]$$

Where, MUm = Marginal utility of money

MUx = Marginal utility of 'x', P_x = Price of 'x'

2. In case of two commodity.

$$\dfrac{\text{MUx}}{\text{Px}} = \dfrac{\text{MUy}}{\text{Py}} = \text{MUm}$$

xy and MU must be decreasing

Units	MUx	MUy	MUx/Px	MUy/Py
1	36	40	12	10
2	33	36	11	9
3	30	32	10	8
4	27	28	9	7
5	24	24	8	6
6	21	20	7	5

Assumption, Px = Rs.3, Py = Rs.4

Y = Rs.20 Here, MUm = 9

(b) **Ordinal approach (Indifference Curve Analysis):** According to this approach utility cannot be measured but can be expressed in order or ranking.

Condition of Equilibrium:

1. $\text{MRSxy} = \dfrac{Px}{Py}\begin{bmatrix} Px = \text{Price of 'x'} \\ Py = \text{Price of 'y'} \end{bmatrix}$

or budget line must be tangent to indifference curve.

2. MRS must be diminishing or,

Indifference curve must be convex to the origin.

2.5 Demand

Demand refers to the amount of goods or services consumers are *willing and able* to purchase at each price.

What a buyer pays for a unit of the specific good or service is called the **price**.

The total number of units purchased at that price is called the **quantity demanded**.

Demand is based on ability to pay. If you can't pay for it, you have no effective demand.

A rise in the price of a good or service almost always decreases the quantity of that good or service demanded. Conversely, a fall in price will increase the quantity demanded.

Economists call this inverse relationship between price and quantity demanded the law of demand.

The law of demand assumes that all other variables that affect demand are held constant.

Law of demand

The law of demand states that, other things being equal,

- More of a good will be bought the lower its price

- Less of a good will be bought the higher its price

Ceteris paribus means "other things being equal."

For example, a consumer may demand 2 kilograms of apples at Rs. 70 per kg; he may, however, demand 1 kg if the price rises to Rs. 80 per kg.

This has been the general human behaviour on relationship between the price of the commodity and the quantity demanded.

Individual demand

Individual demand refers to the quantity of a commodity that a consumer is willing and able to buy, at each possible price during a given period of time.

Market Demand

Market demand refers to the quantity of a commodity that all consumers are willing and able to buy, at each possible price during a given period of time.

To establish the total cost or benefit to society the total value of the private costs and eternal costs needs to be calculated. The sum of the private and external benefits needs to be calculated. If the social cost is greater than the social benefit then the resources & factors of production should be used to produce something else that is more socially beneficial.

2.6 Demand schedule

A demand schedule is a tabulation of the quantity of a good that all consumers in a market will purchase at a given price.

At any given price, the corresponding value on the demand schedule is the sum of all consumers' quantities demanded at that price.

Generally, there is an inverse relationship between the price and the quantity demanded.

In example of a market demand schedule, price in this case is measured in Rupees per Kg of tomato and the quantity demanded is measured in kilograms over some time period.

Price (Rs.)	Quantity demanded (kg)
55	100
45	200
35	300
25	400
15	500

Demand schedule for tomatoes

2.7 Demand Curves

A demand curve shows the relationship between price and quantity demanded on a graph, with quantity on the horizontal axis and the price on the vertical axis.

- Individual demand is how much of a product a consumer will buy at a given price.

- Market demand is the sum of all the individual demand for a product at a given price.

- Demand is based on the actual ability of consumers to purchase the product, not just what they would like but can't afford (sports car, jewellery etc). This is called effective demand.

- Demand curves slope down from left to right - this is because the higher the price the more of a consumer's income must be spent on it & the more satisfaction, they must get from it to justify the opportunity cost.

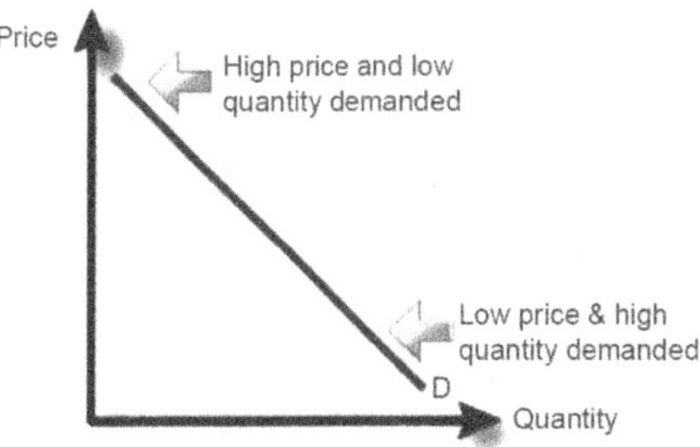

The information from the demand schedule can be used to plot a demand curve on a graph.

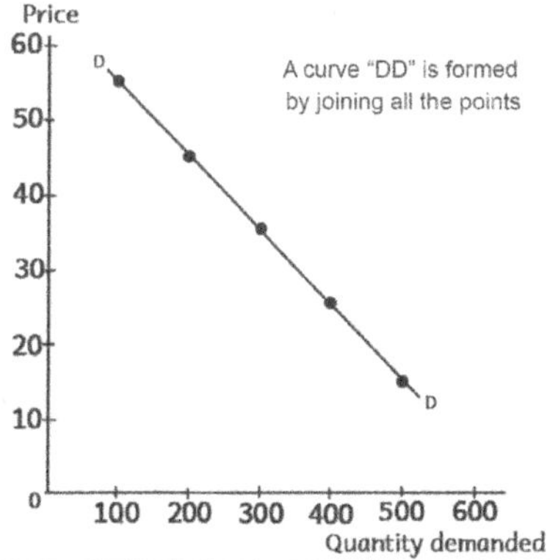

Demand curve for tomatoes

Let us understand with one more example.

Price ($)	Quantity demanded (kg)
5	150
4	225
3	300
2	380
1	460

Demand schedule for burgers in USA

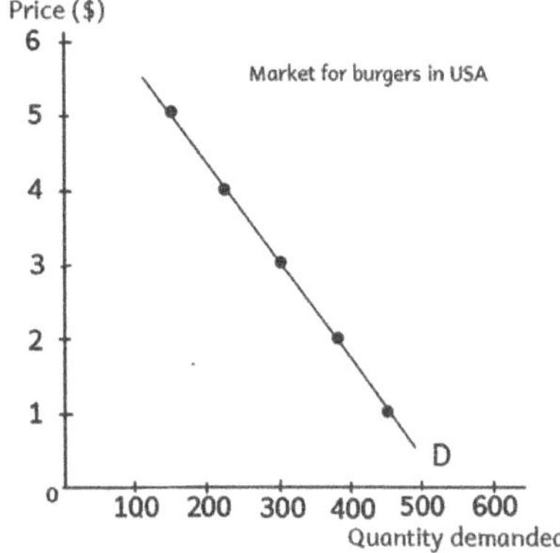

Demand curve for burgers in USA

2.8 Movement along the Demand Curve (Price)

A change in price causes a movement along the curve

- The higher the price of a product, there will be less demand for it.

- If the price rises then demand will fall, this is known as a contraction in demand.

- The lower the price of a product the more it will be demanded.

- If the price falls, then demand will rise, this is known as an extension in demand.

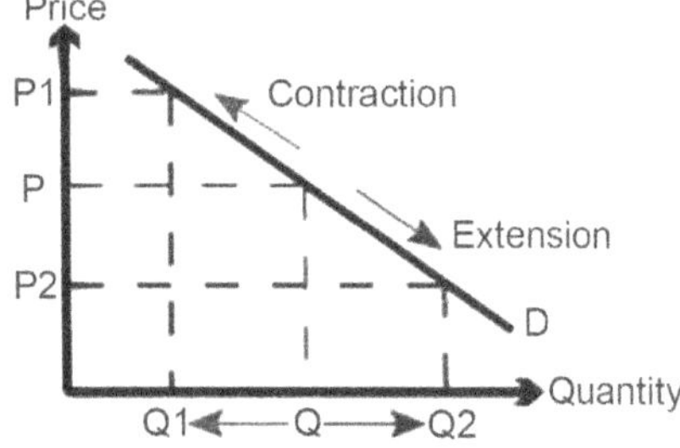

2.9 Shift of the Demand Curve

A shift of the demand curve represents an increase or decrease of demand at a given price level. This may be because of:

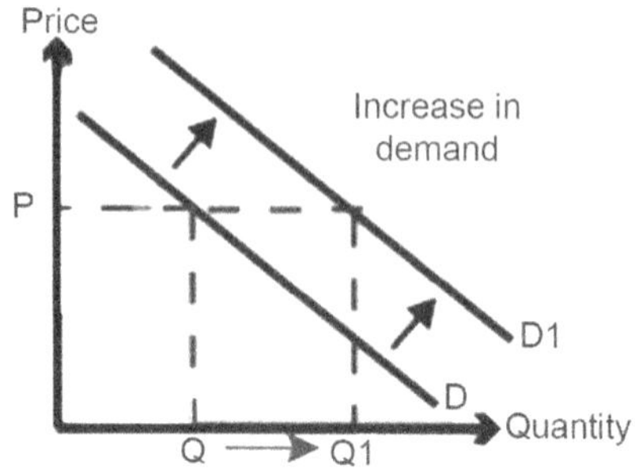

- a change in consumers incomes

- a change in price of competing products

- changes in tastes/fashion

- seasonal factors such as weather

2.10 Price Determination

Market Equilibrium

The equilibrium price is the point at which demand, and supply are equal (where they cross on the diagram). It is also called the *market clearing price* since it is the point at which all the items supplied are demanded - therefor clearing the market of all the stock.

Consumers want low prices & suppliers want higher prices; this leads to adjustments in the price of products until the equilibrium point is reached.

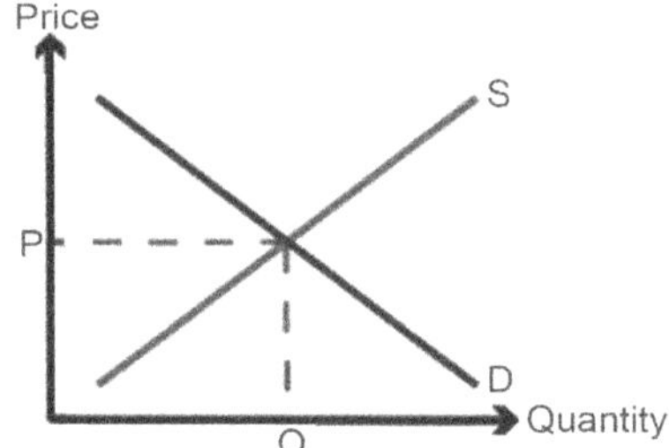

Market Disequilibrium

Disequilibrium price is the price at which market demand and supply curves do not meet, which in this diagram, is any price other than P*.

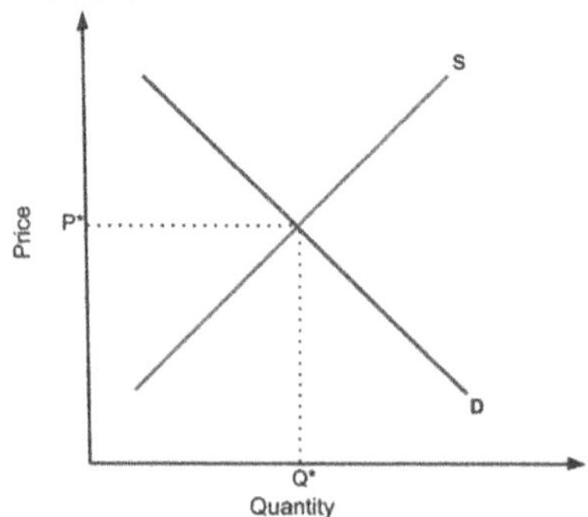

Excess Supply

This situation occurs when the price level is too high which results in a larger quantity supplied than quantity demanded.

Suppliers want to sell the extra stock that they have before it goes bad or out of season so they will lower the price. This leads to an expansion in the quantity demanded and a contraction in the quantity supplied bringing the market back into equilibrium.

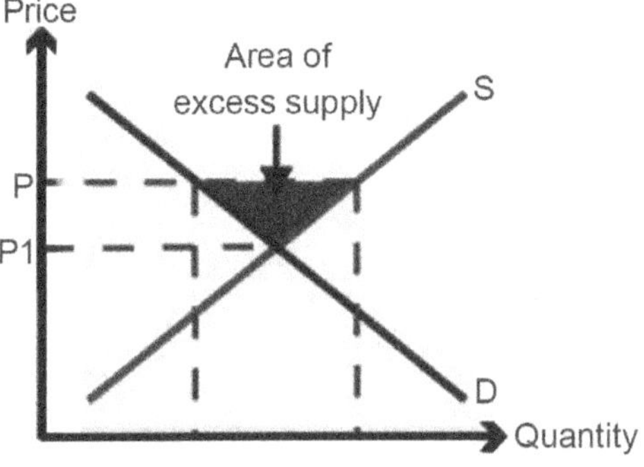

Excess Demand

This occurs when the price is set too low which result in a larger quantity being demanded than there is available from the suppliers.

Suppliers realise that they can charge a higher price and still sell more products, so the price level rises which leads to a contraction in demand (some people won't buy at the higher price) and an extension in supply, bringing the market back into equilibrium.

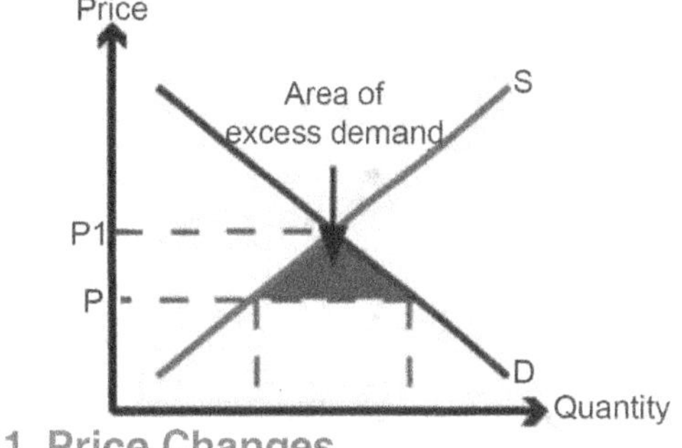

2.11 Price Changes

In most markets, prices are subject to change, whether this be daily, weekly, monthly, or annually. Changing market conditions are the reason for price changes.

Consequences of price changes

Changing market conditions cause prices and sales to change. There are various likely consequences:

- An increase or decrease in demand
- An increase or decrease in supply
- A change in both demand and supply

2.12 A shift in the market demand curve:

▼ **An increase in demand and market price**

An increase in demand for product, because people's income have risen or because the price of a substitute good has gone up, will cause its market demand curve to shift outwards.

In the diagram it shifts from DD to D1D1 as a result, the market price rises from P to P1. The increase in price is a signal to producers to expand or extend the supply for the product from Q1 to Q2 to satisfy the increased quantity consumers want to buy.

The fall in consumer demand will therefore have the opposite effect. Market price will fall, and producers will cut the amount they are willing to supply as their sales and profits fall.

2.13 A shift in the market supply curve:

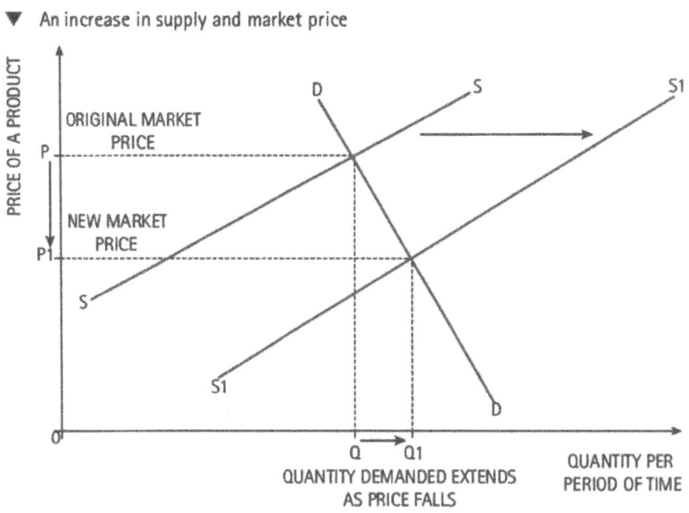

An increase in the amount producers are willing and able to supply of a particular product will cause its market supply curve to shift outwards, from SS to S1S1 in the diagram above. This may occur if there is a fall in the costs of production, for example, due to falling wages or improvements in the speed and accuracy of equipment due to technical progress. As a result of the increase in supply the equilibrium or market price will fall from P to P1. As the market price falls consumers will extend their demand from the product from Q to Q1.

A fall in the supply of a product will cause its market supply curve to shift inverts and market price will rise. Consumer demand for product will contract along the market demand curve as the market price increases until demand equal supply once again.

Changes in demand and supply conditions will result in changes in market price and the allocation of resources to the production of different goods and services. For example, an increase in consumer demand for a product will raise its market price making its production more profitable. As a result, firms will allocate more resources to the production of that product to satisfy the increased consumer demand for it because resources are limited, they will be moved from less profitable products to the production of other profitable products.

2.14 Price Elasticity of Demand (PED)

The PED of a product refers to the responsiveness of the quantity demanded to changes in its price.

$$\text{PED (of a product)} = \frac{\text{\% change in quantity demanded}}{\text{\% change in price}}$$

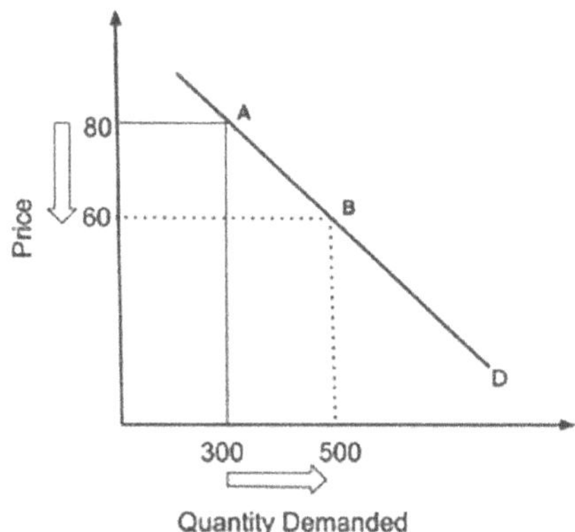

For example, calculate the price elasticity of demand of Coca-Cola from this diagram.

$$\text{PED} = \frac{[(500-300/300)*100]}{[(80-60/80)*100]}$$

$$\text{PED} = \frac{66.67}{25}$$

$$\text{PED} = 2.67$$

In this example, the PED is 2.67, that is, the % change in quantity demanded was higher than the % change in the price. This means, a change in price makes a higher change in quantity demanded. These products have a price elastic demand. Their values are always above 1.

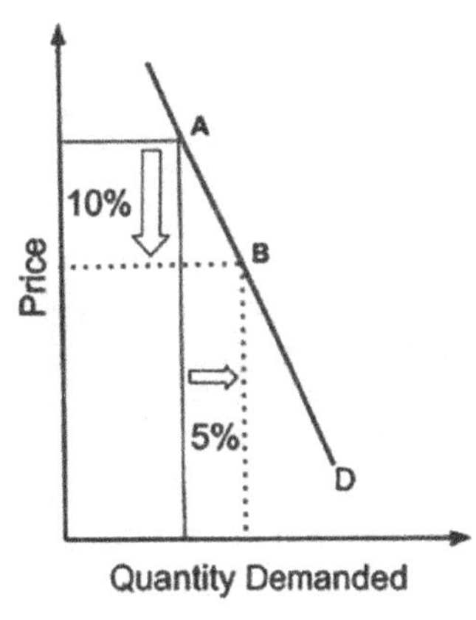

When the % change in quantity demanded is lesser than the % change in price, it is said to have a price inelastic demand. Their values are always below 1. A change in price makes a smaller change in demand.

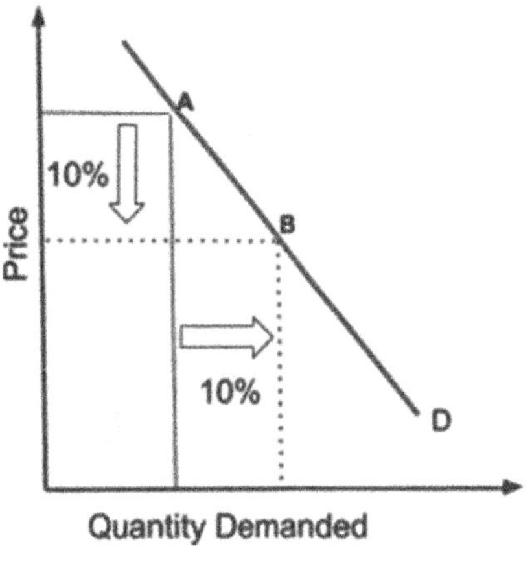

When the % change in demand and price are equal, that is value is 1, it is called unitary price elastic demand.

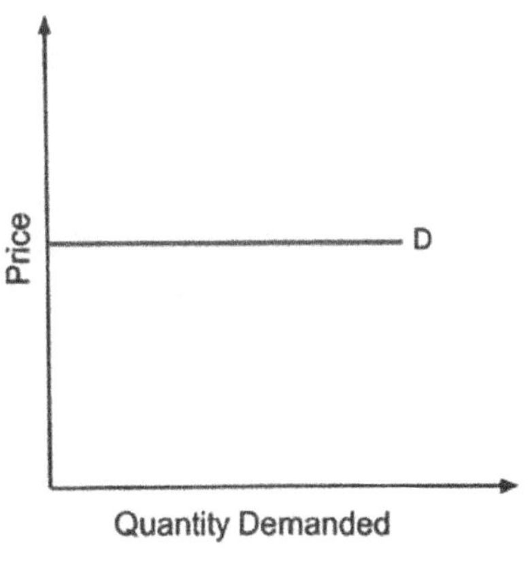

When the quantity demanded changes without any changes in price itself, it is said to have an infinitely price elastic demand. Their values are infinite.

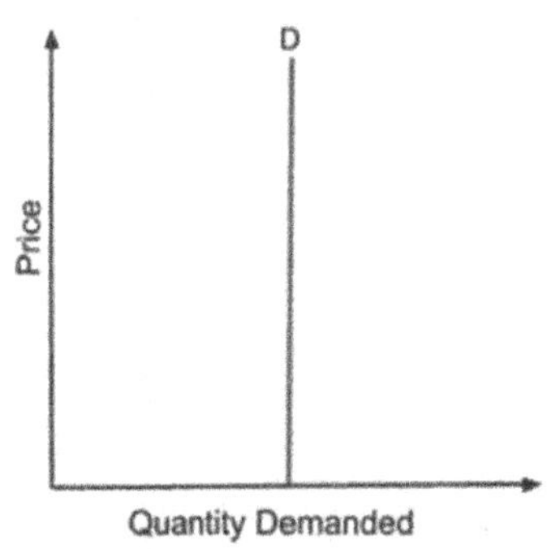

When the price changes have no effect on demand whatsoever, it is said to have a perfect price inelastic demand. Their elasticity is 0.

2.15 Methods of Measurement of Price Elasticity of Demand

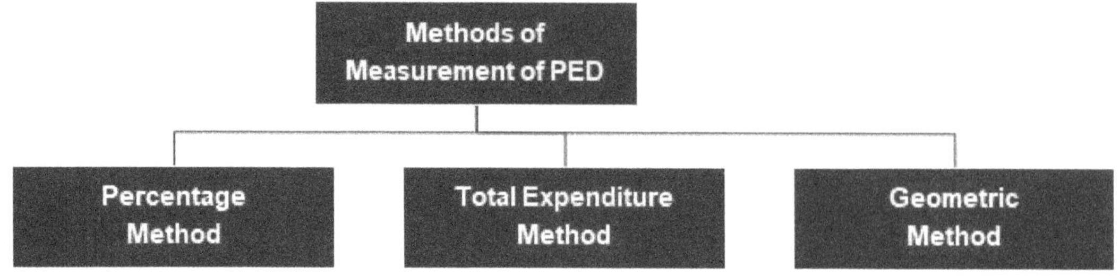

Percentage Method

$$Ep = \frac{\Delta Q}{\Delta P} \times \frac{P}{Q}$$

E_p = Elasticity of Demand

ΔQ = Change in Quantity

ΔP = Change in Price

P = Initial Price

Q + Initial Quantity

OR

$$Ep = \frac{\% \text{ Change In Quantity Demanded of a Commodity}}{\% \text{ Change in Price}}$$

Total Expenditure Method : It measures price elasticity of demand on the basis of change in total expenditure incurred on the commodity by a household due to change in its price.

There are three conditions :

1. E_d=1 When due to rise or fall in price of a good, total expenditure remains unchanged.

2. E_d >1 When due to fall in price, total expenditure goes up and due to rise in price, total expenditure goes down.

3. E_d <1 when due to fall in price, total expenditure goes down and due to rise in price, total expenditure goes up.

Geometric Method : Elasticity of demand at any point is measured by dividing the length of lower segment of the demand curve with the length of upper segment of demand curve at that point.

The value of ed is unity at midpoint of any linear demand curve.

Diagram to show Geometric or point method

Elasticity of demand at given point.

$$Ed = \frac{\text{Lower segment of the demand curve}}{\text{Upper segment of the demand curve}}$$

D is midpoint of the demand curve.

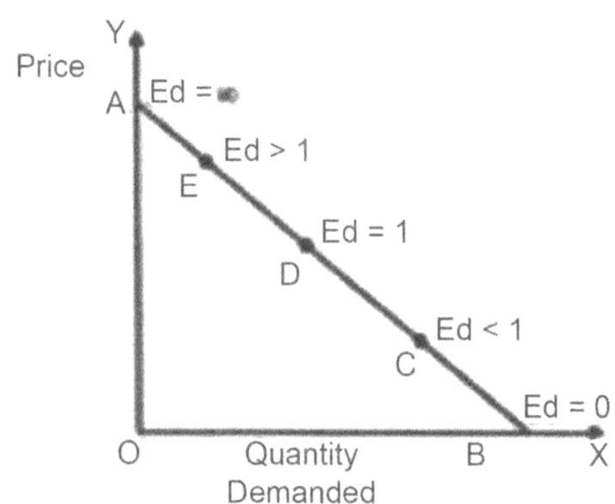

Diagram of total Expenditure Method

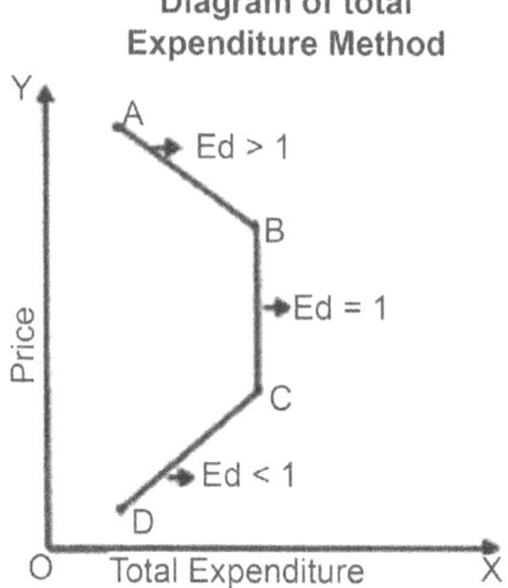

2.16 Factors influencing Price elasticity of Demand

1.   Nature of the Commodity.

2.   Availability of Substitute goods.

3.   Income level of the consumer.

4.   Price level of the commodity.

5.   Time Period.

6.   Different use of the commodity.

7.   Behaviour of the consumer spending .

8.   Postponement of consumption.

2.17 Relationship between PED and revenue and how it is helpful to producers

Producers can calculate the PED of their product and take a suitable action to make the product more profitable.

Revenue is the amount of money a producer/firm generates from sales, i.e., the total number of units sold multiplied by the price per unit. So, as the price or the quantity sold changes, those changes have a direct effect on revenue.

If the product is found to have an elastic demand, the producer can lower prices to increase revenue. The law of demand states that a price fall increases the demand. And since it is an elastic product (change in demand is higher than change in price), the demand of the product will increase highly. The producers get more revenue.

If the product is found to have an inelastic demand, the producer can raise prices to increase revenue. Since quantity demanded wouldn't fall much as it is inelastic, the high prices will make way for higher revenue and thus higher profits.

2.18 The Price Mechanism in a Market Economic System

In a market economic system, consumers and producers signal their preferences through the price mechanism. Government intervention is minimal. The price mechanism works automatically whereby prices are determined by the interaction of demand and supply.

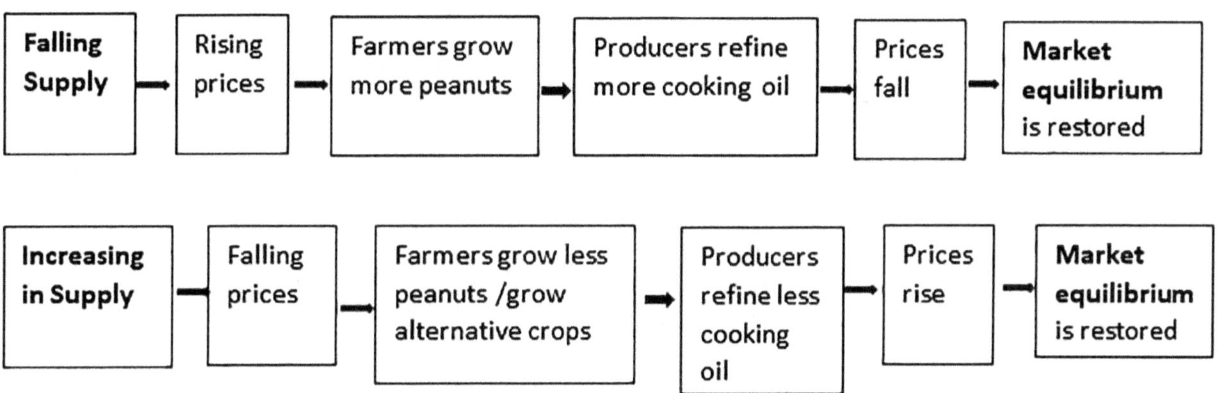

Price mechanism at work in a market economy

Key Statements

Utility: is the power or capacity of a commodity to satisfy human ones. Utility of a commodity means the amount of satisfaction that the person gets from the consumption of a good or service.

Cardinal Utility: It states that the satisfaction the consumer derives by consuming goods and services can be measured with a number.

Ordinal Utility: It uses a ranking system in which a rank is provided to the satisfaction that is derived from the consumption.

Total Utility: It is the total psychological satisfaction of consumer obtains from consuming a given amount of a particular good

Marginal Utility: It is an additional utility derived from consumption of an additional unit of a commodity

Law of Diminishing Marginal Utility: It states that marginal utility derived from the consumption of a commodity declines as more units of that commodity are consumed.

Consumers Equilibrium: It refers to a situation where a consumer gets maximum satisfaction out of his given money income and given market price.

Marginal Rate of Substitution: It is the rate at which a consumer is willing to sacrifice one commodity for an extra unit of another commodity without affecting his total satisfaction.

Demand: the willingness and ability to buy a product.

Supply: the willingness and ability to sell a product.

Giffen Goods: are a special category of inferior goods in which demand for a commodity falls with a fall in its price. In case of certain inferior goods when their prices fall, that demand may not rise because extra purchasing power caused by falling prices diverted on the purchase of superior goods. Example: from purchase of Low Quality Rice to purchase of superior quality Rice(Basmati)

Substitute Goods: are those goods which can be used in place of another goods and give the same satisfaction to a consumer. Example: soaps of different brands

Complementary Goods: Add those which are useless in the absence of other good and which are demanded jointly. Example: coffee, milk and sugar to make coffee

Market equilibrium: a situation where demand is supply or equal at the current price.

Market disequilibrium: a situation where demand and supply are not equal at the current price.

Market is any set of arrangement that brings together all the producers and consumers of a good or service, so they may engage in exchange. Example: a market for soft drinks.

Goods and services are bought and sold in a market at an equilibrium price where demand and supply are equal. This is called the price mechanism. It helps answer the three basic economic questions. Producers will produce the good that consumers demand the most, it will be produced in a way that is cost-efficient and will be produced for those who are willing and able to buy the product.

Social Costs: When considering the cost of production or offering a service we need to take into account more than just the cost to the company. There are wider costs that affect society such as air pollution that are not accounted for on the price.

Private costs: these are the costs to individuals of consuming a product, often the monetary value, but sometimes a health cost such as smoking. They are also the costs to a firm (fixed and variable costs) of production.

Private benefits: the benefit to an individual from consuming a product, often satisfaction, more knowledge etc. In the case of a firm these are likely to be the profits that are made.

External costs: the costs of production or consumption of an item to a third party - litter, air pollution, water pollution are examples, these are often called externalities.

External benefits: the benefits of production or consumption to a third party - other firms & society may benefit from the skills that workers learn through their jobs such as first aid, it skills etc.

Exercise

Frequently asked Questions (FAQ's)

1. What is the difference between law of diminishing marginal utility and consumer's equilibrium?
2. Which curve shows the various combinations of two products that give the same amount of satisfaction to the consumer?
3. What does equilibrium mean?
4. State the law of Equi-Marginal Utility.
5. Is the demand for the following elastic, moderate elastic, inelastic? Give reason.

   1. Demand for petrol

   2. Demand for textbooks

   3. Demand for cars

   4. Demand for milk
6. How is total utility derived from the marginal utility?

Multiple Choice Questions (MCQ's)

1. Which utility is added to the total utility by consuming one additional unit of the commodity?
   (a) Ordinal Utility   (b) Total Utility
   (c) Marginal Utility (d) Average Utility
2. Which of the following statements regarding utility is not true?
   (a) It is the want satisfying power of the commodity
   (b) Utility is measurable
   (c) It helps a consumer to make choices
   (d) It is purely a subjective entity

3. Which of the following utility approaches is based on the theory of Alfred Marshall?
   (a) Ordinal utility approach
   (b) Cardinal utility approach
   (c) Independent utility approach
   (d) None of the above
4. The condition in which market supply matches market demand is called:
   (a) Equalisation
   (b) Normalisation
   (c) Equilibrium
   (d) None of the above
5. Zero Price Elasticity of demand means:
   (a) whatever the change in price, there is absolutely no change in demand
   (b) for a small change in price, there is a small change in demand
   (c) for a small change in price, there is a large change in demand
   (d) for a large change in price, there is a small change in demand
6. What is the law that defines the demand curve to slope downward known as?
   (a) Diminishing Marginal Utility
   (b) Utility Maximisation
   (c) Utility Minimisation
   (d) Consumer Equilibrium

7. Which of the following is the basis of diminishing marginal utility?
   (*a*) Law of Demand   (*b*) Laws Of Return
   (*c*) Law Of Supply   (*d*) None of the above

8. A consumer is in equilibrium when the marginal utilities are ___________ .
   (*a*) Increasing   (*b*) Equal
   (*c*) Minimum   (*d*) Highest

9. Why is a consumer's spending restricted?
   (*a*) Due to the utility maximisation
   (*b*) Due to the budget constraint
   (*c*) Due to the demand curve
   (*d*) Due to the marginal utility

10. When MU is positive, what happens to TU?
    (*a*) It decreases.
    (*b*) It becomes the highest.
    (*c*) It remains constant.
    (*d*) It increases.

11. If $MU_x > P_x$, the consumer ________________
    (*a*) Reaches the equilibrium
    (*b*) Starts incurring losses
    (*c*) Consumes more of X
    (*d*) Stops consuming X

12. Consumer gets maximum satisfaction when the ___________ are the same.
    (*a*) Total utility and marginal utility
    (*b*) Prices of commodity and marginal utility
    (*c*) Price of commodity and total utility
    (*d*) Both (*a*) and (*b*)

13. Utility is generally related to?
    (*a*) Satisfaction   (*b*) Necessary
    (*c*) Useless   (*d*) Useful

14. Which of the following must be true when the marginal is negative?
    (*a*) The average is positive.
    (*b*) The average is negative.
    (*c*) The total is decreasing.
    (*d*) The total is negative.

15. What is the law that defines the demand curve to slope downward known as?
    (*a*) Diminishing Marginal Utility
    (*b*) Utility Maximisation
    (*c*) Utility Minimisation
    (*d*) Consumer Equilibrium

16. What does the term 'marginal' in economics mean?
    (*a*) Additional   (*b*) Unimportant
    (*c*) Minimum unit   (*d*) None of the above

17. Consumer's behaviour is studied in:
    (*a*) Microeconomics (*b*) Macroeconomics
    (*c*) Income Analysis (*d*) None of these

18. Which of the following is a characteristic of utility ?
    (*a*) Utility is a psychological phenomenon
    (*b*) Utility is subjective
    (*c*) Utility is a relative concept
    (*d*) All of the above

19. Elastic demand is shown by:
    (*a*) $\dfrac{\Delta Q}{Q} > \dfrac{\Delta P}{P}$ (*b*) $\dfrac{\Delta P}{P} > \dfrac{\Delta Q}{Q}$
    (*c*) $\dfrac{\Delta P}{P} = \dfrac{\Delta Q}{Q}$ (*d*) None of the above

20. Slope of budget line or price line is:
    (*a*) $-\dfrac{Px}{Py}$ (*b*) $-\dfrac{Py}{Px}$
    (*c*) $+\dfrac{Px}{Py}$ (*d*) $+\dfrac{Py}{Px}$

21. Utility can be measured by:
    (*a*) Money
    (*b*) Exchange of goods
    (*c*) Weight of the good
    (*d*) None of these

22. With a rise in price the demand for 'Giffin' goods:
    (*a*) increases   (*b*) decreases
    (*c*) remains constant (*d*) becomes unstable

23. Which of the following is a formula for measuring the elasticity of demand ?
    (*a*) $\dfrac{\text{Proportionate Change in Demand}}{\text{Propotionate Change in Price}}$
    (*b*) $\dfrac{\text{Proportionate Change in Price}}{\text{Proportionate Change in Demand}}$
    (*c*) $\dfrac{\text{Percentage Change in Demand}}{\text{Percentage Change in Price}}$
    (*d*) $\dfrac{\text{Percentage Change in Price}}{\text{Percentage Change in Demand}}$

24. Following figure shows:

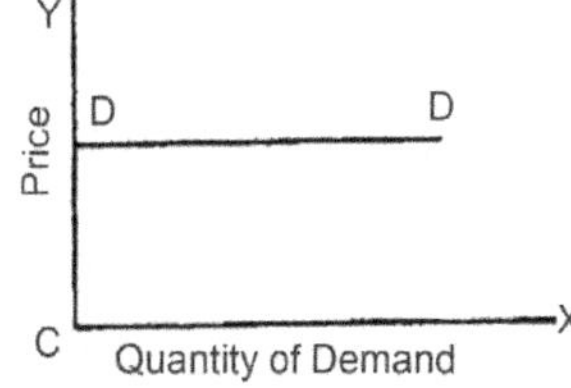

    (*a*) High Elastic Demand
    (*b*) Perfectly Elastic Demand
    (*c*) Perfectly Inelastic Demand
    (*d*) Inelastic Demand

🔑 Solutions

Frequently asked Questions (FAQ's)

1. Law of Diminishing Marginal Utility states that as we consume more and more units of a common the utility derived from each successive unit goes on decreasing. • Consumer's Equilibrium refers to the situation when a consumer is having maximum satisfaction his limited income and has no tendency to change his existing way of expenditure.

2. Indifference Curve

3. Equilibrium means the state of maximum satisfaction.

4. The law of Equi-Marginal Utility refers to a balanced position where a consumer distributes his income between different goods in such a way that the value derived from the last rupees is the same as the first one.

5. (1) The demand for petrol is moderately elastic as when the cost of petrol rises, the customers will decrease the use of it.

   (2) The demand for textbooks is inelastic because even if the price rises the demand will never change.

   (3) The demand for cars is elastic as it is a luxury good so when the price of a car goes up, the demand for it comes down

   (4) The demand for milk is elastic because when the price of the milk increases the consumer starts taking less quantity of milk.

6. The total utility is the total sum of marginal utilities of different units of goods.

   TUn = MU1+MU2+MU3+ _ _ _ _ _ _ MUn

Multiple Choice Questions (MCQ's)

1. (c) Marginal Utility

2. (b) Utility is measurable

3. (b) Cardinal utility approach.

4. **(c)** Equilibrium

5. (a) whatever the change in price, there is absolutely no change in demand

6.

7. (a) Law of Demand

8. (b) Equal

8. (b) Due to the budget constraint

10. (d) It increases.

11. (c) Consumes more of X

12. (b). Price of commodity and marginal utility

13. (a) Satisfaction

14. (c) The total is decreasing.

15. (a) Diminishing Marginal Utility

16. (a) Additional

17. (a) Microeconomics

18. (d) All of the above

19. (a) $\dfrac{\Delta Q}{Q} > \dfrac{\Delta P}{P}$

20. (a) $-\dfrac{Px}{Py}$

21. (a) Money

22. (a) increases

23. (c) $\dfrac{\text{Percentage Change in Demand}}{\text{Percentage Change in Price}}$

24. (b) Perfectly Elastic Demand

Introduction to Macroeconomics

Chief concepts of this chapter –

Macroeconomics – It deals with the aggregate economic variables of the economy.

3.1 Emergence of Macroeconomics

Macroeconomics deals with the overall economy of the market and other systems on a large scale.

3.1.1 Macroeconomics is the part of economic theory that studies the economy as a whole, such as national income, aggregate employment, general price level, aggregate consumption, aggregate investment, etc. Its main instruments are aggregate demand and aggregate supply. It is also called the 'Income Theory' or 'Employment Theory'.

3.1.2 Scope/Subject Matter of Macroeconomics – It is the study of aggregates of the economy. Its study includes:

i) Theory of Employment

ii) Theory of National Income determination

iii) Theory of Money

iv) Theory of International Trade

3.1.3 Importance of Macroeconomics:

i) It helps in government policy formulation.

ii) It facilitates international comparison.

iii) It helps in understanding the distribution of income among different groups of people.

iv) It has special significance in studying monetary problems that affect the economy.

3.1.4 Understanding in what way Macroeconomics differs from Microeconomics:

	Microeconomics		Macroeconomics
1.	It studies the individual unit.	1.	It studies the whole economy or large groups.
2.	Laws related to Marginal analysis are included in its scope.	2.	Problems related to whole economy like employment, public finance, national income etc. are included in its scope.
3.	Microeconomics provides the information relating to the individual prices, individual consumption and production.	3.	Macroeconomics provides the information relating to National Income, total output, total consumption and general price level.
4.	Microeconomics analysis is simple.	4.	Macroeconomics is complex due to the study of large groups.
5.	Microeconomics particularly focus on price analysis.	5.	Macroeconomics particularly focus on income analysis.
6.	Microeconomics studies individual problems and it is less important for comparative study.	6.	Macroeconomics studies the problems relating to the economy and its importance is growing.

3.1.5 Important Terms Related to Macroeconomics:

i) Final Goods

The goods which have crossed the boundary line of production and are ready for use by their final users are known as final goods. Example, clothes, milk, consumed by a consumer et cetera. Expenditure on these goods is referred to as final expenditure.

Final goods are often classified as:

(a) Final Consumer Goods: These are the goods which are consumed by the consumers like milk, bread, etc

(b) Final producer goods: These are the goods which are consumed or used by the producers like machinery, equipment, et cetera.

ii) Intermediate Goods

The goods but she's by your phone for the use in production of other goods or for the purpose of reselling, are known as intermediate goods. Example, Steel used in the production of cars or Wheat purchased by baker of a bakery who sells bread and buns. Expenditure on these goods is referred to as intermediate expenditure.

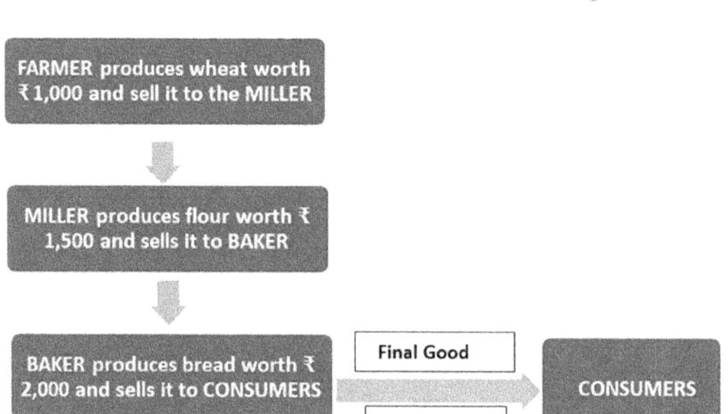

Points of differentiation between Final Goods and Intermediate Goods:

S.No.	Products	Final Goods		Intermediate Goods
		Consumption Goods	**Capital Goods**	
1.	Car	If purchased by a consumer household.	If purchased by a taxi-driver as a taxi.	If purchased by a government for military use. Or If purchased by a car dealer for resale.
2.	Refrigerator	If purchased by a consumer household.	If purchased by a shopkeeper for selling cold drinks.	If purchased by a government for military purpose.
3.	Aeroplanes, Helicopter and Sub-marines		If purchased by air and sea transport companies.	If purchased by a government for military purpose.
4.	Paper, Pens, Pencils, Wheat, Sugar	If used by a consumer household.	If lying unsold with a trader at the end of a year.	If used by producing enterprises (including the government) Or If purchased by producing enterprises (including government) for resale.
5.	Services of Doctors, Lawyers, Teachers.	If used by a consumer household.		If used by the enterprises and government for the production of goods and services.

iii) Consumer Goods

Goods which are directly used for satisfaction of human wants and which are not used in production are known as consumer goods. Example, ice cream and milk used by the households.

Consumer goods are further classified into:

(a) **Durable goods:** these are those goods which can be used several number of times for a considerable period of time. Example, these goods have certain life span like car, AC et cetera.

(b) **Semi-durable goods:** these are those goods which do not have very long-life span, but still, they do not get exhausted in a single use either. Example, crockery, clothing, et cetera.

(c) **Non-durable goods:** these are the goods which have a very short life span and mostly get exhausted in a single use. Example milk, vegetables, et cetera.

(d) **Services:** it refers to the intangible items which cannot be seen however it can be felt. Example, services of a doctor, teacher, et cetera.

iv) Capital Goods

These goods are repeatedly used in the process of production. They are the fixed assets of the producer. Example, building, plant and machinery et cetera. They help to convert intermediate goods into final goods.

v) Investment

It is the process of capital formation by a firm or increase in the existing capital stock.

Investment can be classified as:

(a) **Gross investment:** Gross investment of an economy constitutes that part of an economy constitutes that part of final output that comprises of capital goods. i.e., expenditure on fixed assets or on inventory stock. Symbolically,

Gross investment = Expenditure on the Purchase of Fixed Asset in an Accounting Year + Expenditure on Inventory Stock in an Accounting Year.

(b) **Net investment:** It is the net increase in stock of capital, adjusted against depreciation, during an accounting year. It is also termed as new capital formation. Symbolically,

Net investment = Gross investment - Depreciation

Components of investments are

(a) **Fixed investment:** In a specific time period (generally in an accounting year), the increase in the stock of fixed assets of the producers is termed as fixed investment.

(b) **Inventory investment:** During a specific time period (generally an accounting year), the change in inventory stock, i.e., the sum of unsold goods, semi-finished goods and raw materials is termed as inventory investment. It is also called as change in stock and calculated as,

Change in stock = Closing stock – Opening Stock

vi) Depreciation

It is the loss or fall in value of fixed assets in use on account of normal wear and tear, normal rate of accidental damage is unexpected or foreseen absolute obsolescence. Depreciation is also called consumption of fixed capital.

vii) Depreciation Reserve Fund

It is a font created by the producers to meet the upcoming depreciations losses in the process of production.

viii) Inventory

It is termed as a stock of unsold finished goods, semi-finished goods (goods which are in the process of production) and raw materials, Witcher form carries from one year to the next year.

ix) Stock

It can be defined as any quantity measured at a particular point of time. Example, number of machines in a plant on 31st March, amount in the bank account on 20th November

x) Flow

These are defined as any quantity measured boy unit at a particular period of time. Example, income or expenditure over a period of one month or one year.

3.1.6 Structure of Macroeconomy: As we know, Macroeconomics is concerned with economic problems at the level of an economy as a whole. Structure of Macroeconomics implies study of different sectors of the economy.

An economy may be divided into different sectors depending on the nature of study.

(a) Producer sector engaged in the production of goods and services.

(b) Household sector engaged in the consumption of goods and services.

Note: Households are taken as the owners of factors of production.

(c) The government sector engaged in activities like taxation and subsidies

(d) Rest of the world sector engaged in exports and imports.

(e) Financial sector (or financial system) engaged in the activity of borrowing and lending.

3.2 Circular flow of income

It refers to flow of money, income or the flow of goods and services across different sectors of the economy in a circular form.

There are two types of Circular flow:

(a) Real/Product/Physical Flow

(b) Money/Monetary/Nominal Flow

(a) Real flow

(i) Real flow of income implies the flow of factor services from the household sector to the producing sector and corresponding flow of goods and services from the producing sector to the household sector.

(ii) Let us consider a simple economy consisting only of 2 sectors:

- Producer Sector.
- Household Sector.

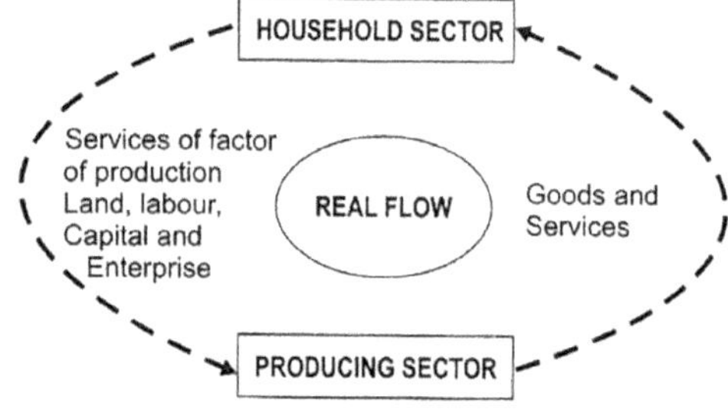

(iii) These two sectors are dependent on each other in the following ways:

- Producers supply goods and services to the households.
- Household (as the owners of factors of production) supplies factors of production (or factor services) to the producers.

This interdependence can be explained with the help of the diagram given here.

(b) Money Flow

(i) Money flow refers to the flow of factor income, as rent, interest, profit and wages from the producing sector to the household sector as monetary rewards for their factor services as shown in the flowchart.

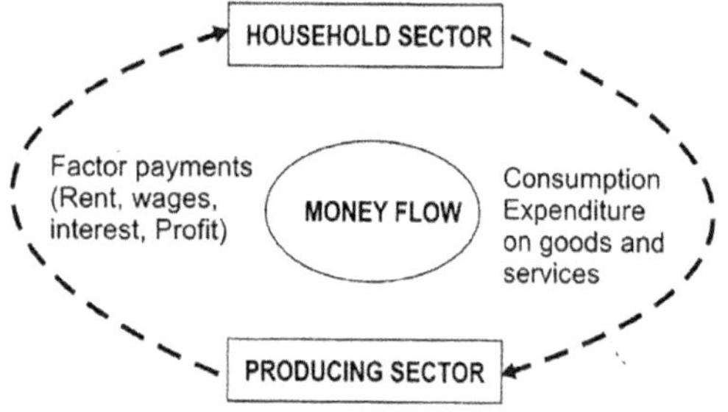

(ii) The households spend their incomes on the goods and services produced by the producing sector. Accordingly, money flows back to the producing sector as household expenditure as shown in the flowchart.

Circular Flow Of Income in Two Sector Model:

The following assumptions with regard to a simple economy with only two sector of economics activity are:

(i) There are only two sectors in the economy; that is, household and firms.

(ii) Household supply factor services to firms.

(iii) Firms hire factor services from Households.

(iv) Households spend their entire income on consumption.

(v) Firms sell all that is produced to the households.

(vi) There is no government or foreign trade.

Such an economy described above has two types of markets.

(i) Market for goods and services, that is product market.

(ii) Market for factors of production, factor market.

As a result we can derive the following, in the case of our simple economy:

(i) Total production of goods and services by firms = Total consumption of goods and services by Household Sector.

(ii) Factor Payments by Firms = Factor Incomes of Household Sector.

(iii) Consumption expenditure of Household sector = Income of Firm.

(iv) Hence, Real flows of production and consumption of Firms and households = Money flows of income and expenditure of Firms and Households.

Phases Of Circular Flow:

There are three types of phases of Circular flow.

(i) **Production Phase:**
- It deals with the production of goods and services by the producer sector.
- If we study it in term of the quantity of goods and services produced, it is a Real Flow. But, it is a Money flow, if we study it in terms of the market value of the goods produced.

(ii) **Distribution Phase:** It means the flow of income in the form of rent, interest, profit and wages, paid by producer sector to the household sector. It is a Money Flow.

(iii) Disposition Phase:

- Disposition means expenditure made. This phase deals with expenditure on the purchase of goods and services by households and other sectors.

- This is a Money Flow from other sectors to the producer sector. These phases are illustrated in the figure given here.

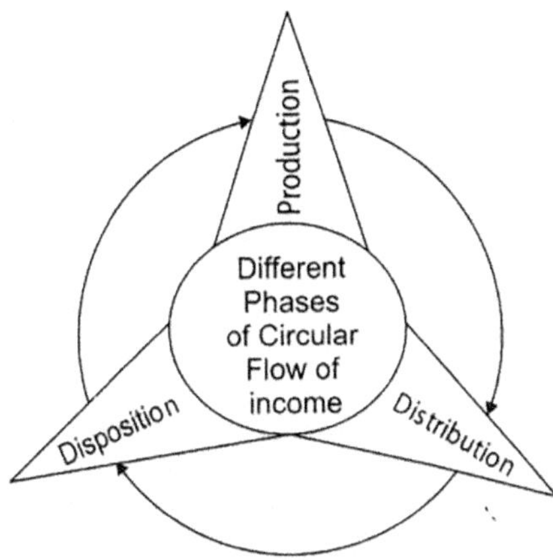

3.3 Some Basic Concepts Of Macroeconomics

1. Factor Income

(a) Income earned by factor of production by rendering their productive services in the production process is known as Factor Income.

(b) It is a bilateral Two–Sided Concept.

(c) It is included in National Income as it contributes something in the flow of goods and services.

Examples: Rent, interest, wages and profit.

2. Transfer Income

(a) Income received without rendering any productive services is known as transfer income.

(b) It is a unilateral one–sided concept.

(c) It is not included in National Income as it does not contribute anything in the flow of goods and services.

Examples: Old Age Pension, Scholarship, Unemployment allowance.

There are two types of transfers:

(i) Current transfers

(ii) Capital transfers

(i) Current Transfers

- Transfers made from the income of the payer and added to the income of the recipient (who receive) for consumption expenditure are called current transfers.

- It is recurring or regular in nature.

  For example, scholarships, gifts, old age pension, etc.

(ii) Capital Transfers

- Capital transfers are defined as transfers in cash and in kind for the purpose of investment to recipients, made out of the wealth or saving of the donor.

- It is non recurring or irregular in nature.

  For example, investment grant, capital gains tax, war damages, etc.

3. Economic territory or Domestic Territory

(a) According to the United Nations, economic territory is the geographical territory administered by a government within which persons, goods and capital circulate freely.

(b) The above definition is based on the criterion "freedom of circulation of persons, goods and capital". Clearly, those parts of the political frontiers (or boundaries) of a country where the government of that country does not enjoy the above "freedom" are not to be included in economic territory of that country.

(i) One example is embassies. Government of India does not enjoy the above freedom in the foreign embassies located within India. So, these are not treated as a part of economic territory of India. They are treated as part of the economic territories of their respective countries. For example the U.S. embassy in India is a part of economic territory of the U.S.A. Similarly, the Indian embassy in Washington is a part of economic territory of India.

(ii) International organizations like UNO, WHO, etc. located within the geographical boundaries of a country.

(iii) In layman terms, the domestic territory of a nation is understood to be the territory lying within the political frontiers (or boundaries) of a country. But in national income accounting, the term domestic territory is used in a wider sense. Based on 'freedom' criterion, the scope of economic territory is defined to cover:

- Ships and aircrafts owned and operated by normal residents between two or more countries. For example, Indian Ships moving between china and India regularly are part of domestic territory of India. Similarly, planes operated by Air India between Russia and Japan are part of the domestic territory of India. Similarly, planes operated by Malaysian Airlines between India and Japan are a part of the domestic territory of Malaysia.

- Fishing vessels, oil and natural gas rigs and floating platforms operated by the residents of a country in the international waters where they have exclusive rights of operation. For example, Fishing boats operated by Indian fishermen in international waters of Indian Ocean will be considered a part of domestic territory of India.

- Embassies, consulates and military establishments of a country located abroad. For example, Indian Embassy in Russia is a part of the domestic territory of India. 'Consulate' is an office or building used by consul (an officer commissioned by the government to reside in a foreign country to promote the interest of the country to which he belongs).

4. Citizenship

(a) Citizenship is basically a legal concept based on the place of birth of the person or some legal provisions allowing a person to become a citizen.

(b) It means, Indian citizenship can arise in two ways:
  (i) When a person is born in India, he acquires automatic citizenship of India.
  (ii) A person born outside India applies for citizenship and Indian Law allows him to become Indian Citizen.

5. Normal Resident/Resident

(a) A Normal resident, whether a person or an institution, is one whose centre of economic interest lies in the economic territory of the country in which he lives.

(b) The centre of economic interest implies in two things:
  (i) The resident lives or is located within the economic territory for more than one year and
  (ii) The resident carries out the basic economic activities of earnings, spending and accumulation from that location

(c) There is a difference between the terms normal resident (resident) and citizen (or national).
  (i) A person becomes a national of a countiy because he was born in the country or on the basis of some other legal criterion.
  (ii) A person is treated resident of a country on the basis of economic criterion.
  (iii) It is not necessary that a resident must also be the national of that country. Even foreigners can be the residents if they pass the above stated economic criterion.

  For example, a large number of Indian nationals have settled in U.S.A., England, Australia, etc. as residents (and not as nationals) of these countries. For India, they are Non-resident Indians (NRI) but continue to remain Indian nationals.

Following are not included under the category of Normal residents:

(i) Foreign visitors in the country for such purposes as recreation, holidays, medical treatment, study tours, conferences, sports events, business etc. (they are supposed to stay in the host country for less than one year. In case they continue to stay for one year or more in the host country, they will be treated as normal residents of the host country).

(ii) Crew members of foreign vessels, commercial travellers and seasonal workers in , the country (Foreign workers who work part of the year in the country in response to the varying seasonal demand for labour and return to their households and border workers who regularly cross the frontier each day or somewhat less regularly, (i.e. each week) to work in the neighbouring country are the normal residents of their own countries. Example: Nepal.

(iii) Officials, diplomats, and members of the armed forces of a foreign country.

(iv) International bodies like World Bank, World Health Organisation or International Monetary Fund are not considered residents of the country in which these organisations operate but are treated as residents of international territory. However, the staffs of these bodies are treated as normal residents of the country in which the international body operates. For example, international body like World Health Organisation located in India is not normal resident of India but Americans working in its office for more than a year will be treated as normal residents of India.

(v) Foreigners who are the employees of non-resident enterprises and who have come to the country for purposes of installing machinery or equipment purchased from their employers. (They are supposed to stay for less than one year. In case they continue to stay for one year or more, they will be treated as normal residents of the host country).

Key Statements

Circular flow of income: It refers to flow of money income or the flow of goods and services across different sectors of the economy in a circular form.

Money flow (nominal flow): Money flow refers to the flow of factor income, as rent, interest, profit and wages from the producing sector to the household sector as monetary rewards for their factor services.

Real flow or physical flow: Real flow of income implies the flow of factor services from the household sector to the producing sector and corresponding flow of goods and services from the producing sector to the household sector.

Factor income: Income earned by factor of production by rendering their productive services in the production process is known as Factor Income.

Transfer income: Income received without rendering any productive services is known as Transfer Income.

Current transfers: Transfers made from the current income of the payer and added to the current income of the recipient (who receive) for consumption expenditure are called current transfers.

Capital transfers: Capital transfers are defined as transfers in cash and in kind for the purpose of investment to recipient made out of the wealth or saving of a donor.

Final goods: These are those which are used for:

(a) Personal consumption (like bread purchased by consumer household), or

(b) Investment or capital formation (like building, machinery purchased by a firm)

Intermediate goods: These are those, which are used for:

(a) Further processing (like sugar used for making sweets), or

(b) Resale in the same year (If car purchased by a car dealer for resale).

Consumption goods: Consumption goods are those goods which satisfy the wants of consumers directly.

Capital goods: Capital goods are defined as all goods produced for use in future productive processes.

Economics Agents: By economic units or economic agents, we mean those individuals or institutions which take economic decisions. They can be -

Consumers who decide what and how much to consume.

Producers of goods and services who decide what and how much to produce.

Entities like the government, corporation, banks which take decisions like how much to spend, what interest rate to charge on credits, how much to tax, etc.

Few Facts about emergence of Microeconomics and Macroeconomics:

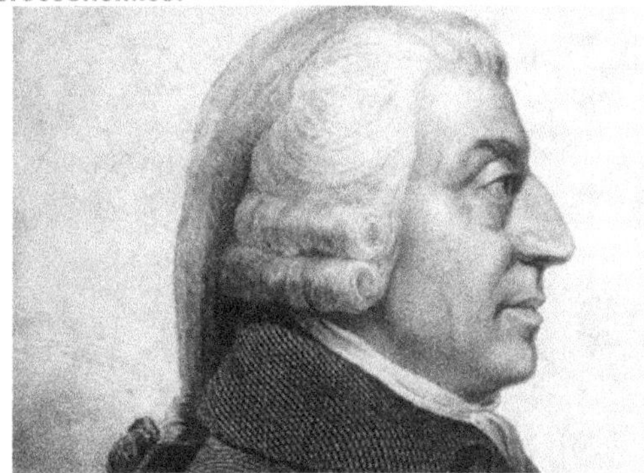

ADAM SMITH : 1723 – 17901

Adam Smith – Is regarded as the founding father of modern economics (it was known as political economy at that time). He was a Scotsman and a professor at the University of Glasgow. Philosopher by training, his well-known work *An Enquiry into the Nature and Cause of the Wealth of Nations* (1776) is regarded as the first major comprehensive book on the subject. The Physiocrats of France but prominent thinkers of political economy before Smith Adam Smith, had suggested that is the buyers and sellers in each market take the decisions following only their self-interest, economists will not need to think of the wealth and welfare of the country as a whole separately. But economists gradually discovered that they had to look further

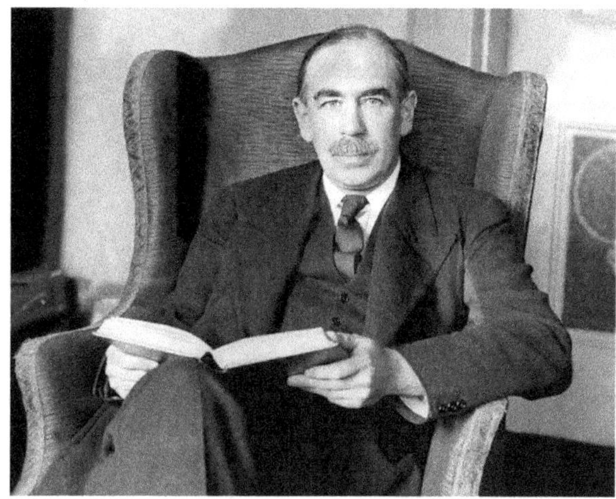

JOHN MAYNARD KEYNES : 1883 – 1946

John Maynard Keynes- macroeconomics, emerged as a separate branch of economics, after the British economist John Maynard Keynes published his celebrated book in 1936. The dominant thinking in economics before Keynes was that all the labourers who are ready to work will find employment and all the factories will be working at their full capacity. This school of thought is known as the classical tradition

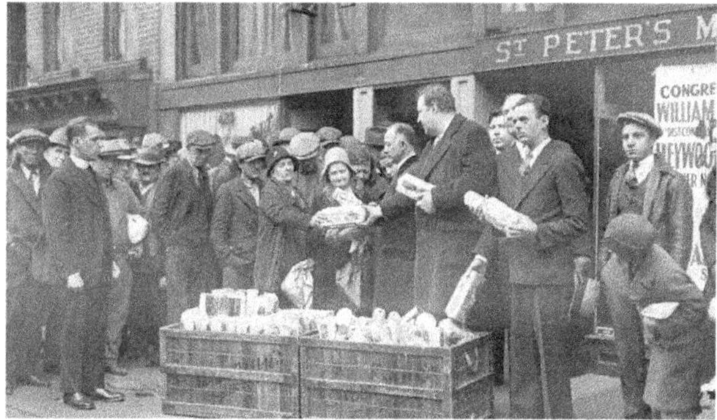

GREAT DEPRESSION: Started in 1929 and lasted until late 1930s

The Great Depression 1929- The Great Depression of 1929 was one of the worst economic depressions in the history of the world. It began when the U.S. stock market crashed in 1929 and lasted until the end of the 1930s. Several causes are considered to be responsible for this period of economic downturn. Raising debt levels, fall in profits and the gold standard system are some attributed causes.

The Great Depression led to a series of problems for the economy and the people. There was a drastic decrease in production and consumption in the economy. The rate of unemployment skyrocketed resulting in hardships across the population. A lot of prominent banks failed and ran out of business. Eventually, the great depression shaped the politics of the U.S. and laid the foundations for The New Deal.

Exercise

Frequently asked Questions (FAQ's)

1. What is the difference between microeconomics and macroeconomics?

2. What are the important features of a capitalist economy?

3. Describe the four major sectors in an economy according to the macroeconomic point of view.

Multiple Choice Questions (MCQ's)

1. The branches of the subject Economics is
   (a) Wealth and welfare
   (b) Production and consumption
   (c) Demand and supply
   (d) Micro and macro

2. Who coined the word 'macro'?
   (a) Adam Smith   (b) J M Keynes
   (c) Ragnar Frìsch   (d) Karl Marx

3. Who is regarded as Father of Modern Macro Economics?
   (a) Adam smith   (b) J M Keynes
   (c) Ragnar Frisch   (d) Karl Marx

4. Identify the other name for macro Economics. .
   (a) Price Theory   (b) Income Theory
   (c) Market Theory   (d) Micro Theory

5. Macroeconomics is a study of ....
   (a) individuals
   (b) firms
   (c) a nation
   (d) aggregates

6. Indicate the contribution of J M Keynes to economics
   (a) Wealth of nations
   (b) General Theory
   (c) Capital
   (d) Public Finance

7. A steady increase in general price level is termed as ....
   (a) Wholesale price index
   (b) Business Cycle
   (c) Inflation
   (d) National Income

8. Identify the necessity of Economic policies.
   (a) to solve the basic problem
   (b) to overcome the obstacles
   (c) to achieve growth
   (d) all the above

9. Indicate the fundamental economic activities of an economy.
   (a) Production and Distribution
   (b) Production and Exchange
   (c) Production and Consumption
   (d) Production and Marketing

10. An economy consists of
   (a) Consumption sector
   (b) Production sector
   (c) Government sector
   (d) All the above

11. Identify the economic system where only private ownership of production exists.
   (a) Capitalistic Economy
   (b) Socialistic Economy
   (c) Globalist Economy
   (d) Mixed Economy

12. Economic system representing equality in distribution is
   (a) Capitalism
   (b) Globalism
   (c) Mixed
   (d) Socialism

13. Macroeconomics study the economy as a whole or in aggregates. Which of the following are the macroeconomic study aggregates/variables?
    (*a*) Aggregate demand, aggregate supply, individual income and price level.
    (*b*) Individual demand, individual supply, national income and price level.
    (*c*) Aggregate demand, aggregate supply, national income and price level.
    (*d*) None of the above.

14. The country following Capitalism is ....
    (*a*) Russia   (*b*) America
    (*c*) India   (*d*) China

15. Identity The Founding Father of economics
    (*a*) J M Keynes   (*b*) Karl Marx
    (*c*) Adam smith   (*d*) Samuelson

16. An economic system where the economic activities of a nation are done both by the private and public together is termed as ....
    (*a*) Capitalistic Economy
    (*b*) Socialistic Economy
    (*c*) Globalist Economy
    (*d*) Mixed Economy

17. Quantity of a commodity accumulated at a point of time is termed as ....
    (*a*) production   (*b*) stock
    (*c*) variable   (*d*) flow

18. Identity the flow variable
    (*a*) money supply
    (*b*) assets
    (*c*) income
    (*d*) foreign exchange reserves

19. Identity the sectors of a Two sector Model.
    (*a*) Households and Firms
    (*b*) Private and Public ,
    (*c*) Internal and External
    (*d*) Firms and Government

20. The Circular Flow Model that represents an open Economy,
    (*a*) Two sector Model
    (*b*) Three sector Model
    (*c*) Four sector Model
    (*d*) All the above

21. Which of the following is the reason of depreciation of fixed assets?
    (*a*) Normal wear and tear an unforeseen obsolescence.
    (*b*) Normal wear and tear foreseen obsolescence.
    (*c*) Abnormal wear and tear and foreseen obsolescence.
    (*d*) Abnormal wear and tear an unforeseen obsolescence.

22. Real flow includes:
    (*a*) Factor services and production of goods and services
    (*b*) Factor payments and production of goods and services
    (*c*) Factor services and expenditure on goods and services
    (*d*) Factor payments and expenditures on goods and services

23. From the following, which is not the part of injection?
    (*a*) Investment
    (*b*) Savings
    (*c*) Exports
    (*d*) None of these

24. Money flow includes:
    (*a*) Factor services and production of goods and services
    (*b*) Factor services and expenditure of goods and services
    (*c*) Factor payment and production of goods and services
    (*d*) Factor payment and expenditure on goods and services

25. The fiscal deficit is a:
    (*a*) Flow variable
    (*b*) Stock variable
    (*c*) the ratio of a flow variable to a stock variable
    (*d*) The ratio of a stock variable to a flow variable

🔑 Solutions

Frequently asked Questions (FAQ's)

1. **Microeconomics**
   - Deals with the behaviour, choices and incentives of individuals or individual companies.
   - Pioneered by economists such as Alfred Marshall
   - Can be used to explain consumer behaviour, the theory of price and marketing principles.

   Macroeconomics
   - Deals with the whole economy, including governments, corporations, and regulatory institutions.
   - Pioneered by economists such as John. Maynard. Keynes
   - Can be used to explain aggregate market performance, unemployment, growth, and overall market predictions.

2. These are the important features of a capitalist economy
   - The means of production are privately owned.
   - The maximization of profit is the main motive for the producers.
   - The market determines the price of the product based on demand and supply.
   - There is competition among the producers and free enterprise is ensured.

3. These are the four major sectors in the economy according to the macroeconomic point of view.
   i) The production sector that is responsible for the production of goods and services
   ii) The household sector that consumes the goods and services produced in the economy
   iii) The government sector that is responsible for framing laws and regulating policies that affect the economy and the people.
   iv) The external sector that refers to the rest of the world which is interconnected through trade. (Exports and Imports)

Multiple Choice Questions (MCQ's)

1. (d) Micro and macro
2. (c) Ragnar Frìsch
3. (b) J M Keynes
4. (b) Income Theory
5. (d) aggregates
6. (b) General Theory
7. (c) Inflation
8. (d) all the above
9. (c) Production and Consumption
10. (d) All the above
11. (a) Capitalistic Economy
12. (d) Socialism
13. (c) Aggregate demand, aggregate supply, national income and price level.
14. (b) America
15. (b) Adam Smith
16. (d) Mixed Economy
17. (b) stock
18. (c) income
19. (a) Households and Firms
20. (c) Four sector Model
21. (b) Normal wear and tear foreseen obsolescence.
22. (a) Factor services and production of goods and services
23. (b) Savings
24. (d) After payment and expenditure on goods and services
25. (a) Fiscal deficit is a flow variable, and it is defined with reference to a period of time

National Income and Related Aggregates

Chief concepts of this introductory chapter –

- Aggregate related to National Income
- Gross National Product GNP
- Net National Product NNP
- Gross Domestic Product GDP
- Net domestic product NDP
- At market price, at factor cost, Nominal and Real GDP.
- GDP and Welfare

Aggregate Of National Income

In an economy, where is types of goods and services are produced by different productive units during a period of one year. Such goods and services cannot be added together in terms of quantity. Therefore, these are expressed in terms of money there are many aggregates in national income to measure the value of goods and services in terms of money.

4.1 The related aggregates of national income are:-

i)   Gross Domestic Product at Market price (GDP_{MP})

ii) Gross Domestic Product at Factor Cost (GDP_{FC})

iii) Net Domestic Product at Market Price (NDP_{MP})

iv) Net Domestic Product at FC or (NDP_{FC})

v)   Net National Product at FC or National Income (NNP_{FC})

vi) Gross National Product at FC (GNP_{FC})

vii) Net National. Product at MP (NNP_{MP})

viii) Gross National Product at MP (GNP_{MP})

(i) **Gross Domestic Product at Market Price** : It is the money value of all the final goods and services produced within the domestic territory of a country during an accounting year.

GDP_{MP} = Net domestic product at FC (NDP_{FC}) + Depreciation + Net Indirect tax.

(ii) **Gross Domestic Product at FC** : It is the value of all final goods and services produced within domestic territory of a country which does not include net indirect tax.

$GDP_{FC} = GDP_{MP}$ – Indirect tax + Subsidy

or $GDP_{FC} = GDP_{MP}$ – NIT

(iii) **Net Domestic Product at Market Price** : It is the money value of all final goods and services produced within domestic territory of a country during an accounting year and does not include depreciation.

$NDP_{MP} = GDP_{MP}$ – Depreciation

(iv) **Net Domestic Product at FC** : It is the value of all final goods and services which does not include depreciation charges and net indirect tax. Thus, it is equal to the sum of all factor incomes (compensation of employees, rent, interest, profit and mixed income of self-employed) generated in the domestic territory of the country.

$NDP_{FC} = GDP_{MP}$ – Depreciation – Indirect tax + Subsidy

(v) **Net National Product at FC (National Income) :** It is the sum total of factor incomes (compensation of employees + rent + interest + profit) earned by normal residents of a country in an accounting year.

or

$NNP_{FC} = NDP_{FC} +$ Factor income earned by normal residents from abroad – factor payments made to abroad.

(vi) **Gross National Product at FC:** It is the sum total of factor incomes earned by normal residents of a country along with depreciation, during an accounting year.

$$GNP_{FC} = NNP_{FC} + Depreciation$$

OR

$$GNP_{FC} = GDP_{FC} + NFIA$$

(vii) **Net National Product at MP :** It is the sum total of factor incomes earned by the normal residents of a country during an accounting year including net indirect taxes.

$$NNP_{MP} = NNP_{FC} + Indirect\ tax - Subsidy$$

(viii) **Gross National Product at MP :** It is the sum total of factor incomes earned by normal residents of a country during an accounting year including depreciation and net indirect taxes.

$$GNP_{MP} = NNP_{FC} + Depreciation + NIT$$

4.2 Domestic Aggregates

Gross domestic Product at Market Price (GDP_{MP}) is the market value of all the final goods and services produced by all producing units located in the domestic territory of a country during an accounting year. It includes the value of depreciation or consumption of fixed capital.

Net Domestic Product at Market Price (NDP_{MP}) :

$NDP_{MP} = GDP_{MP} -$ Depreciation (consumption of Fixed capital).

It is the market value of final goods and services produced within the domestic territory of the country during a year exclusive of depreciation.

Domestic Income: NDP_{FC} :

It is the factor income accruing to owners of factors of production for suppling factor services within domestic territory during an accounting year.

4.3 National Aggregates

Gross National Product at Market Price (GNP_{MP}): is the market value of all the final goods and services produced by normal residents (in the domestic territory and abroad) of a country during an accounting year.

$$GDP_{MP} + NFIA = GNP_{MP}\ (NNP_{FC})$$

National Income NNP_{FC} : It is the sum total of all factors incomes which are earned by normal residents of a country in the form of wages. rent, interest and profit during an accounting year.

$$NNP_{FC} = NDP_{FC} + NFIA = National\ Income.$$

4.4 Methods of Estimation of National Income

4.4.1 Value Added Product Method

Step 1: Gross Domestic Product at Market Price (GDP_{MP}):

Gross Value Added (GVA_{MP}) Primary Sector + Gross Value Added (GVA_{MP}) of Secondary Sector

+ Gross Value Added (GVA_{MP}) of Tertiary Sector

Step 2: Net National Product at Factor Cost (NNP_{FC}):

First calculate Net Domestic Income :

$$NDP_{FC} = GDP_{MP} - Depreciation - Net\ Indirect\ Taxes.$$

Then   National Income $(NNP_{FC}) = NDP_{FC} + NFIA$

4.4.2 Income Method

Step 1: Net Domestic Product at Factor Cost (NDP_{FC}):

Compensation of employees + Operating Surplus + Mixed income for self - employed person

Step 2: National Income (NNP_{FC}):

$NDP_{FC} +$ Net Factor Income Earned from Abroad (NFIA)

4.4.3 Expenditure Method also known as "Income Disposal Method"

Step 1: Gross Domestic Product at Market Price (GDP_{MP}):

Private Final Consumption (PFCE) + Government Final Consumption Expenditure (GFCE)

+ Gross Domestic Capital Formation (GDCF)

+ Net Exports (X – M)

$$GDP_{MP} = PFCE + GFCE + GDCF + (X - M)$$

Step 2: Net National Product at Factor Cost (NNP_{FC})

First calculate Net Domestic Income :

$$NDP_{FC} = GDP_{MP} - Depreciation - Net\ Indirect\ Taxes.$$

National Icome $(NNP_{FC}) = NDP_{FC} + NFIA$

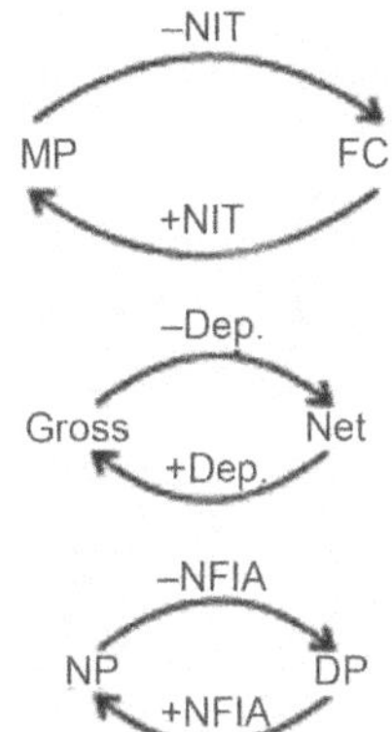

Conversion Hints

Where:

NIT : Net Indirect Tax (Indirect Taxes – Subsidies)

MP = Market Price

FC = Factor Cost

Dep = Depreciation – Consumption of Fixed Capital

NP = National Product

DP = Domestic Product

NFIA = Net Factor income from Abroad

4.5 National Income at Current Prices

It is also called nominal National income. When goods and services produced by normal residents within and outside of a country in a year valued at current years prices i.e., current prices is called national income at current prices.

$Y = Q \times P$

Y = National income at current prices

Q = Quantity of goods and services produced during an accounting year

P = Prices of goods and services prevailing during the current accounting year

4.5.1 National Income at Constant Prices

It is also called as real national income. When goods and services produced by normal residents within and outside of a country in a year valued at constant price i.e., base year's price is called National Income at Constant Prices.

National Income at Constant Price

$$= \frac{\text{National Income at Current Price}}{\text{Current Price Index}} \times 100$$

Value of Output :Market value of all goods and services produced by an enterprise during an accounting year.

Value added :It is the difference between value of output of a firm and value of inputs bought from the other firms during a particular period of time.

4.6 Problem of Double Counting

Counting the value of a commodity more than once while estimating national income is called double counting. It leads to overestimation of national income. So, it is called problem of double counting.

4.6.1 Ways to solve the problem of double counting

(a) By taking the value of only final goods.

(b) By value added method.

Components of $GDP_{MP} = \Sigma$ Values Added by all 3 sectors

1. Value Added by Primary Sector(=VO-IC)

2. Value Added by Secondary Sector(=VO-IC)

3. Value Added by Tertiary Sectors(=VO-IC)

Hints

VO = Value of output

IC = Intermediate Consumption

VO = Price X quantity OR

Sales + Change in stock

(Change in stock = Closing Stock – Opening Stock)

4.7 Components of Final Expenditure

4.7.1 Final Consumption Expenditure

a. Private Final Consumption Expenditure(C)

b. Government Final Consumption Expenditure(G)

4.7.2 Gross Domestic Capital Formation

a. Gross Domestic Fixed Capital Formation

    i. Gross business Fixed Investment

    ii. Gross Residential Construction Investment

    iii. Gross public Investment

b. Change in Stock or Inventory Investment

4.7.3 Net Export (X-M)

a. Export(X)

b. Import(M)

4.8 Components of Domestic Income

1. Compensation of Employees

    a. Wages and salaries(Cash/or kinds)

    b. Employers Contribution of Social security Schemes

2. Operating surplus

    a. Rent

b.   Interest

c.   Profit

d.   Corporate Tax

e.   Dividend

f.   Undistributed corporate profit

3.   Mixed Income for self-Employed person

4.9 Net Factor Income

from Abroad NFIA = It is difference between factor income received/earned by normal residents of a country and factor income paid to non-residents of the country.

4.9.1 Components of NFIA

1.   Net Compensation of Employees

2.   Net Income from Property and entrepreneurship

3.   Net Retained earnings of resident companies abroad

Hints :

NFIA : Net Factor Income Earned from Abroad.

NFIA = Factor Income Received from Abroad – Factor Income Paid to Abroad.

4.10. Net National Disposable Income (NNDI)

It is defined as net national product at Market price NNP_{MP} plus net current transfer from rest of the world.

$NNDI = NNP_{MP}$ + Net current transfers from rest of the world.

= National income + net indirect tax + net current transfers from the rest of the world.

4.11 Gross National Disposable Income

(Gross NDI) = GNP_{MP} + Net current Transfers from rest of the world.

4.12 Net National Disposable Income

(Net NDI) = NNP_{MP} + Net current Transfers from rest of the world.

OR

= Gross NDI – Depreciation.

4.12.1 NNP_{FC} from Personal Disposable Income

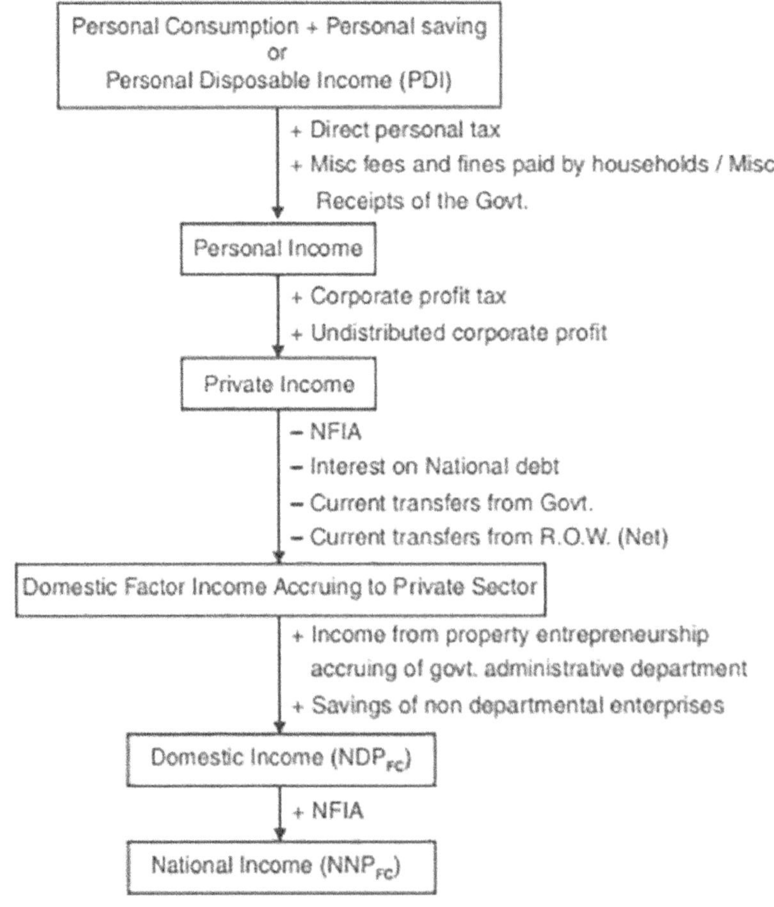

Concept of Value Added of One Sector or One Firm

1. Value output = Sales + Change in Stock. or value of output = price × qty. sold + Δ Stock.

2. Gross value added at market price (GVA_{MP}) = Value of output – Intermediate consumption.

3. Net value added at market price (NVA_{MP}) = GVA_{MP} – Depreciation.

4. Net value added at factor cost NVA_{FC} = NVA_{MP} – Net Indirect Tax.

Note: By adding up NVA_{FC} of all the sectors, we get NDP_{FC} or Domestic Income.

4.12.2 Personal Disposable Income from National Income (NNP_{FC})

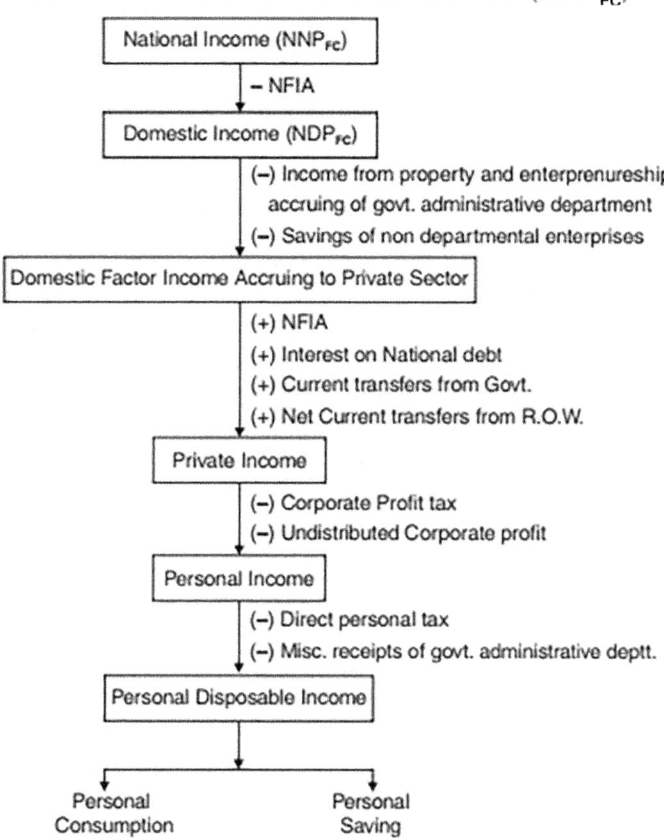

Private Income: Private income is estimated income of factor and transfer incomes from all sources to private sector within and outside the country.

Personal Income: It refers to income received by household from all sources. It includes factor income and transfer income.

Personal Disposable Income: It is that part of Personal income which is available to the households for disposal as they like.

4.13 GDP and Welfare

In general GDP and Welfare are directly related with each other. A higher GDP implies that more production of goods and services. It means more availability of goods and services. But more goods and services may not necessarily indicate that the people were better off during the year. In other words, a higher GDP may not necessarily mean higher welfare of the people. There are two types of GDP:

- **Real GDP:** When the goods and services are produced by all producing units in the domestic territory of a country during an a/c. year and valued these at base year's prices or constant price, it is called real GDP or GDP at constant prices. It changes only by change in physical output not by change price level. It is called a true indicator of economic development.

- **Nominal GDP:** When the goods and services are produced by all producing units in the domestic territory of a country during an a/c. year and valued these at current year's prices or current prices, it is called Nominal GDP or GDP at current prices. It is influenced by change in both physical output and price level. It does not consider a true indicator of economic development.

4.13.1 Conversion of national GDP into real GDP

$$\text{Real GDP} = \frac{\text{Nominal GDP}}{\text{Price Index}} \times 100$$

Price index plays the role of deflator deflating current price estimates into constant price estimates. In this way it may be called GDP deflator.

Welfare mean material wellbeing of the people. It depends on many economic factors like national income, consumption level quality of goods etc and non-economic factor like environmental pollution, law and order etc. the welfare which depends on economic factors is called economic welfare and the welfare which depends on non-economic factor is called non-economic welfare. The sum total of economic and non-economic welfare is called social welfare. Conclusion thus GDP and welfare directly related with each other but this relation is incomplete because of the following reasons.

4.13.2 Limitation of per capita real GDP/ GDP as an indicator of Economic welfare :

- Non-monetary exchange
- Externalities not taken into GDP but it affects welfare.
- Distribution of GDP.
- All product may not contribute equally to economic welfare.
- Contribution of some products may be negative.
- Inflation may give falls impression of growth of GDP.

Key Statements

Goods: In economics a goods is defined as any physical object, manmade, that could command a price in the market and these are the materials that satisfy human wants and provide utility

Consumption Goods: Those final goods which satisfy human wants directly. ex- ice-cream and milk used by the households.

Capital Goods: Those final goods which help in production. These goods are used for generating income. These goods are fixed assets of the producers. Example: plant and machinery.

Final Goods are those goods which are used either for final consumption or for investment.

Intermediate Goods refers to those goods and services which are used as a raw material for further production or for resale in the same year. These goods do not fulfil needs of mankind directly.

Investment: Addition made to the physical stock of capital during a period of time is called investment. It is also called capital formation.

Capital formation: Change in the stock of capital is also called capital formation.

Depreciation: means fall in value of fixed capital goods due to normal wear and tear and expected obsolescence. It is also called consumption of fixed capital.

Gross Investment: Total addition made to physical stock of capital during a period of time. It includes depreciation. OR Net Investment + Depreciation

Net Investment: Net addition made to the real stock of capital during a period of time. It excludes depreciation.Net Investment = Gross investment – Depreciation.

Stocks: Variables whose magnitude is measured at a particular point of time are called stock variables. Example: National Wealth, Inventory etc.

Flows: Variables whose magnitude is measured over a period of time are called flow variable. Example: National income, change in stock etc.

Value of Output:

i) When the entire output is sold in an accounting year, then: Value of Output = Sales.

ii) When the entire output is not sold in an accounting year, then the unsold stock is added to the value of sales. Unsold stock is the excess of closing stock over operating stock and is termed as Change in Stock-ΔS.

Base Year is a normal year which is free from price fluctuations. Presently, 2011-12 is taken as the base year in India.

Circular flow of income: It refers to continuous flow of goods and services and money income among different sectors in the economy. It is circular in nature. It has neither any end and nor any beginning point. It helps to know the functioning of the economy.

Leakage: It is the amount of money which is withdrawn from circular flow of income. For e.g., Taxes, Savings and Import. It reduces aggregate demand and the level of income.

Injection: It is the amount of money which is added to the circular flow of income. For e.g., Government Expenditure, investment and exports. It increases the aggregate demand and the level of income.

Economic Territory: Economic (or domestic) Territory is the geographical territory administrated by a Government within which persons, goods, and capital circulate freely.

Scope of Economic Territory :

(a) Political frontiers including territorial waters and airspace.

(b) Embassies, consulates, military bases etc. located abroad.

(c) Ships and aircraft operated by the residents between two or more countries.

(d) Fishing vessels, oil and natural gas rigs operated by residents in the international waters.

Normal Resident of a country is a person or an institution who normally resides in a country and whose Centre of economic interest lies in that country.

Exceptions:

(a) Diplomats and officials of foreign embassy.

(b) Commercial travellers, tourists' students etc.

(c) People working in international organizations like WHO, IMF, UNESCO etc. are treated as normal residents of the country to which they belong.

Exercise

Frequently asked Questions (FAQ's)

1. Is machine purchased always a final good ?

2. Are the following included in domestic productive India:

   - Profits earned by a branch of foreign bank in India

   - Payment of salaries to its staff by embassy located in New Delhi

   - Interest received by an Indian resident from its abroad firms

3. Explain the meaning of non – market activities.

4. Give one example of 'externality' which reduces welfare of the people.

5. What are externalities? Give an example of a positive externality and its impact on welfare of the people.

Multiple Choice Questions (MCQ's)

1. Those goods which satisfy human wants directly are called:
   (*a*) Intermediate goods
   (*b*) Consumer goods
   (*c*) Capital goods
   (*d*) None of the above

2. In the production of sugar, sugar cane is:
   (*a*) A final good
   (*b*) Capital good
   (*c*) An intermediate good
   (*d*) None of the above

3. Which of the following is a semi-durable good?
   (*a*) Radio (*b*) Clothes
   (*c*) Milk (*d*) Petrol

4. Capital goods are those goods:
   (*a*) Which are used in the production process for several years
   (*b*) Which are used in the production process for few years
   (*c*) Which involve depreciation losses
   (*d*) Both (*a*) and (*c*)

5. Increase in the stock capital is known as:
   (*a*) Capital loss
   (*b*) Capital gain
   (*c*) Capital formation
   (*d*) None of the above

6. Next investment is equal to:
   (*a*) Gross investment + depreciation
   (*b*) Gross investment - depreciation
   (*c*) Gross investment x depreciation
   (*d*) Gross investment depreciation

7. Net capital formation causes:
   (*a*) Increase in production capacity
   (*b*) Increase in depreciation
   (*c*) Increase in profits
   (*d*) Increase in cost

8. Which of the following leads to depreciation?
   (*a*) Normal wear and tear
   (*b*) Damages due to floods
   (*c*) Damages due to market crash
   (*d*) None of the above

9. Income of the family is the example of which variable?
   (*a*) Stock
   (*b*) Flow
   (*c*) Both Stock and Flow
   (*d*) Neither Stock nor Flow

10. Domestic product is equal to:

   (*a*) National product + Net Factor Income from abroad

   (*b*) National product – Net Factor Income from abroad

   (*c*) National product × Net Factor Income from abroad

   (*d*) National product ÷ Net Factor Income from abroad

11. Which of the following is not correct?

   (*a*) NNP at Market Price = GNP at Market Price + Depreciation

   (*b*) NDP at Market Price = NNP at Market Price – Net Factor Income from Abroad

   (*c*) NDP at Factor Cost = NDP at Market Price - Indirect taxes + Subsidies

   (*d*) GDP at Factor Cost = NDP at Factor Cost + Depreciation

12. Which one is correct?

   (*a*) National income = NDP at Factor Cost - Net Factor Income from Abroad

   (*b*) GNP at Factor Cost = GNP at Market Price + Net Indirect Tax

   (*c*) Personal Income = Private Income – Corporate Tax – Corporate Saving

   (*d*) Disposable Income = Saving of Household Sector – Consumption of Household Sector

13. Which one includes depreciation?

   (*a*) GNP at Market Price

   (*b*) NNP at Market Price

   (*c*) NNP at Factor Cost

   (*d*) None of the above

14. Market price of the final goods and services (including depreciation) produced within the domestic territory of a country during an accounting here is called:

   (*a*) GDP at Market Price

   (*b*) GNP at Factor Cost

   (*c*) NNP at Factor Cost

   (*d*) GDP at Factor Cost

15. GNP at market prices measured as:

   (*a*) GDP at Market Price – Depreciation

   (*b*) GDP at Market Price + Net Factor Income from Abroad

   (*c*) GNP at Market Price + Subsidies

   (*d*) NDP at Factor Cost + Net Factor Income from Abroad

16. Value added method measure the contribution of which of the following within the domestic territory of a country?

   (*a*) One producing enterprise only

   (*b*) All producing enterprises

   (*c*) A few producing enterprises

   (*d*) None of the above

17. As a result of double counting, National Income is:

   (*a*) Over-estimated

   (*b*) Under-estimated

   (*c*) Correctly estimated

   (*d*) Not estimated for the entire year of accounting

18. Which of these is a limitation in the measurement of social welfare using GDP at constant prices as an index?

   (*a*) Increase in population size

   (*b*) change in working conditions

   (*c*) Composition of production

   (*d*) All of the above

19. Which of the following is not transfer payment?

   (*a*) Interest on National debt

   (*b*) Retirement pensions

   (*c*) Old age pensions

   (*d*) Donations

20. Which of the following items is not included while estimating GNP of a country at Market Prices?

   (*a*) Salaries and wages before taxes

   (*b*) Indirect taxes

   (*c*) Remittances by NRIs

   (*d*) Subsidy

21. Which of the following items is not included while estimating National Income by Income Method ?

   (*a*) Rent

   (*b*) Mixed income

   (*c*) Fixed investment

   (*d*) Undistributed profits

22. Real national income means:

   (*a*) National income at current prices

   (*b*) National income at factor prices

   (*c*) National income at constant prices

   (*d*) National income at average prices of the past ten years

23. Which of the following is not included in final consumption expenditure ?
    (a) Household expenditure on food
    (b) Government final consumption expenditure
    (c) Household expenditure on education
    (d) Expenditure on raw material

24. Which one refers to Net Indirect Taxes ?
    (a) Indirect taxes + subsidies
    (b) Indirect taxes - subsidies
    (c) Direct taxes - subsidies
    (d) None of the above

25. Basis of the difference between concepts of Market Price and Factor Cost is:
    (a) Direct taxes
    (b) Indirect taxes
    (c) Subsidy
    (d) Net indirect taxes

🔑 Solutions______________________________________

Frequently asked Questions (FAQ's)

1. It depends on the user that will decide if a machine is a finished product or not. When a machine is purchased by a household, it is referred to as a final good. On the other hand, if a machine is purchased by a business for using it to produce other goods, that is also referred to as a final good. However, if it is purchased buy a company for resale, then it is referred to as an intermediate good.

2. 1. Profits earned by a foreign bank branch in India are included in India's domestic income because they earned within the country's borders.

   2. Since the embassy in New Delhi is not part of India's domestic territory, salaries paid to its employees will not be included in the country's domestic income.

   3. Interest received by an Indian resident from his or her foreign enterprises is not included in India's domestic income because it is a factor income.

3. Non – market are those that are gained as a result of the purchase of a large number of finished goods and services. They are really not bought and sold in the open market. For example, vegetables grown in the house kitchen garden.

4. When the activities of one result in harm to others with no payment made for the harm done, such activities are called negative externalities, e.g., factories produce goods but at the same time creates water and air pollution. Production of goods increases welfare but at the same time pollution reduces the welfare.

5. Externalities refer to the benefits or harms a firm or an individual causes to another for which they are not paid. These externalities can be positive as well as negative. A positive externality exists when an individual or firm making a decision does not receive the full benefit of the decision, e.g., Immunisation prevents an individual from getting a disease, but has the positive effect of the individual not being able to spread the disease to other. It enhances the overall welfare of the society and creates positive externalities.

Multiple Choice Questions (MCQ's)

1. (b) Consumer goods
2. (c) An intermediate good
3. (b) Clothes
4. (d) Both (a) and (c)
5. (c) Capital formation
6. (b) Gross investment – depreciation
7. (a) Increase in production capacity
8. (a) Normal wear and tear
9. (b) Flow
10. (b) National product – Net Factor Income from abroad
11. (a) NNP at Market Price = GNP at Market Price + Depreciation
12. (c) Personal Income = Private Income – Corporate Tax – Corporate Saving
13. (a) GNP at Market Price
14. (a) GDP at Market Price
15. (b) GDP at Market Price + Net Factor Income from Abroad
16. (b) All producing enterprises
17. (a) Over-estimated
18. (d) All of the above
19. (b) Retirement pensions
20. (c) Remittances by NRIs
21. (c) Fixed investment
22. (c) National income at constant prices
23. (d) Expenditure on raw material
24. (b) Indirect taxes – subsidies
25. (d) Net indirect taxes

Determination of Income and Employment

Chief concepts of this chapter –

* Aggregate demand and its components.

* Propensity to consume and propensity to save (average and marginal).

* Short - run equilibrium output, investment multiplier and its mechanism.

* Meaning of full employment and involuntary unemployment.

* Problems of excess demand and deficient demand; measures to correct them- changes in government spending, taxes and money supply through Bank Rate, CRR, SLR, Repo Rate and Reverse Repo Rate, Open Market Operations, Margin Requirement.

In this chapter, we study the determination of National Income under the assumption of a fixed price of final goods and a constant rate of interest in the economy.

5.1 Aggregate Demand and its Components

Aggregate Demand refers to total value of all final goods and services that are planned to buy by all the sectors of the economy at a given level of income during a period of time. AD represents the total expenditure on goods and services in an economy during a period of time.

The Components of Aggregate Demand are

a. Private consumption demand (C)
b. Private investment demand (I)
c. Purchase of goods and services by the government (G)
d. Demand for net exports (X–M)

Thus, $AD = C + I + G + NEAD = C + I + G + NE$ (sum of four components: consumption, investment, government purchase and net export).

Aggregate Demand is very important for economists as it provides the tool to measure the strength of an economy. Usually, economists evaluate the total market for things produced in an economy for a year. So, if the aggregate demand is high then the economy is strong, meaning it can sell many products.

5.2 Determination of Income In two sector economy

$$AD = C + I$$

The Aggregate Demand Curve

Aggregate demand, or *AD*, refers to the amount of total spending on domestic goods and services in an economy. Strictly speaking, AD is what economists call total planned expenditure. We'll talk about that more in other articles, but for now, just think of aggregate demand as total spending.

Aggregate demand includes all four components of demand:

* Consumption

* Investment

* Government spending

* Net exports—exports minus imports

This demand is determined by a number of factors; one of them is the price level. An *aggregate demand curve* shows the total spending on domestic goods and services at each price level.

You can see an example aggregate demand curve below. Just like in an aggregate supply curve, the horizontal axis shows real GDP and the vertical axis shows price level. But there's a big difference in the shape of the AD curve—it slopes down. This downward slope indicates that increases in the price level of outputs lead to a lower quantity of total spending.

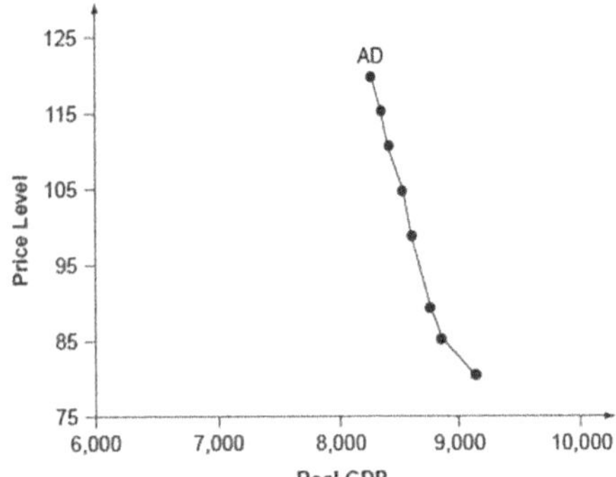

The aggregate demand curve

The graph shows a downward sloping aggregate demand curve, showing that, as the price level rises, the amount of total spending on domestic goods and services declines.

Let's dig a little deeper. To fully understand why price level increases lead to lower spending, we need to understand how changes in the price level affect the different components of aggregate demand. Remember, the following components make up aggregate demand: consumption spending, C; investment spending, I; government spending, G; and spending on exports, X, minus imports M.

Aggregate demand = C + I + G + X – M

The wealth effect holds that as the price level increases, the buying power of savings that people have stored up in bank accounts and other assets will diminish, eaten away to some extent by inflation. Because a rise in the price level reduces people's wealth, consumption spending will fall as the price level rises.

The interest rate effect explains that as outputs rise, the same purchases will take more money or credit to accomplish. This additional demand for money and credit will push interest rates higher. In turn, higher interest rates will reduce borrowing by businesses for investment purposes and reduce borrowing by households for homes and cars—thus reducing both consumption and investment spending.

The foreign price effect points out that if prices rise in the United States while remaining fixed in other countries, then goods in the United States will be relatively more expensive compared to goods in the rest of the world. US exports will be relatively more expensive, and thus the quantity of exports sold will fall. Imports from abroad will be relatively cheaper, so the quantity of imports will rise. Thus, a higher domestic price level, relative to price levels in other countries, will reduce net export expenditures.

Truth be told, among economists, all three of these effects are controversial, in part because they do not seem to be very large.

For this reason, the aggregate demand curve in our example aggregate demand curve above slopes downward fairly steeply. The steep slope indicates that a higher price level for final outputs does reduce aggregate demand for all three of these reasons, but the change in the quantity of aggregate demand as a result of changes in price level is not very large.

5.3 Aggregate Supply

Aggregate Supply is the money value of all final goods and services available for purchase by an economy during a given period. It is the flow of goods and services in the economy. Since, money value of final goods and services is equal to net value added, AS is nothing but the national income.

AS = C + S

Aggregate supply represents the national income of the country.

AS = Y (National Income)

The Aggregate Supply Curve

Firms make decisions about what quantity to supply based on the profits they expect to earn. Profits, in turn, are also determined by the price of the outputs the firm sells and by the price of the inputs—like labour or raw materials—the firm needs to buy. *Aggregate supply*, or *AS*, refers to the total quantity of output—in other words, real GDP—firms will produce and sell. The *aggregate supply curve* shows the total quantity of output—real GDP—that firms will produce and sell at each price level.

The graph below shows an aggregate supply curve. Let's begin by walking through the elements of the diagram one at a time: the horizontal and vertical axes, the aggregate supply curve itself, and the meaning of the potential GDP vertical line.

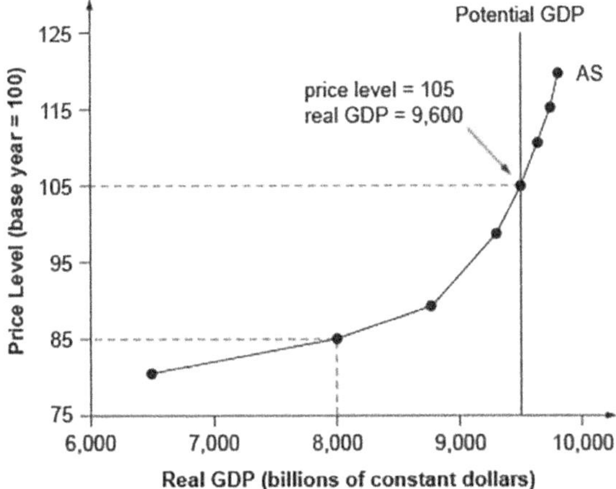

The aggregate supply curve

The graph shows an upward sloping aggregate supply curve. The slope is gradual between 6,500 and 9,000 before becoming steeper, especially between 9,500 and 9,900.

The horizontal axis of the diagram shows real GDP—that is, the level of GDP adjusted for inflation. The vertical axis shows the price level. Price level is the average price of all goods and services produced in the economy.

Consumption function shows functional relationship between consumption and Income.

$C = f(Y)$

Where:

C = Consumption, Y = Income , f = Functional relationship.

Equation of Consumption Function

$C = \overline{C} + MPC * Y$

Where: C = Consumption, $\overline{C}$ = Autonomous consumption

$\overline{C}$ does not change/affected by change in income. It is minimum level of consumption, even when income is zero. Consumption expenditure at zero level of income is called autonomous consumption. It is income inelastic.

Induced consumption is the expenditure which is affected by change in income. It is indicated by MPC × Y. Induced consumption is the portion of consumption that varies with disposable income.

Average Propensity to consume: It is a schedule that shows consumption expenditure at different levels of income in an economy.

Consumption function (propensity to consume) is of two types:

    (a) Average propensity to consume (APC)

    (b) Marginal propensity to consume (MPC)

Average propensity to Consume (APC): It refers to the ratio between total consumption (C) and total income (Y) at given level of income in the economy.

$$APC = \frac{\text{Consumption (C)}}{\text{Income (Y)}} = \frac{C}{Y}$$

Important Points about APC

    (i) APC is more than 1: as long as consumption is more than national income before the break-even point, APC > 1.

    (ii) APC = 1, at the break-even point, consumption is equal to national income.

    (iii) APC is less than 1: beyond the break-even point. Consumption is less than national income.

    (iv) APC falls with increase in income.

    (v) APC can never be zero: because even at zero level of national income, there is autonomous consumption.

Marginal Propensity to Consume (MPC): Marginal propensity to consume refers to the ratio of change in consumption expenditure to change in income.

$$MPC = \frac{\text{Change in Consumption}}{\text{Change in Income}} = \frac{\Delta C}{\Delta Y}$$

Important Points about MPC

    (1) Value of MPC varies between O and 1: If the entire additional income is consumed, then $\Delta C = \Delta Y$, making MPC = 1. However, if entire additional income is saved, than $\Delta C = 0$, making MPC = 0

    (2) MPC is the slope of consumption curve and remain constant throughout in the short run.

    (3) Value of APC > MPC

Saving function refers to the functional relationship between saving and national income.

$S = f(y)$

Where   S = saving

           Y = National Income

           f = Functional relationship.

Saving function (Propensity to Save) is of two types.

    (i) Average Propensity to Save (APS)

    (ii) Marginal propensity to Save (MPS)

Average Propensity to Save (APS): Average propensity to save refers to the ratio of savings to the corresponding level of income

$$APS = \frac{\text{Savings}}{\text{Income}} = \frac{S}{Y}$$

Important Point about APS

    (1) APS can never be 1 or more than 1 :As saving can never be equal to or more than income.

    (2) APS can be zero: At break-even point C = Y, hence S = 0

    (3) APS can be negative: At income levels which are lower than the break-even point, APS can be negative when consumption exceeds income.

    (4) APS rises with increase in income.

Marginal Propensity to Save (MPS): Marginal propensity to save refers to the ratio of change in savings to change in total income.

$$MPS = \frac{\text{Change in Savings}}{\text{Change in Income}} = \frac{\Delta S}{\Delta Y}$$

MPS varies between 0 and 1

(i)   MPS = 1 if the entire additional income is saved. In such a case, $\Delta S = \Delta Y$, then MPS = 1

(ii) MPS = 0 If the entire additional income is consumed. In such a case, $\Delta S = 0$, then MPS = 0

(iii) MPS is the slope of saving curve.

(iv) MPS remains constant throughout in short run.

Relationship between APC and APS The sum of APC and APS is equal to one. It can be proved as under we know

APC + APS = 1

Y = C + S

Dividing both sides by Y, we get

$$\frac{Y}{Y}=1; \frac{C}{Y}=APC; \frac{S}{Y}=APS$$

1 = APC + APS

Because income is either used for consumption or for saving.

Relationship between MPC and MPS

MPC + MPS = 1 because total increment in income is either used for consumption or for saving.

We know: $\Delta Y = \Delta C = \Delta S$

Dividing both sides by ΔY, we get:

$$\frac{\Delta Y}{\Delta Y}=1; \frac{\Delta C}{\Delta Y}=MPC; \frac{\Delta S}{\Delta Y}=MPS$$

1 = MPC + MPS

Consumption function expresses the level of consumer spending depending on three factors.

- Yd = disposable income (income after government intervention – e.g. benefits, and taxes)

- a = autonomous consumption (consumption when income is zero. e.g. even with no income, you may borrow to be able to buy food)

- b = marginal propensity to consume (the % of extra income that is spent). Also known as induced consumption.

Graph of the basic Consumption Function

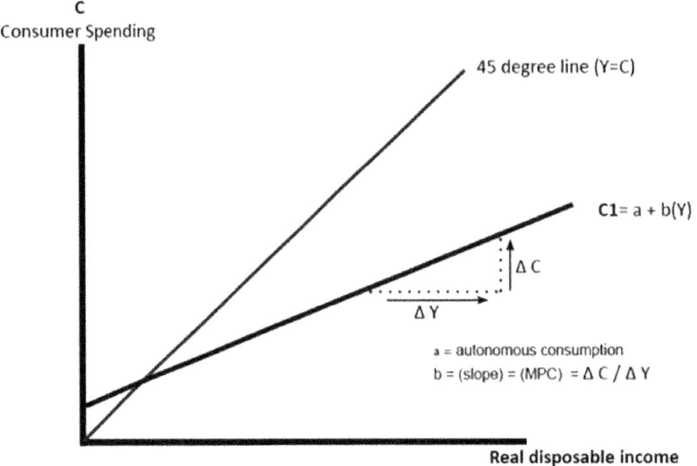

Consumption function formula

- C = a + b Yd

  This suggests consumption is primarily determined by the level of disposable income (Yd). Higher Yd leads to higher consumer spending.

  This model suggests that as income rises, consumer spending will rise. However, spending will increase at a lower rate than income.

- At low incomes, people will spend a high proportion of their income. The average propensity to consume could be one or greater than one. This means people spend everything they have. When you have low income, you don't have the luxury of being able to save. You need to spend everything you have on essentials.

- However, as incomes rise, people can afford the luxury of saving a higher proportion of their income. Therefore, as incomes rise, spending increases at a lower rate than disposable income. People with high incomes have a lower average propensity to spend.

Implications of consumption function

If you cut income tax for those on low income, they tend to have a higher marginal propensity to consume this extra income. Therefore, there is a large increase in spending. People with high incomes will tend to have a lower marginal propensity to consume. If they benefit from a tax cut, they will save a greater proportion.

Graph for the Shift in the consumption function

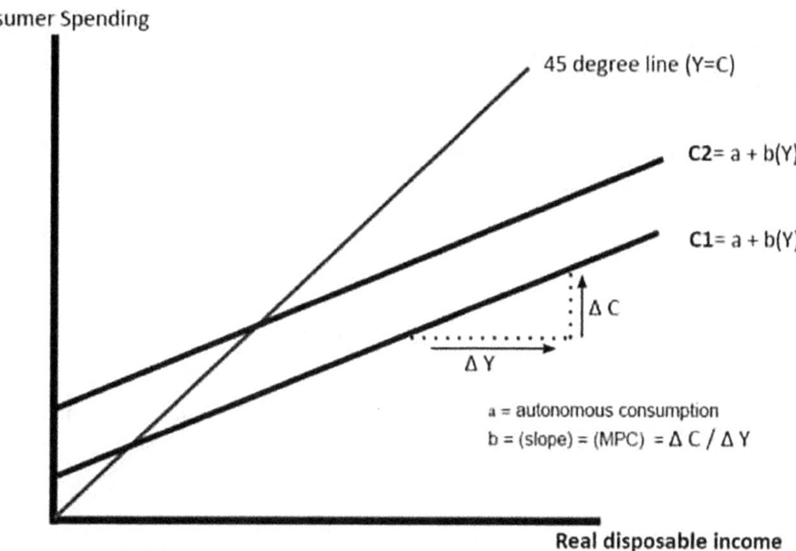

In this diagram, the consumption function has shifted to the upwards (to the left. (C1 to C2). This means consumers are spending a higher % of their income. This could be due to a rise in property prices which increases consumer confidence and lead to higher consumer spending.

Graph for the Increased Marginal Propensity to Consume

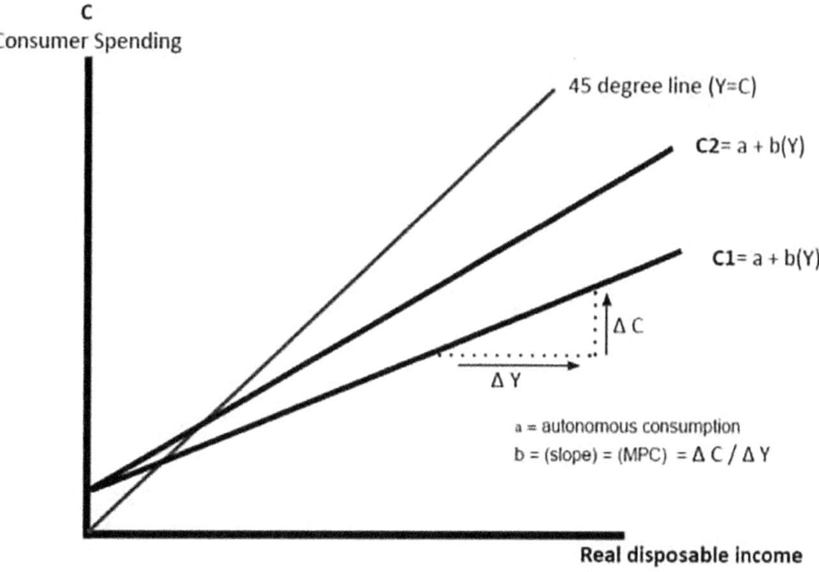

In this diagram, the consumption function has become steeper. This means the value of b (MPC) has increased. Therefore, people are spending a higher % of their additional income. This could be due to rising confidence, lower saving and easier availability of credit.

5.4 Investment

Investment refers to the expenditure incurred on creation of new capital assets.

The investment expenditure is classified under two heads:

    (i)   Induced investment

    (ii) Autonomous investment.

Induced Investment: Induced investment refers to the investment which depends on the profit expectations and is directly influenced by income level (only for reference).

Autonomous Investment: Autonomous investment refers to the investment which is not affected by changes in the Level of income and is not induced solely by profit motive. It is income inelastic.

$$I = \bar{I}$$

Where $\bar{I}$ is a positive constant which represents the autonomous investment in the economy in a given year.

5.5 Determination of Equilibrium Income in the Short-run

Investment Multiplier

The Initial increment in the investment causes additional income (output) in the economy.

But as per the concept of Investment Multiplier, the increment in the income is many times more than the initial increase in the investment.

The factor by which the increase in output/income is greater than the increase in investment is called investment Multiplier.

The different Names of Investment Multiplier.

    1.   Investment Multiplier

    2.   Output Multiplier

Definition of Investment Multiplier

"It refers to the number of times by which the increase in output/income exceeds the increase in investment. It is measured as the ratio between the change in output/income and change in investment."

Formula of Investment Multiplier

$$K = \frac{\Delta Y}{\Delta I}$$

Where :

    K = Multiplier

    ΔY = Change in Output/Income

    ΔI = Change in Investment

Example of Investment Multiplier

Illustration:

If investment increases by Rs. 20 crores and as a consequence, income increases by Rs. 60 crores. What is the investment multiplier?

Solution:-

ΔI = 20 crores

ΔY = 60 crores

Investment multiplier is

$$K = \frac{\Delta Y}{\Delta I}$$

$$K = \frac{60}{20} = 3 \text{ times}$$

Relationship between Investment Multiplier and MPC (Marginal Propensity to consumer).

Not only an Increase in Income depends on the initial increase in investment. It only depends on the Marginal propensity to consume (MPC).

It is on the concept of expenditure of one is the income of the other.

Higher is the consumption of one, higher would be the income of the other.

Thus, the Investment multiplier has a direct relationship with MPC. Higher the value of MPC, the higher the multiplier, and vice-versa.

Formula of Investment multiplier with MPC

$$K = \frac{1}{1 - MPC}$$

Formula of Investment Multiplier with MPS

We know:

$$K = \frac{1}{1 - MPC}$$

We also know :

$$MPS = 1 - MPC$$

$$\text{So, } K = \frac{1}{MPS}$$

Explain the working of Multiplier

As we already have discussed, the higher is the MPC, the higher would be the investment multiplier.

It is based on the fact that one person's expenditure is another person's income. Higher is the expenditure of first-person, higher would be the income of the second one.

The higher is the income of the second one more is the expenditure, the higher would be the income of the third one.

So, overall additional income generates in several rounds.

Let's have an example to illustrate it.

How much would be the generation of additional income depends on the two factors

1.   Initial autonomous investment

2.   Value of MPC.

Let's Suppose

1.   Initial increase in autonomous Investment is = Rs. 100

2.   MPC = 0.80

The total increase in income takes several rounds.

First-round increase

Investment refers to the expenditure on producer goods. So as an investment in Rs. 100 crore raises the income of suppliers of such goods by Rs. 100 crores. This is the first-round increase.

Second round increase

As MPC is 0.80, the people spend 80% of the increase in income on consumption. This raises the income of the producers of consumer goods by Rs. 80 crores.

This is the second-round increase. It equals to 80% of the first-round increase.

Now, total income generated in both two round is (100 + 80) = Rs. 180 crore

Third round increase

In the third round, people who received income in the second round, i.e, 80% of Rs. 80 crores = Rs. 64 crores on consumption.

This leads to another increase in the income of producers of consumer goods.

The income generated in this round is Rs. 64 crore.

Thus, the total income generated up to third round is (100 + 80 + 64 = Rs. 244 crore)

This is the third-round increase.

All-round increase

Thus, income generated goes on increasing round after round.

But in each successive rounds of income generation goes on decreasing by 20% by previous rounds.

The whole process goes on until Initial investment becomes equal to the total savings of all rounds.

As in each successive round, there is an increase of saving by 20% of the previous round.

Let's understand this whole process with the following table.

Round	Increase in Income	Increase in consumption expenditure	Increase in savings
I	100	80	20
II	80	64	16
III	64	51.20	12.80
IV	51.20	40.96	10.24
-			
-			
-			
Total rounds	500	400	100

In the above table total increase in Income is given

$$K = \frac{1}{1-MPC}$$

MPC = 0.8

$$K = \frac{1}{1-0.8}$$

$$K = \frac{1}{0.2}$$

$$K = \frac{10}{2} = 5 \text{ times}$$

Diagrammatical representation

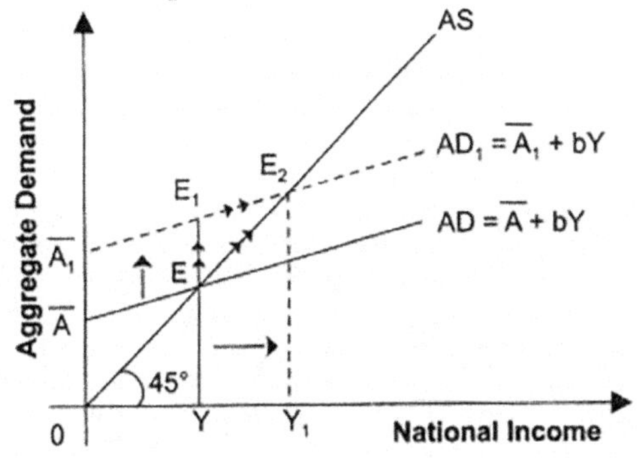

In the above mentioned diagram, aggregate demand is measured on vertical axis and national income is measured on horizontal axis. Initially, at autonomous expenditure $\overline{A}$, the equilibrium level of national income OY is determined at point E. But due to increase in autonomous expenditure from $\overline{A}$ to $\overline{A}_1$, the aggregate demand curve shifts upward from AD to AD1 and at the same level of national income, i.e., OY, aggregate demand is greater than aggregate supply. Production will have to be increased to meet the excess demand. Consequently, national income will increase from OY to OY_1.

Y1 as, we know positive relationship exists between national income and consumption, so consumption will increase which will, increase the new aggregate demand AD_1.

Range of Values of Investment Multiplier

The range of Investment Multiplier is from 1 to infinity. The reason is the value of MPC ranges from 1 to 0.

If the MPC maximum value is 1. The value of Investment Multiplier is infinity. As when all income is 100% expand. There is an unlimited rise in Income.

But, When the MPC maximum value is 0. The value of Investment Multiplier is 1. As all income is saved. The income is multiplier only one time in 1st round only.

5.5.1 Short-Run Equilibrium Output

Short-run According to JM Keynes, 'A period of time during which level of output is determined exclusively by the level of employment in the economy, is termed as short-run.'

Equilibrium Output It refers to the level of output where the Aggregate Demand is equal to the Aggregate Supply (AD = AS) in an economy. It signifies that whatever the producers intend to produce during the year is exactly equal to what the buyers intend to buy during the year.

Where: AD = C + I (for a two-sector economy)

and   AS = C + S

Where:

AD = Aggregate Demand

AS = Aggregate Supply

C = Consumption

I = Investment

S = Saving

Determination of Equilibrium Output

We have two approaches to study the determination of equilibrium output/income.

(i)   AD = AS Approach

According to the modern theory, income and employment are determined at the level, where Aggregate Demand is equal to Aggregate Supply.

It is illustrated with the help of a diagram

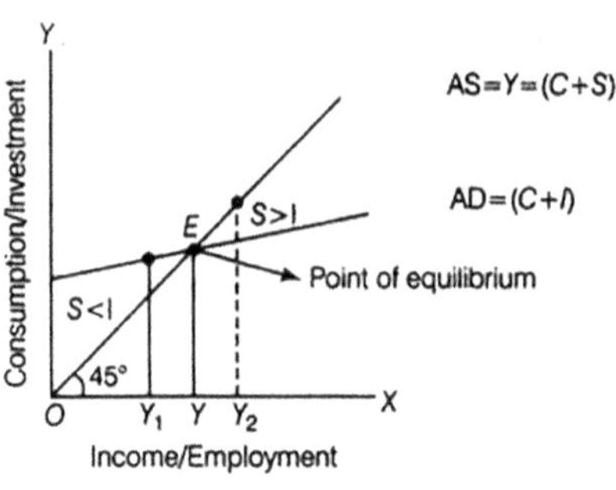

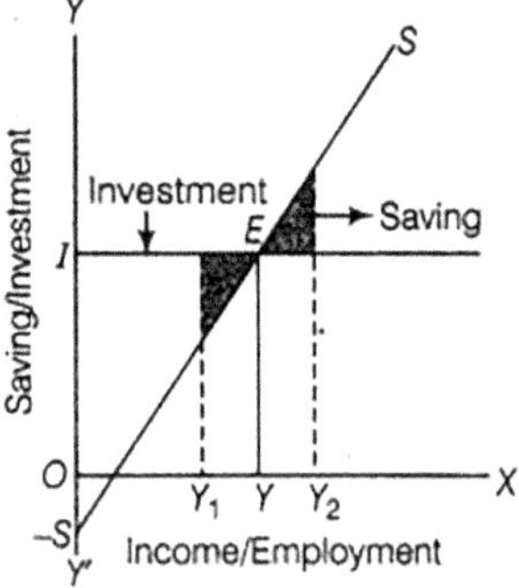

This is illustrated with the help of the above diagram.

Ex-ante Saving The planned or desired saving during an accounting year is termed as ex-ante saving. These are desired savings by the people for one year.

Ex-ante Investment The planned or desired investment expenditure which is intended to be made in an economy during an accounting year, is termed as ex-ante Investment.

Ex-post Saving The actual saving in the economy during a period of one year is termed as ex-post saving.

Ex-post Investment The actual investment expenditure during a period of one year is termed as ex-post investment.

Shifts in Equilibrium In an economy, the flow of income changes due to injections and withdrawals in the circular flow of income. Injections boosts the flow of income and cause positive multiplier effect. On the other hand, withdrawals reduces the flow of income and cause a negative multiplier effect. Investment is considered as an injection and savings is treated as a withdrawal from the circular flow.

5.5.3 Multiplier Mechanism

Investment Multiplier The ratio between change in income and the change in investment is termed as investment multiplier. It is denoted by K.

$$\text{Multiplier } (K) = \frac{\Delta Y}{\Delta I}$$

Where, ΔY = Change in income

                     ΔI = Change in investment

It represents the responsiveness of income to change in the investment.

Relationship between Multiplier (K) and Marginal Propensity to Consume (MPC) There is a direct relationship between multiplier and MPC. Higher the value of MPC, higher the multiplier and vice-versa.

Infact, multiplier can also be estimated using the following formula, K = 1/1 – MPC

Relationship between Multiplier (K) and Marginal Propensity to Save (MPS) There is an inverse relationship between multiplier and MPS. Higher the values of MPS, lower the multiplier and vice-versa.

In fact, multiplier can be estimated using the following formula, K = 1/MPS

Derivation of Investment Multiplier

$$K = \frac{1}{1 - MPC}$$

As $$MPC = \frac{\Delta C}{\Delta Y}$$

We can write the above equation as :

$$K = \frac{1}{1 - \dfrac{\Delta C}{\Delta Y}}$$

$$= \frac{1}{\dfrac{\Delta Y - \Delta C}{\Delta Y}} = \frac{1}{\dfrac{\Delta I}{\Delta Y}} \quad [\text{As } Y = C = I \text{ and } Y - C = I]$$

$$= \frac{\Delta Y}{\Delta I}$$

$$K = \frac{\Delta Y}{\Delta I}$$

Methods to control excess demand or deficient demand:

1. **Fiscal Measures or Fiscal Policy**

    (a) Change in Tax

    (b) Change in Public expenditure

    (c) Change in Public borrowing

    (d) Deficit financing (Printing new notes)

2. **Monetary Measures or Monetary Policy**

    (a) Quantitative measures

        (i) Bank rate

        (ii) Cash Reserve Ratio

        (iii) Statutory Liquidity Ratio

        (iv) Open Market operation

    (b) Qualitative/Selective measures

        (i) Marginal requirement

        (ii) Rationing of credit

        (iii) Direct Action

        (iv) Moral Suasion

Key Statements

Full employment is a situation when all those who are able and willing to work at prevailing wage rate, get the opportunity to work.

Voluntary unemployment is a situation where person is able to work but not willing to work at prevailing wage rate.

Involuntary unemployment is a situation where worker is able and willing to work at prevailing wage rate but does not get work.

Under employment is a situation where all those who are able to work at existing wage rates, are not getting jobs. It refers to that situation in the economy where AS = AD or S = I, but without fuller utilisation of labour force.

Investment multiplier (K) is the ratio of change in income (ΔY) due to change in investment ΔI.

$$K = \frac{\Delta Y}{\Delta I} \text{ or } K = \frac{1}{1 - MPC} \text{ or } K = \frac{1}{MPS}$$

Value of investment multiplier lies b/w 1 to infinitive.

Excess demand refers to a situation when aggregate demand exceeds aggregate supply corresponding to full employment.

Inflationary gap is the gap by which actual aggregate demand exceeds the level of aggregate demand required to establish full employment. It measures the extent of excess demand.

Deficient Demand: When AD falls short of AS at full employment it is called deficient demand. In other words, AD < AS at the level of full employment. It is called deficient demand.

Deflationary gap is the gap by which actual aggregate demand is less than the level of aggregate demand required to establish full employment. It measures the extent of deficient demand.

Paradox of Thrift It is defined as a situation in which people tend to save more money, and this increased saving leads to reduced consumption, resulting in a decrease in aggregate consumption. Such a savings system reduces employment levels, reduces total economic savings, and slows economic growth. This is regarded as a crucial component of Keynesian economics.

Exercise

Frequently asked Questions (FAQ's)

1. What is meant by effective demand?
2. Define the term 'multiplier'. How do we measure it?
3. An increase of Rs. 1,000 crore in investment leads to a rise of Rs. 5,000 crore in the national income. Calculate the value of multiplier.
4. If the value of marginal propensity to consume is 0.6, calculate the value of multiplier.
5. When will there be equilibrium level of National Income?

Multiple Choice Questions (MCQ's)

1. If in an economy investment is greater than saving, national income of the economy,
   - (*a*) increases
   - (*b*) decreases
   - (*c*) remains constant
   - (*d*) None of the above

2. What happens to the level of national income, when aggregate supply falls short of aggregate demand?
   - (*a*) Increases
   - (*b*) Decreases
   - (*c*) Constant
   - (*d*) None of the above

3. What happens to the level of national income, when aggregate supply exceeds aggregate demand?
   - (*a*) Increases
   - (*b*) Decreases
   - (*c*) Remains constant
   - (*d*) None of the above

4. If MPC and MPS are equal, value of multiplier is,
   - (*a*) 2
   - (*b*) 1
   - (*c*) 5
   - (*d*) 3

5. What is the relationship between MPS and Multiplier?
   - (*a*) Positive
   - (*b*) Negative
   - (*c*) Constant
   - (*d*) None of the above

6. What can be the minimum value of investment multiplier?
   - (*a*) 0
   - (*b*) 1
   - (*c*) 2
   - (*d*) 5

7. What can be the maximum value of investment multiplier?
   - (*a*) 5
   - (*b*) ∞
   - (*c*) 4
   - (*d*) 2

8. If marginal propensity to save is 0.1 and increase in national income is Rs. 500 crore, calculate increase in investment.
   - (*a*) Rs. 50 crore
   - (*b*) Rs. 40 crore
   - (*c*) Rs. 10 crore
   - (*d*) Rs. 2 crore

9. The value of multiplier is:
   - (*a*) $\dfrac{1}{MPC}$
   - (*b*) $\dfrac{1}{MPS}$
   - (*c*) $\dfrac{1}{1-MPS}$
   - (*d*) $\dfrac{1}{MPC-1}$

10. If MPC = 1, the value of multiplier is:
    - (*a*) 0
    - (*b*) 1
    - (*c*) Between 0 and 1
    - (*d*) Infinity

11. Which is the determining factor for investment ?
    - (*a*) Marginal Efficiency of Capital
    - (*b*) Interest Rate
    - (*c*) Both (*a*) and (*b*)
    - (*d*) None of the above

12. Increase in aggregate demand of equilibrium level of income and employment causes increase in :
    - (*a*) Employment
    - (*b*) Production
    - (*c*) Income
    - (*d*) All of the above

13. Which or is true ?
    - (*a*) MPC + MPS = 0
    - (*b*) MPC + MPS < 1
    - (*c*) MPC + MPS = 1
    - (*d*) MPC + MPS > 1

14. The main component of aggregate demand is :
    - (*a*) Individual consumption
    - (*b*) Public consumption
    - (*c*) Investment
    - (*d*) All of the above

15. IF MPC = 0.5, then Multiplier (k) will be:
    - (*a*) 1/4
    - (*b*) = 0
    - (*c*) 1
    - (*d*) 2

16. According to saving-investment viewpoint, income employment equilibrium will be determined at a point where:
    - (*a*) S > I
    - (*b*) I > S
    - (*c*) S = I
    - (*d*) None of these

17. Increase in aggregate demand of equilibrium level of income and employment causes increase in:
    - (*a*) Employment
    - (*b*) Production
    - (*c*) Income
    - (*d*) All of the above

18. Which one is correct ?

 (a) $K = \dfrac{1}{MPC}$ (b) $K = \dfrac{1}{MPS}$

 (c) $K = \dfrac{1}{1-MPS}$ (d) $K = \dfrac{1}{1+MPS}$

19. Which of the following is correct ?

 (a) MPC and multiplier have direct relationship

 (b) MPS and multiplier have inverse relationship

 (c) Both (a) and (b)

 (d) None of the above

20. If MPC = 0.5 and initial investment is Rs. 100 crores, the income generation in the economy will be :

 (a) Rs. 5 crores   (b) Rs. 100 crores

 (c) Rs. 200 crores   (d) Rs. 500 crores

21. If income equilibrium level in the economy is determined at the level before full employment, it is known as the state of:

 (a) Deficit Demand

 (b) Surplus Demand

 (c) Partial Demand

 (d) None of the above

22. What are the characteristics of Deficit Demand ?

 (a) Aggregate Demand falls short of Aggregate Demand required at full employment

 (b) Aggregate Demand remains short of Aggregate Supply required of full employment level

 (c) Both (a) and (b)

 (d) None of the above

23. Deflationary Gap shows the measurement of:

 (a) Deficit Demand

 (b) Surplus Demand

 (c) Full Employment

 (d) None of the above

24. Which one is the reason of appearing Deficit Demand condition ?

 (a) Fall in the money supply in the country

 (b) Fall in investment demand as a result of rise in bank rate

 (c) Fall in disposable income and consumption demand due to increase in taxes

 (d) All of the above

25. Income and employment are determined by:

 (a) Total demand

 (b) Total supply

 (c) Total demand and total supply both

 (d) By market demand.

🔑 Solutions

Frequently asked Questions (FAQ's)

1. The level at which the economy is in equilibrium, i.e., where aggregate demand = aggregate supply, is called effective demand.

2. The ratio of change in national income (ΔY) due to change in investment (ΔI) is known as multiplier (K).

$$K = \dfrac{\Delta Y}{\Delta I}$$

3. Multiplier (K) = $\dfrac{\text{Change in Income}}{\text{Change in Investment}}$

$$K = \dfrac{5000}{1000} = Rs.\ 5$$

4. Multiplier $K = \dfrac{1}{1-MPC}$

$$K = \dfrac{1}{0.6}$$
$$K = 2.5$$

5. When Aggregate Demand is equal to Aggregate Supply (AD = AS) in an economy at full employment level, then it is termed as the equilibrium level of National Income.

Multiple Choice Questions (MCQ's)

1. (a) increases

2. (a) Increases

3. (b) Decreases

4. (a) 2

5. (b) Negative

6. (b) 1

7. (b) ∞

8. (a) Rs. 50 crore

9. (b) $\dfrac{1}{MPS}$

10. (d) Infinity

11. (c) Both a)Marginal Efficiency of Capital and (b) Interest Rate
12. (d) All of the above
13. (c) MPC + MPS = 1
14. (d) All of the above
15. (d) 2
16. (c) S = I
17. (d) All of the above

18. (b) $K = \dfrac{1}{MPS}$
19. (c) Both (a) and (b)
20. (c) Rs. 200 crores
21. (a) Deficit Demand
22. (c) Both (a) and (b)
23. (a) Deficit Demand
24. (d) All of the above
25. (c) Total demand and total supply both

Money and Banking

Chief concepts of this chapter –

- Money – meaning and supply of money - Currency held by the public and net demand deposits held by commercial banks.
- Money creation by the commercial banking system
- Central bank and its functions (example of the Reserve Bank of India): Bank of issue, Government Bank, Bankers Bank, Control of Credit.

Barter System

It is a system of exchange, where good are exchanged for goods. It is also known as C-C economy, which means that commodity is exchanged for commodity.

Drawbacks of Barter System of Exchange

i) Lack of double coincidence of wants

ii) Lack of common measures of value

iii) Lack of store value

iv) Lack of standard for deferred payments

v) Lack of divisibility

6.1 Meaning and Definition of Money

Money is anything which is generally used as a medium of exchange, measure of value, store of value and means so of standard deferred payment.

It covers all types of money: coins, paper notes, cheques, digital money, plastic money, etc. It can be used to buy anything as it is legally accepted by everyone. It removes the problem of double coincidence of wants as anyone can buy anything he needs.

6.2 Evolution of Money

Money finds its origin to facilitate the need of exchange and to overcome the drawbacks of barter system. Next time the various forms that we took during the process of evolution where:

i) **Commodity money**: all sorts of commodities like pearls, sea-shells, salt et cetera have been used as a medium of exchange.

ii) **Animal money**: animals such as cow, goat, etc will used as a medium of exchange.

iii) : money made from metals like gold, silver, copper, et cetera where called metallic money.

It can be further classified as:

(a) **Full-bodied money**: whose value is commodity equals its value as money.

(b) **Token-coins**: whose value is money exceeds its value as commodity.

iv) **Paper money**: money made of paper is known as paper money and is further classified as-

(a) **Representative paper money**: which is backed by equivalent amount of gold and silver reserves

(b) **Convertible paper money**: for which the government or central bank assures convertibility to either gold or silver, at a fixed rate.

(c) **Inconvertible paper money**: for which government does not give any assurance for conversion into gold or silver.

v) **Credit money**: It refers to bank deposits with banks which are withdrawable through a cheque.

vi) **Plastic money**: It is the modern form of money in the form of debit and credit cards.

6.3 Functions of Money

The functions of money a broadly classified as:

1. Primary Functions
2. Secondary Functions

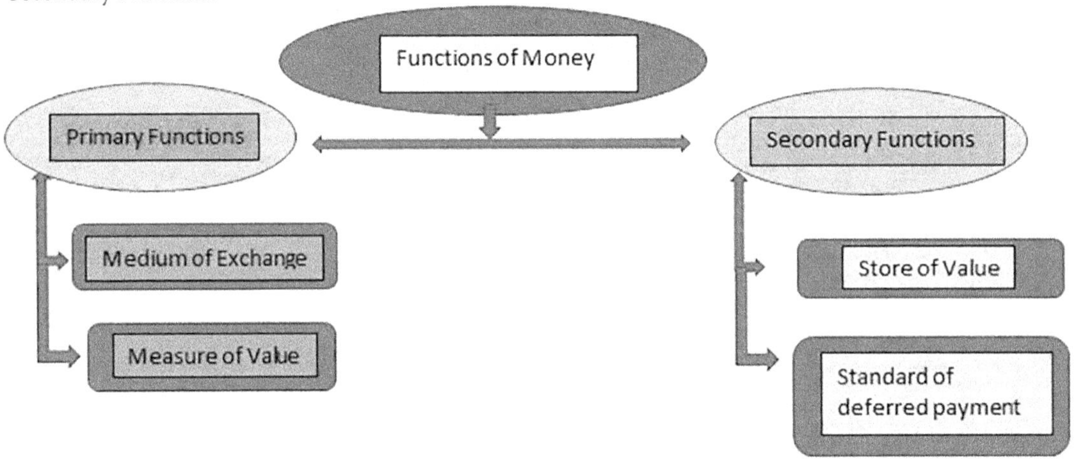

Functions of Money

Primary Functions — Medium of Exchange — Measure of Value

Secondary Functions — Store of Value — Standard of deferred payment

Due to the deficiencies of the barter system, money came into existence which acts as a medium of exchange, unit of account, store of value and standard of deferred payment.

i) **Legal definition of money**: According to this definition, money is anything which has the legal power to act as a medium of exchange and to discharge debts. Legally money can be of two types:

    (a) **Legal tender money of Fiat money**: The money issued by the legal authority of an economy, suggest coins and currency notes are referred to as legal tender money Fiat money. This can be further classified as limited an unlimited legal tender.

    (b) **Non-legal tender or fiduciary money**: The form of money which is backed by the trust between the two parties i.e., payer and payee, is termed as fiduciary money. Example, cheques issued by one party to another, promissory notes, et cetera.

ii) **Functional definition of money**: According to this definition, money is anything that is generally accepted as a means of exchange and at the same time, at as a measure and as a store of value.

6.4 Monetary System in India

❖ In India, Monetary Authority is 'Reserve Bank of India'.

❖ Paper currency standard is followed in India.

❖ Coins are regarded as limited legal tender money.

❖ RBI has sold monopoly to issue currency in India.

❖ Ministry of Finance issues 1-rupee coins and notes in India.

❖ India follows Minimum Reserve System for issuing notes. It means that RBI has to keep a minimum of rupees 200 crores as gold and foreign exchange with the World Bank for issuing coins and notes.

6.5 Demand for Money

The demand for money tells us What makes people desire a certain amount of money Since money is the medium of exchange it will determine the money people will want to keep for their transactions

6.6 Money Supply

The total stock of money in circulation among the public at a particular point of time is called money supply. Stock of money held by supplier of money is not part of money supply. Meaning by the government or banking system.

6.7 Measures of Money Supply in India

There are four measures of money supply in India as follows:

i) M_1 = Currency and coins with public + Demand deposits with commercial Banks + Other deposits with RBI

ii) M_2: It is a broader concept of money supply as compared to M_1. It also includes savings deposits with the post office saving bank.

   $M_2 = M_1$ + Saving deposits with Post Office saving bank

iii) M_3: It also includes net time deposits in addition to M_1 picture of money supply.

   $M_3 = M_1$ + Net time deposits with banks

iv) M_4: It includes total deposits with post office Savings Bank in addition to M_3 measure of money supply.

   $M_4 = M_3$ + Total Post Office Deposits excluding NSCs (National Saving Certificates)

  ❖ M_1 is the most liquid form of money supply while M_4 is the least liquid.

  ❖ M_1 and M_2 are considered the narrow concept of money supply while M_3 and M_4 are the broader concept of money supply.

6.8 High Powered Money

High powered money is the liability off the Monetary Authority of the country. This is also called the monetary base and is created by the RBI. High powered money includes currency notes and coins, deposits with the government and reserves of commercial banks with RBI. Thus, high powered money is

   $H = C + R$

Where: H = High powered money

   C = Currency

   R = Cash Reserves Commercial banks

6.9 Bank

The word bank has been derived from the French word 'banque' Or 'banco', which means bench or money exchange table.

It is an institution which accepts deposits from the public and gives loans and advances to those who need them. In a modern economy money comprises cash and bank deposits. The banking system comprises of two types of institutions: central bank of the economy and the commercial banking system of an economy

6.9.1 Commercial Banks

A profit making financial institution which accepts chequeable and non-chequeable deposits from the people and offers different kind of loans for the purpose of consumption or investment, is termed as commercial banks. These institutions are a part of money-creating system of the economy. The interest rate paid by the commercial bank to depositor's is lower than the rate charged from the borrowers. This difference between the two types of interest rates, called the 'spread' is the profit appropriated by the bank.

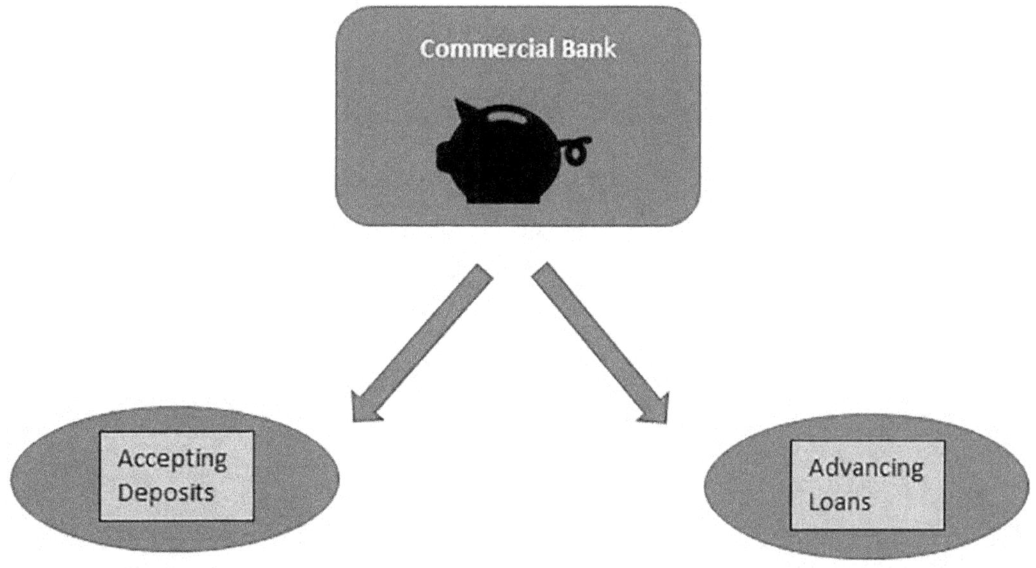

6.9.2 Functions of Commercial Banks

i)   Acceptance of deposits

    (a)   Chequeable Deposits

    (b)   Non-chequeable Deposits

ii)   Advancement of loans

    (a)   Overdraft facility

    (b)   Discounting bills of exchange

6.9.3 Money or Credit Creation by Commercial Banks

This is an important activity of commercial bank. Through this process, commercial banks create credit, which is created through excess reserves of the initial deposits.

Commercial banks increase the flow of money in an economy my credit creation. This process of credit creation is an outcome of its two primary functions, i.e., acceptance of deposits and advancement of loans. The banks issue loans from their cash reserves with the confidence on the historical experience that all depositor's will not withdraw their funds at the same time.

In this way, commercial banks create credit many more times than their cash reserves and contribute to increase money supply in the economy. But There is a limit to money or credit creation by banks. The RB I decides a certain percentage of deposits which every bank must keep as reserves. This is done to ensure that no bank is 'over lending'. This is a legal requirement and is binding on the banks put stop this is called the 'Required Reserve Ratio' or the 'Reserve Ratio' or 'Cash Reserve Ratio' (CRR).

Credit creation depends on initial level of deposits and money multiplier.

For the credit creation, commercial banks are legally required to keep a certain fraction of deposits with RBI and themselves. This fraction is called Legal Reserve Ratio (LRR).

6.9.4 Money Multiplier

"Money Multiplier" or deposit multiplier measures the number of deposits the commercial banks are able to create through the deposits of public kept with them as reserves.

$$\text{Money Multiplier} = \frac{1}{\text{LRR}}$$

$$\text{Money Creation} = \text{Initial Deposits} \times \frac{1}{\text{LRR}}$$

6.10 Central Bank

It is an apex banking institution which controls and regulates the entire banking system and money supply of a country. Reserve Bank of India is the central Bank of India.

6.11 Functions of Central Bank

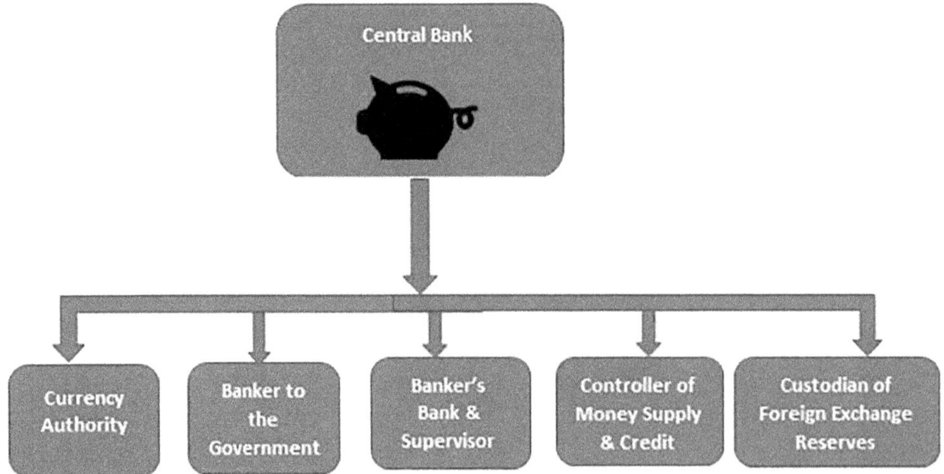

As the central Bank of the country, the Reserve Bank of India performs the following functions:

    i)   Authority for issuing of currency notes

    ii)   Banker to the government

    iii)   Banker's bank

    iv)   Lender of the last resort

    v)   Supervision of all Commercial Banks

    vi)   Maintains the custody of nations foreign currency reserves

    vii)   Clearing house

    viii) Controls the supply of credit

    ix)   Collect statistical information

6.12 Credit Control Policy/Monetary Policy of Central Bank

The Central Bank's policy to control and regulate the supply of money or credit within an economy, is termed as monetary policy.

The following instruments are used in monetary policy to control the flow of credit:

i) **Quantitative instruments**

These instruments affect the overall supply of money in an economy. These are

(a) Bank rate policy

(b) Open market operations

(c) Cash reserve ratio

(d) Statutory liquidity ratio

(e) Repo rate

(f) Reverse repo rate

iii) **Qualitative instruments**

These instruments affect the flow of money in selected or intended sectors these are:

(a) Margin requirement

(b) Rationing of credit or selective credit control

(c) Direct action

(d) Moral Suasion

Difference between Commercial Bank and Central Bank

BASIS	CENTRAL BANK	COMMERCIAL BANK
MEANING	Central bank is the 'apex' body that controls, regulates and operates the entire banking system in the country.	A Commercial Bank is a bank which accept deposits and advance loans for the purpose of earning profits.
OWNERSHIP	Owned and governed by government.	Owned and governed generally by private sector.
OBJECTIVE	Operates in public interest.	Operates to maximise profits.
ISSUE OF CURRENCY	Sole monopoly to issue currency.	No powers to issue currency.
PUBLIC DEALING	Does not deal directly with public.	Deals directly with public directly.
NUMBER OF BANKS	There is only one Central Bank in every country	There are multiple Commercial Banks in our country
EXAMPLES	Reserve Bank of India (RBI)	SBI, Kotak Mahindra, ICICI,ETC.

Key Statements

Repo rate: the rate at which the Central Bank offers loans to other Commercial Banks against security pledged for the loan.

Reverse repo rate: the interest rate at which commercial banks can deposit their surplus funds with Central Bank, or in other words the rate at which Central Bank borrows from Commercial Banks.

Cash Reserve Ratio (CRR): The percentage of total deposits, which Commercial Bank needs to keep as reserves with the Central Bank, this term does Cash Reserve Ratio.

Statutory Liquidity Ratio (SLR): Every Commercial Bank is required to maintain a fixed percentage of its assets in the form of cash or other liquid assets. This is termed as Statutory Liquidity Ratio.

Legal Reserve Ratio (LRR): It refers to that legal minimum fraction of total deposits which the Commercial Banks are required to keep. It is some of CRR and SLR.

Bank Rate: The rate at which Commercial Banks can borrow money from RBI without any security, when they run short of reserves, is termed as Bank Rate.

Open market operation: To sell or purchase of government bonds and securities by the central bank in open market is termed as open market operation.

Margin Requirement: It refers to the difference between the value of security and the amount of loan granted. Banks never grant loan equal to the amount of security.

Lender of the Last Resort: When Commercial Banks fail to meet the needs of the public, then RBI helped the Commercial Banks and the public by advancing loans to them and acts as a lender of last resort.

Clearing House: central bank has the reserves of commercial banks with themselves. All commercial banks have their accounts with the RBI. Therefore, RBI can make settlement of claims of various banks against each other by editing the entries in their accounts.

Supervisor: central bank regulates and controls the commercial banks. It exercises regular inspection of these banks and entries passed by them.

Moral Suasion: this is a combination of persuasion and pressure that Central Bank applies on other banks to get them to act, in a manner, in line with its policy.

Selective Credit Controls: under selective credit controls, the RBI gives directions to other banks to give or not to give credit for certain purposes to particular sectors. This method can be applied in both positive and negative manner what stop if positive, it means using measures to channelise credit to priority sectors which includes small scale industry, agriculture, exports, etc. If negative, it means using measures to restrict flow of credit to particular sectors.

Custodian of Foreign Exchange Reserves: caught the central bank acts as a custodian of the country stock of gold and reserves of foreign exchange. According to regulations of foreign exchange, all foreign exchange transactions must be routed through RBI. Centralisation of foreign exchange transactions with the Reserve Bank serves two objectives:

i) It helps the bank in stabilising the external value of currency.

ii) It helps in pursuing a coordinated policy towards the balance of payments situation of the country.

Demonetization: was a new initiative taken by the Government of India in November 2016 to tackle the problem of corruption, black money, terrorism and circulation of fake currency in the economy. Old currency notes of Rs. 5000 rupees thousand were no longer legal tender. New currency notes in the denomination of Rs. 500 and Rs. 2000 were launched. The public were advised to deposit old currency notes in their bank account till 31st November 2016 without any declaration and up to 31st March 2017 with the RBI with declaration. This move received both appreciation and criticism.

Exercise

Frequently asked Questions (FAQ's)

1. Why is modern currency accepted as a medium of exchange without any use of its own?

2. What is the role of money in the economy?

3. What is the difference between money multiplier and reserve?

4. What is the difference between a commercial bank and a central bank? .

5. How does the open market work?

Multiple Choice Questions (MCQ's)

1. The system, where in trade can be carried out through the exchange of goods and services is called the:
   (a) Barter system (b) Monetary system
   (c) Goods system (d) None of the above

2. Rakesh, a fruit seller, exchanged full mangoes with Sunil, a baker for 5 loafs of bread. This is an example of:
   (a) Barter system (b) Monetary system
   (c) Goods system (d) None of the above

3. Which of the following, solves the problem of "Double coincidence of wants"?
   (a) Goods
   (b) Banks
   (c) Money
   (d) All of the above

4. Double coincidence of one's refers to the _______ fulfilment of _____launch of the buyer and seller:
   (a) Simultaneous; Mutual
   (b) Sequential; Mutual
   (c) Mutual; Simultaneous
   (d) Mutual; Sequential

5. Which of the following is a function of money?
   (a) Medium of exchange
   (b) Store value
   (c) Measure of value
   (d) All of the above

6. Which of the following is the thing that is generally accepted by everyone as a medium of exchange?
   (a) Money (b) Goods
   (c) Services (d) None of the above

7. Money, comprises is of which of the following, which assistant conducting business transactions:
   (a) Coins (b) Currency notes
   (c) Cheques (d) All of the above

8. Money supply is which ___________ concept?
   (a) Stock
   (b) Flow
   (c) Monetary
   (d) None of the above

9. The ratio of total deposits that a commercial bank has to keep with Reserve Bank of India is called:
   (*a*) Statutory liquidity ratio
   (*b*) Deposit ratio
   (*c*) Cash reserve ratio
   (*d*) Legal reserve ratio

10. What will be the effect of increase in the Repo Rate on the money supply?
    (*a*) Money supply will increase
    (*b*) Money supply will decrease
    (*c*) Money supply will remain same
    (*d*) Money supply will initially increase and then it will decrease

11. If the total deposits created by commercial bank is Rs. 10,000 crores and legal reserve requirement is 40%, then amount of the initial deposits will be __________.
    (*a*) Rs. 4,000 crores
    (*b*) Rs. 6,000 crores
    (*c*) Rs. 11,000 crores
    (*d*) Rs. 14,000 crores

12. What is the other name for Money Multiplier?
    (*a*) Credit multiplier
    (*b*) Cash reserve ratio
    (*c*) Deposit multiplier
    (*d*) None of the above

13. The one rupee note and coins are issued by:
    (*a*) RBI central bank
    (*b*) Ministry of Finance
    (*c*) Commercial bank
    (*d*) Central government

14. What is the value of money multiplier when initial deposits are rupees 500 crores and LRR is 10% ?
    (*a*) 0.1   (*b*) 0.2
    (*c*) 10   (*d*) 20

15. Which of the following is not the function of the central bank?
    (*a*) Banking facilities to public
    (*b*) Banking facilities to government
    (*c*) Lending to government
    (*d*) Lending to commercial banks

16. Name the credit control method which refers to difference between the amount of loan and market value of the security offered by the borrower against the loan.
    (*a*) Moral suasion
    (*b*) Margin requirements
    (*c*) Legal reserve requirements
    (*d*) Selective credit controls

17. Which institution(s) performs the activity of credit creation?
    (*a*) Commercial banks
    (*b*) Central Bank
    (*c*) Both (*a*) and (*b*)
    (*d*) Neither (*a*) nor (*b*)

18. Demand deposits include (Choose the correct alternative):
    (*a*) Saving account deposits and fixed deposits
    (*b*) Saving account deposits and current account deposits
    (*c*) Current account deposits and fixed deposits
    (*d*) All types of deposits

19. Reverse Repo Rate is the rate at which central bank:
    (*a*) Lends money to Commercial banks for short term
    (*b*) Lends money to Commercial bank for long term
    (*c*) Accepts deposits from the Commercial banks
    (*d*) None of these

20. Name the institution which performs the functions of accepting deposits, granting loans and making investments, with the aim of earning profits.
    (*a*) Commercial Banks
    (*b*) Central Bank
    (*c*) Neither (*a*) nor (*b*)
    (*d*) Both (*a*) and (*b*)

21. The function of central bank involves buying and selling of government securities from or to the public and commercial banks.
    (*a*) Selective Credit Controls
    (*b*) Open Market Operations
    (*c*) Legal Reserve Requirements
    (*d*) None of these

22. Which bank controls the banking and monetary structure in India?
    (*a*) Reserve Bank of India
    (*b*) State Bank of India
    (*c*) Axis Bank
    (*d*) World Bank

23. Which of the following is not a quantitative method of credit control ?
    (*a*) Open Market Operation
    (*b*) Margin Requirements
    (*c*) Variable Reserve Ratio
    (*d*) Bank Rate Policy

24. Credit creation by commercial bank is determined by: (Choose the correct alternative)
    (*a*) Cash Reserve Ratio (CRR)
    (*b*) Initial Deposits
    (*c*) Statutory Liquidity Ratio (SLR)
    (*d*) All of the above

25. Repo Rate is the rate at which:
    (*a*) Commercial banks purchase government securities from the central bank
    (*b*) Commercial banks can take loans from the central bank
    (*c*) Commercial banks can keep their deposits with the central bank
    (*d*) Short term loans are given by commercial banks

 ## Solutions

Frequently asked Questions (FAQ's)

1. 1) Modern currency is authorized by the government of a country.
   2) In India, the Reserve Bank of India issues all currency notes on behalf of central Government.
   3) No other individual or organization is allowed to issue currency.

2. Money actually serves several different key functions in our economy. It is a medium of exchange, a unit of account, and a store of value. ... Money helps to facilitate trade because people in the economy generally recognize it as valuable.

3. Money multiplier is the amount of money that banks generate with each dollar of reserves. Reserve is the amount of deposits that the federal reserve require to hold not lend. It is the ratio of stock of money to the stock of high powered money in an economy.

4. While central bank serves the other banks along with the government, commercial banks serve the general public, including individuals and business organizations. The primary objective of the central bank is credit control and economic stability.

5. Open market operations work by selling and buying government securities by the central bank of a nation. To increase the money supply, the central bank buys back securities, while to reduce the money supply it sells securities to the commercial banks.

Multiple Choice Questions (MCQ's)

1. (a) incr
1. (a) Barter System
2. (a) Barter System
3. Money
4. (a) Simultaneous; Mutual
5. (d) All of the above
6. (a) Money
7. (d) All of the above
8. (a) Stock
9. (c) Cash reserve ratio
10. (b) Money supply will decrease
11. (a) Rs. 4,000 crores
12. (c) Deposit multiplier
13. (b) Ministry of Finance
14. (c) 10
15. (a) Banking facilities to public
16. (c) Margin requirements
17. (a) Commercial banks
18. (b) Saving account deposits and current account deposits
19. (c) Accepts deposits from the Commercial banks
20. (a) Commercial Banks
21. (b) Open Market Operations
22. (a) Reserve Bank of India
23. (b) Margin Requirements
24. (d) All off the above
25. (b) Commercial Banks can take loans from the Central Bank

CHAPTER 7

Government Budget and The Economy

LEARNING OBJECTIVES

❖ Government budget and its components.

❖ Measures of budgetary deficits.

Chief concepts of this chapter –

- Government budget – meaning, objectives and components.

- Classification of receipts – revenue receipts and capital receipts.

- Classification of expenditure-revenue expenditure and capital expenditure.

- Measures of government deficit- revenue deficit, fiscal deficit, primary deficit their meaning.

7.1 Government Budget – Meaning and its components

Budget is a financial statement showing the expected receipt and expenditure of Govt. for the coming fiscal or financial year.

There **are two components** of budget:

(a) **Revenue budget:** Revenue Budget consists of revenue receipts of government and expenditure met from such revenue.

(b) **Capital budget:** Capital budget consists of capital receipts and capital expenditure.

7.1.1 Objectives of Government Budget

Main objectives of budget are:

(i) Reallocation of resources.

(ii) Redistribution of income and wealth

(iii) Economic Stability

(iv) Management of public enterprises.

(v) Economic Growth

(vi) Generation of employment

7.1.2 Classification of Receipts

1. **Revenue Receipts** are those receipts that do not lead to a claim on the government. They are therefore termed non- redeemable. They are divided into tax and non-tax revenues.

   - Tax

     a. Direct Tax

       i. Income tax

       ii. Corporate Tax

       iii. Wealth and Property Tax

     b. Indirect Tax

       i. Value added Tax

       ii. Service Tax

       iii. Excise Duty

       iv. Custom Duty

       v. Entertainment Tax

   - Non-Tax

     a. Commercial Revenue

     b. Interest

     c. Dividend, Profits

     d. External Grants

     e. Administrative Revenues

     f. Fees

     g. License Fee

     h. Fines, Penalties

     i. Cash grants-in-aid from foreign countries and international organisations.

2. **Capital Receipts** the government also receives money by way of loans or from the sales of its assets. Loans will have to be returned to the agencies from which they have been borrowed. Thus, they create liability. sale of government assets, like sale of shares in public sector undertakings PSUs which is referred do a PSU disinvestment, reduce the total amount of financial assets of the government. All those receipts of the government which create liability or reduce financial assets are termed as capital receipts. When government takes fresh loans it will mean that in future these loans will have to be returned and interest will have to be paid on these loans. Similarly, when government sells an asset, then it means that in future its earnings from that asset, will disappear. Thus, these receipts can be debt creating or non-debt creating.

A. Borrowing and Other liabilities

B. Recovery of Loans

C. Other receipts (Disinvestments)

Direct Tax: A direct tax is one whose burden cannot be shifted to others i.e., the impact and incidence of the tax is on the same person. Example - income tax, wealth tax, gift tax.

Indirect Tax: An indirect tax is one whose burden can be shifted to others or the impact and incidence of an indirect tax falls on different people. ex- excise duty, VAT, service tax.

Revenue Receipts:

(i) Neither creates liabilities for Govt.

(ii) Nor causes any reduction in assets.

Capital Receipts:

(i) It creates liabilities or

(ii) It reduces financial assets

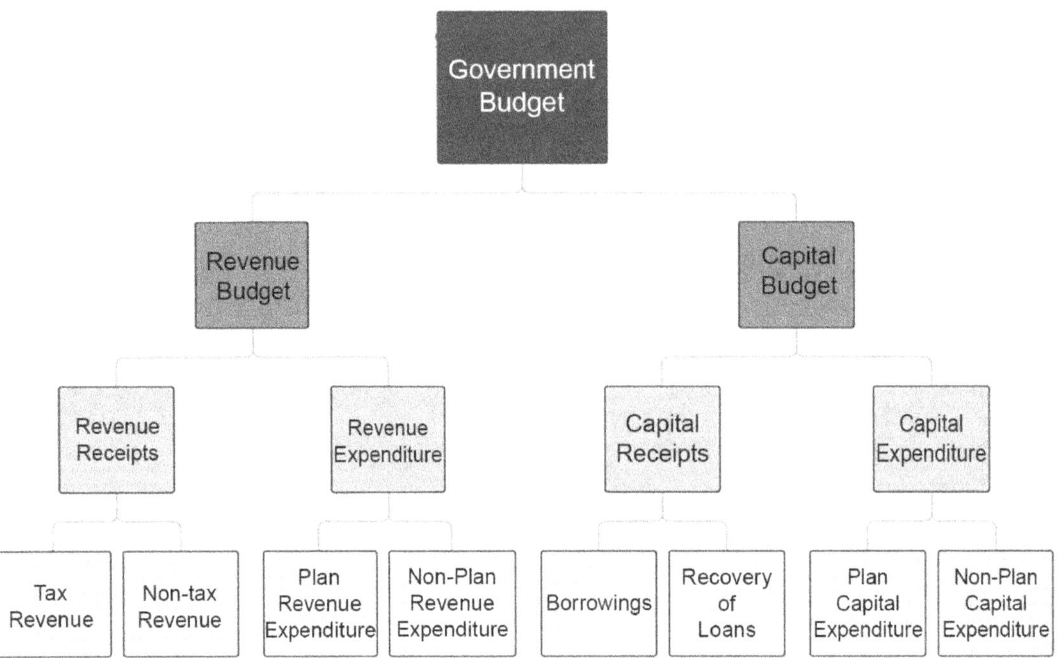

7.1.3 Classification of Expenditure

1. Revenue Expenditure

(i) Neither creates assets

(ii) Nor reduces liabilities. e.g., Interest Payment, subsidies etc.

2. Capital Expenditure:

(i) It creates assets

(ii) It reduces liabilities. e.g., Construction of school building Repayment of loans etc.

7.2 Balanced, Surplus and Deficit budget

Budget Deficit: It refers to a situation when budget expenditure of a government are greater than the government receipts.

Budgetary Deficit: Total Expenditure > Total Receipts.

Revenue Deficit: It is the excess of government revenue expenditure over revenue receipts.

Implications of Revenue Deficit are:

• A high revenue deficit shows fiscal indiscipline.

• It shows wasteful expenditures of Govt. on administration.

- It implies that government is dissaving, i.e., government is using up savings of other sectors of the economy to finance its consumption expenditure.

- It reduces the assets of the govt. due to disinvestment.

- A high revenue deficit gives a warning signal to the government to either curtail its expenditure or increase its revenue.

Fiscal Deficit: When total expenditure exceeds total receipts excluding borrowing.

Fiscal Deficit = Total expenditures > Total Receipts excluding borrowing.

Implications of Fiscal Deficits are:

(i) It leads to inflationary pressure.

(ii) A country has to face debt trap.

(iii) It reduces future growth and development.

(iv) It increases liability of the government.

(v) It increases foreign dependence.

7.2.1 Measures of Government Deficit

Revenue Deficit: Total revenue expenditure > Total revenue receipts

The revenue deficit refers to the excess of government revenue expenditure over revenue receipts.

Revenue deficit = Revenue expenditure - Revenue receipts

Fiscal deficit – Is the difference between the government's total expenditure and its total receipts excluding borrowing.

Gross fiscal deficit = Total expenditure – (Revenue receipts + Non- debt creating capital receipts)

The fiscal deficit will have to be financed through borrowing. Thus, it indicates the total borrowing requirements of the government from all sources. From the financing side:

Gross fiscal deficit = Net borrowing at home + Borrowing from RBI + Borrowing from abroad

Primary Deficit: By deducting Interest payment from fiscal deficit, we get primary deficit.

Gross primary deficit = Gross fiscal deficit – Net interest liabilities

Implications of Primary Deficits are: It indicates, how much of the government borrowings are going to meet expenses other than the interest payments.

7.3 GST: One Nation, One Tax, One Market

"ONE NATION, ONE MARKET AND ONE TAX": A TAX REFORM IN INDIA MACRO ECONOMICS Indian economy faced a drastic change in the year of 2017. As the Goods and Service Tax (GST) was implemented, it has replaced all the previous existing indirect tax such as Value

Added Tax. GST is implemented with the aim of "ONE NATION, ONE MARKET AND ONE TAX". problem of double taxing or tax on tax. GST has also changed the market value of many goods and services as it is functioning in five slabs, namely 0%, 5%, 12%, 18%, and 28%. The 0%slab is for the basic necessary goods and services and 28% for the luxurious goods and services. It has impacted the various sectors of Indian economy.

Five petroleum products have been kept out of GST for the time being but with passage of time, they will get subsumed in GST. State governments will continue to levy VAT on alcoholic liquor for human consumption. Tobacco and tobacco products will attract both GST and Central Excise Duty.

Many critics are still criticizing this move of the government. Among the critics some are criticizing only for political purpose but some do have a point, for example still many fields in the GST are ambiguous, more clarifications are needed for some goods, somethings which are exempted from paying tax should be taxed, etc. Moreover, there is a need for the awareness program by the government for the better understanding of GST.

Key Statements

Government Budget: A government budget is an annual financial statement showing item wise estimates of expected revenue and anticipated expenditure during a fiscal year.

Balanced Budget: If the government revenue is just equal to the government expenditure made by the general government, then it is known as balanced budget.

Unbalanced budget: If the government expenditure is either more or less than a government receipts, the budget is known as Unbalanced budget.

Surplus Budget: If the revenue received by the general government is more in comparison to expenditure, it is known as surplus budget.

Deficit Budget: If the expenditure made by the general government is more than the revenue received, then it is known as deficit budget.

Budget receipt: It refers to the estimated receipts of the government from various sources during a fiscal year.

Budget expenditure: It refers to the estimated expenditure of the government on its "development and non-development programmes or "plan and non-plan programmes during the fiscal year.

Revenue Budget: Revenue Budget contains both types of the revenue receipts of the government, i.e., Tax revenue and No-tax revenue ; and the Revenue expenditure.

Revenue Receipts: Government receipts, which

(a) Neither create any liabilities for the government; and

(b) Nor cause any reduction in assets of the government, are called revenue receipts.

Tax Revenue: Tax revenue refers to receipts from all kinds of taxes such as income tax, corporate tax, excise duty etc.

Tax: A tax is a legally compulsory payment imposed by the government on income and profit of persons and companies without reference to any benefit.

Non-tax revenue: It refers to government revenue from all sources other than taxes called non-tax revenue.

Revenue Expenditure: An expenditure that (a) Neither creates any assets (b) nor causes any reduction of liability.

Capital Budget: Capital budget contains capital receipts and capital expenditure of the government.

Capital Receipts: Government receipts that either creates liabilities (of payment of loan) or reduce assets (on disinvestment) are called capital receipts.

Capital Expenditure: Government expenditure of the government which either creates physical or financial assets or reduction of its liability.

Direct Tax: When (a) liability to pay a tax (Impact of Tax), and (b) the burden of that tax (Incidence of tax), falls on the same person, it is termed as direct tax.

Indirect Tax: When (a) liability to pay a tax (Impact of tax) is on one person; and (b) the burden of that tax (Incidence of tax), falls on the other person, it is termed as indirect tax.

Progressive Tax: A tax the rate of which increases with the increase in income and decreases with the fall in income is called a progressive tax.

Proportional Taxation: A tax is called proportional when the rate of taxation remains constant as the income of the taxpayer increases.

Regressive Tax: In a regressive tax system, the rate of tax falls as the tax base increases.

Plan expenditure: It refers to that expenditure which is incurred by the government to fulfil its planned development programmes.

Non-Plan Expenditure: This refers to all such government expenditures which are beyond the scope of its planned development programmes.

Developmental Expenditure: Developmental expenditure is the expenditure on activities which are directly related to economic and social development of the country.

Non-developmental expenditure: Non-developmental expenditure of the government is the expenditure on the essential general services of the government.

Budgetary deficit: It refers to the excess of total budgeted expenditure (both revenue expenditure and capital expenditure) over total budgetary receipts (both revenue receipt and capital receipt).

Revenue Deficit: Revenue deficit refers to the excess of revenue expenditure of the government over its revenue receipts.

Fiscal deficit: It is defined as excess of total expenditure over total receipts (revenue and capital receipts) excluding borrowing. Fiscal deficit indicates capacity of a country to borrow in relation to what it produces. In other words, it shows the extent of government dependence on borrowing to meet its budget expenditure.

Debt Trap: A vicious circle set wherein the government takes more loans to repay earlier loans, which is called Debt Trap.

Primary deficit: It is defined as fiscal deficit minus interest payments.

Exercise

Frequently asked Questions (FAQ's)

1. State any one objective of government budget.
2. Define surplus budget.
3. Define a balanced budget.
4. Define a deficit budget.
5. Why is entertainment tax an indirect tax?
6. What is meant by revenue deficit?
7. What are the objectives of a budget?

Multiple Choice Questions (MCQ's)

1. An annual statement of the estimated receipts and expenditure of the government over the fiscal year is known as
   (*a*) Budget
   (*b*) Income estimates
   (*c*) Account
   (*d*) Expenditure

2. When government spends more than it collects by way of revenue, it incurs ______
   (a) Budget surplus
   (b) Budget deficit
   (c) Capital expenditure
   (d) Revenue expenditure

3. The fiscal deficit is the difference between the government's total expenditure and its total receipts excluding ______
   (a) Interest   (b) Taxes
   (c) Spending   (d) Borrowings

4. Which of the following is the component of a budget?
   (a) Fiscal budget   (b) Capital budget
   (c) Both of these   (d) None of these

5. The amount collected by the government as taxes and duties is known as ______
   (a) Capital receipts
   (b) Tax revenue receipts
   (c) Non-tax revenue receipts
   (d) All of the above

6. Borrowing in the government budget is:
   (a) Revenue deficit   (b) Fiscal deficit
   (c) Primary deficit   (d) Deficit in taxes

7. The non-tax revenue in the following is:
   (a) Export duty   (b) Import duty
   (c) Dividends   (d) Excise

8. Direct tax is called direct because it is collected directly from:
   (a) The producers on goods produced
   (b) The sellers on goods sold
   (c) The buyers of goods
   (d) The income earners

9. Which objectives government attempts to obtain by Budget
   (a) To Promote Economic Development
   (b) Balanced Regional Development
   (c) Redistribution of Income and Wealth
   (d) All of the above

10. Which is a component of the Budget Receipt?
    (a) Revenue Receipt
    (b) Capital Receipt
    (c) Both (a) and (b)
    (d) None of the above

11. Tax revenue of the Government includes :
    (a) Income Tax   (b) Corporate Tax
    (c) Excise Duty   (d) All of the above

12. Which is included in the Direct Tax?
    (a) Income Tax   (b) Gift Tax
    (c) Both (a) and (b) (d) Excise Duty

13. Which is included in Indirect Tax?
    (a) Excise Duty   (b) Sales Tax
    (c) Both (a) and (b) (d) Wealth Tax

14. The expenditures which do not create assets for the government is called :
    (a) Revenue Expenditure
    (b) Capital Expenditure
    (c) Both (a) and (b)
    (d) None of the above

15. Capital budget consist of:
    (a) Revenue Receipts and Revenue Expenditure
    (b) Capital Receipts and Capital Expenditure
    (c) Direct and Indirect Tax
    (d) None of the above

16. Which type of expenditure is made in bridge construction?
    (a) Capital Expenditure
    (b) Revenue Expenditure
    (c) Both (a) and (b)
    (d) None of the above

17. Which of the following budget is suitable for developing economies?
    (a) Deficit Budget
    (b) Balanced Budget
    (c) Surplus Budget
    (d) None of the above

18. What is the duration of a Budget?
    (a) Annual   (b) Two Years
    (c) Five Years   (d) Ten Years

19. Which of the following is included in fiscal policy?
    (a) Public Expenditure
    (b) Tax
    (c) Public Debt
    (d) All of the above

20. Which of the following statement is true?
    (a) Fiscal deficit is the difference between total expenditure and total receipts
    (b) Primary deficit is the difference between total receipt and interest payments
    (c) Fiscal deficit is the sum of primary deficit and interest payment
    (d) All of the above

21. In an unbalanced budget:
    (*a*) Income is greater than expenditure
    (*b*) Expenditure is higher relative to income
    (*c*) Deficit is covered by loans or printing of notes
    (*d*) Only (*b*) and (*c*)

22. Which of the following is not a revenue receipt?
    (*a*) Recovery of Loans
    (*b*) Foreign Grants
    (*c*) Profits of Public Enterprise
    (*d*) Wealth Tax

23. Which of the following is a correct measure of the primary deficit?
    (*a*) Fiscal deficit minus revenue deficit
    (*b*) Revenue deficit minus interest payments
    (*c*) Fiscal deficit minus interest payments
    (*d*) Capital expenditure minus revenue expenditure

24. Budget is presented in the Parliament by:
    (*a*) Prime Minister
    (*b*) Home Minister
    (*c*) Finance Minister
    (*d*) Defence Minister

25. Which one of the following is a pair of direct tax?
    (*a*) Excise duty and Wealth Tax
    (*b*) Service Tax and Income Tax
    (*c*) Excise Duty and Service Tax
    (*d*) Wealth Tax and Income Tax

Solutions

Frequently asked Questions (FAQ's)

1. One of the primary objectives of the government budget is to mobilise resources for the purpose of rapid development.

2. A surplus budget is the one where the estimated revenues of the government are greater than the estimated expenditures.

3. A balanced budget is the one where the estimated revenue of the government equals the estimated expenditure.

4. A deficit budget is the one where the estimated revenue of the government is less than the estimated expenditure.

5. The entertainment tax is an indirect tax because the seller of the service passes the burden of tax on to the buyer of the service.

6. Revenue deficit in the government budget represents the excess of current revenue expenditure over the current revenue receipts.

7. The objectives of a budget are as follows:
   • Reallocation of Resources
   • Reducing Inequalities in Income and Wealth
   • Economic Stability
   • Management of Public Enterprises
   • Economic Growth
   • Reducing Regional Disparities

Multiple Choice Questions (MCQ's)

1. (a) Budget
2. (b) Budget Deficit
3. (d) Borrowings
4. (c) Both of these
5. (b) Tax revenue receipts
6. (b) Fiscal deficit
7. (c) Dividends
8. (d) The income earners
9. (d) All of the above
10. (c) Both (a) and (b)
11. (d) All of the above
12. (c) Both (a) and (b)
13. (c) Both (a) and (b)
14. (a) Revenue Expenditure
15. (b) Capital Receipts and Capital Expenditure
16. (a) Capital Expenditure
17. (a) Deficit Budget
18. (a) Annual
19. (d) All of the above
20. (c) Fiscal deficit is the sum of primary deficit and interest payment
21. (d) Only (b) and (c)
22. (a) Recovery of Loans
23. (c) Fiscal deficit minus interest payments
24. (c) Finance Minister
25. (d) Wealth Tax and Income Tax

Open Economy Macroeconomics

Chief concepts of this chapter –

- Balance of payments accounts – meaning and components.
- Foreign Exchange rate – meaning of fixed and flexible rates and managed floating

Open Economy: It is one that conducts business with other countries in a range of methods. The majority of modern economies are open.

8.1 The Balance of Payments

Balance of Payment (BOP): It is a record of all transactions that occurred between firms in a particular country and the rest of the world over a certain time period, such as a quarter or a year.

Accounts of Balance of payment:

8.1.1 Current Account

Current Account: It is the record of goods and services traded as well as transfer payments. It encompasses a country's most important activities, such as capital markets and services.

Two components of the Current Account:

- **Balance of Trade (BOT):** It is the difference between the value of a country's exports and imports of goods over a specified timeframe. The export of products is recorded as a credit in the BOT, whereas the import of goods is recorded as a debit. It is also referred to as the Trade Balance.
- **Balance of Invisibles:** The difference between a country's exports and imports of invisible over a certain time frame is known as the balance of invisible. Services, transfers, and income movements between countries are all examples of invisible.

8.1.2 Capital Account

Capital Account: All overseas asset transactions are recorded in the Capital Account. An asset is any type of wealth that may be held, such as money, stocks, bonds, government debt, and so on. The purchase of assets is recorded as a debit item on the capital account.

Components of Capital Account:

- **Investments:**
    a. **Direct Investment:** Equity Capital, Foreign Direct Investment (FDI), Reinvested Earning, and other Direct Capital Flows.
    b. **Portfolio Investment:** Offshore Funds. Foreign Institutional Investors (FII)
- **External Borrowings:** Includes Short-term Debt, External Commercial Borrowings.
- **External Assistance:** Multilateral and Bilateral Loans, Government Aid, Inter governmental Aid.

8.1.3 Balance of Payments Surplus and Deficit

Deficit of Balance of Payment Account:

- When a country has a balance of payments deficit, it imports more goods, capital, and services than it exports. It must take from other countries in order to pay for its imports.
- A deficit in the balance of payment happens when total payment surpasses total receipts; ergo BOP = Credit < Debit.
- A deficit of the balance of payment can be amended through an official reserve deal which signifies the sale of foreign exchange by the Reserve Bank.

Autonomous Transactions:

- When international economic transactions are made for reasons other than bridging the balance of payments gap, they are referred to as autonomous transactions.

- One reason might be to make money. In the balance of payment, these items are referred to as "above the line" items.

- This type of transactions are free of the condition of the balance of payment account.

- Autonomous items allude to those international economic exchanges, which happen because of some economic intention, for example, profit maximisation.

Accommodating Transactions:

- The gap in the balance of payments, or whether there is a deficit or surplus in the balance of payments, determines accommodating transactions, also known as "below the line" items. In other words, the net consequences of autonomous transactions determine them.

- Accommodating transactions are repaying capital exchanges that are intended to address the disequilibrium in the balance of payments, i.e., the autonomous items.

- If the balance of payment has a surplus or deficit, accommodating transactions are carried out on purpose to balance the balance of payment's surplus or deficit.

Errors and Omissions:

- It is difficult to keep accurate records of all international transactions. As a result, in addition to the current and capital accounts, there is a third element of the balance of payment called errors and omissions, which reflects this.

- The entries made under this head relate for the most part to leads and lags in the detailing of exchanges.

- It is a balancing entry that is expected to counterbalance the exaggerated or underestimated components.

8.2 The Foreign Exchange Market

Foreign Exchange Market:

- The foreign exchange market is the market where national currencies are exchanged for one another.

- Commercial banks, foreign exchange brokers, other authorised dealers, and monetary authorities are the main participants in the foreign exchange market.

- The foreign exchange markets are the first and most established financial markets and remain the premise whereupon the remainder of the financial edifice is built. It provides global liquidity, ideally with reasonable stability.

8.2.1 Foreign Exchange Rate

Foreign Exchange rate: An exchange rate is the worth of a country's currency versus that of another nation or an economic zone, also termed as Forex rate. Most of the trade rates are free-floating and will rise or fall based on market interest on the lookout. A few monetary forms are not free-floating and have limitations. It connects different countries' currencies and allows for cost and price comparisons across territorial boundaries.

8.2.2 Determination of the Exchange Rate

1. **Demand for Foreign Exchange:** People require foreign exchange because they want to buy goods and services from other countries, send gifts abroad, and buy financial assets from a specific country. The demand for foreign exchange falls as the flexible exchange rate rises and vice versa.

2. **Supply of Foreign Exchange:** Foreign currency flows into the home country for the following reasons - a country's exports lead to foreigners purchasing its domestic goods and services; foreigners send gifts or make transfers, and foreigners purchase a home country's assets. The foreign exchange supply has a positive relationship with the foreign exchange rate. When the foreign exchange rate rises, so does the supply of foreign exchange, and vice versa.

8.2.3 Merits and Demerits of Flexible and Fixed Exchange Rate Systems

Flexible Exchange Rate: The market forces of demand and supply determine this exchange rate. It is also referred to as a floating exchange rate.

- An increase in the exchange rate indicates that the price of foreign currency (dollar) in terms of domestic currency (rupees) has risen. This is referred to as depreciation of the domestic currency (rupees) in terms of foreign currency (dollars).

- Appreciation of the domestic currency (rupees) in terms of foreign currency (dollars) occurs when the price of domestic currency (rupees) increases in relation to foreign currency (dollars).

Merits of Flexible Exchange Rate:

a. There is no need to keep foreign exchange reserves.

b. As a result, the 'balances of payments' are automatically adjusted.

c. To remove impediments to capital and trade transfers.

d. Improves resource allocation efficiency.

e. It eliminates the issue of currency undervaluation or overvaluation.

f. It encourages foreign exchange-based venture capital.

Demerits of Flexible Exchange Rate:

   a. Future exchange rate fluctuations.

   b. Is a deterrent to international trade and investment.

   c. Promotes speculation.

   d. It contributes to market uncertainty.

Fixed Exchange Rate: The government fixes the exchange rate at a specific level in this exchange rate system. The goal of a fixed exchange rate system is to maintain the value of a currency within a narrow spectrum.

- **Devaluation** occurs in a fixed exchange rate system when a government action raises the exchange rate, causing the domestic currency to become cheaper.

- In a fixed exchange rate system, a **revaluation** occurs when the government lowers the exchange rate, making the domestic currency more expensive.

Merits of Fixed Exchange Rate:

   a. Exchange rate stability.

   b. There is no room for speculation.

   c. Encourages capital mobility and international trade.

   d. Attracts foreign investment. e. It forces the government to keep inflation under control.

Demerits of Fixed Exchange Rate:

   a. In relation to the balance of payments, there are no automatic adjustments i.e., it forestalls changes for monetary standards that become under-or over-esteemed.

   b. Requiring a huge pool of reserves to help the currency of a country in the event that it goes under pressure.

   c. It could lead to currency undervaluation or overvaluation.

   d. It undercuts the goal of free markets.

Determination of Equilibrium Foreign Exchange Rate: The equilibrium foreign exchange rate is the rate at which demand and supply of foreign exchange are equitable. It is determined by market forces, i.e., demand for and supply of foreign exchange, in a free market situation. The demand for foreign exchange and the exchange rate has an inverse relationship.

There is a direct relationship between foreign exchange supply and exchange rate. Because of the aforementioned reasons, the demand curve is sloped downward, and the supply curve is sloped upward.

The equilibrium foreign exchange rate is determined graphically by the intersection of the demand and supply curves.

Demand Curve for Foreign Exchange:

The demand curve of foreign exchange is 'Downward Sloping' because of inverse relationship between demand foreign exchange and foreign exchange rate. When the foreign exchange rate decreases, people demand more of foreign exchange. When the foreign exchange rate rises, its demand and decreases.

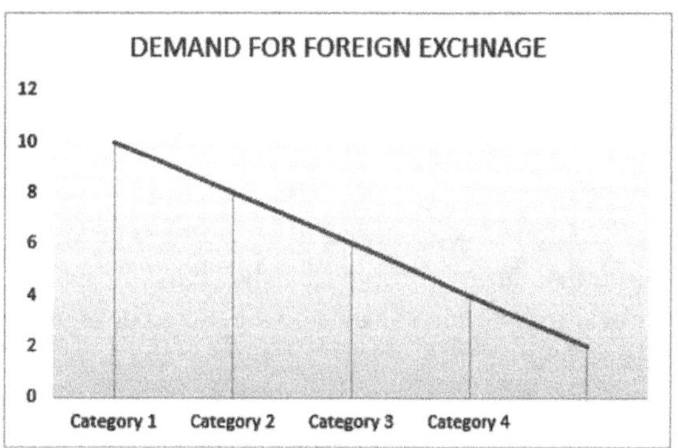

Supply Curve for Foreign Exchange:

The supply of foreign exchange arises when people demand for the foreign exchange to purchase goods or services from their country. The supply of foreign exchange arises because of the following reasons export of goods and services foreign investment speculations unilateral transfers from abroad.

There exists a positive relationship between foreign exchange rate and supply of foreign exchange. When the foreign exchange rate decreases, its supply also falls full stop when foreign exchange rate rises, its supply also increases.

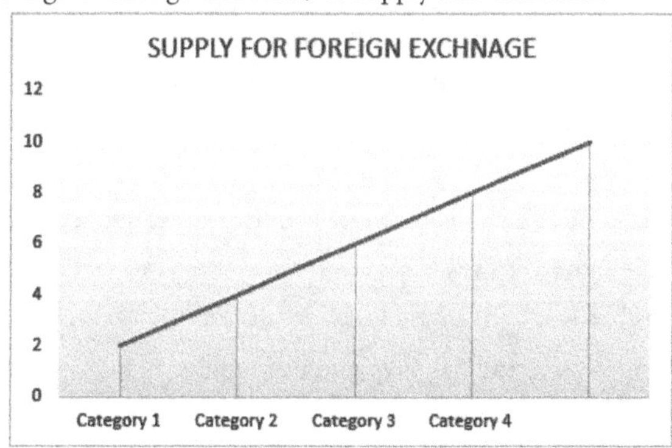

8.2.4 Managed floating

Managed Floating: It is a hybrid of a flexible exchange rate system, known as the float, and a fixed rate system, known as the managed part. This exchange rate system enables a country's central bank to intervene on a regular basis in foreign exchange markets to moderate exchange rate movements whenever such actions are deemed appropriate.

8.3 Exchange Rate Management: the Indian Experience

India's exchange rate policy has evolved in line with international and domestic developments. The exchange rate off the rupee is market determined, with the Reserve Bank ensuring orderly conditions in the foreign exchange market through its sales and purchases.

Key Statements

Open Economy It is one in which trading is done with other nations in goods and service and most often in financial assets.

Output Market an economy can trade in goods and services with other countries. This widens choice in the sense that consumers and producers can choose between domestic and foreign goods.

Financial Market most often an economy can buy financial assets from other countries. This gives investors the opportunity to choose between domestic and foreign assets.

Labour Market Firms can choose where to locate production and workers to choose where to work. There are various immigration laws which restrict the movement of labour between countries.

Leakage and injection: When Indians buy foreign goods, this spending escapes as from the circular flow of income decreasing aggregate demand. Our exports to foreigners enter as an injection into the circular flow, increasing aggregate demand of goods produced within the domestic economy.

Balance of Payment It is a systematic record of all economic transaction between the residents of a country, and the rest of the world during a year.

Current Account Transactions relating to trade in goods and services and transfer payment constitute the current account.

Components of Current Account
(i) Visible Trade (ii) Invisible Trade (iii) Transfer Payment

Capital Account It represents international capital transactions which include sale and purchase of assets such as bonds equities, lands , loans, bank account etc.

Components of capital account

(i) Foreign Investment

(ii) Loans

(iii) Banking Capital Transaction.

Balance of Trade It means the systematic records of visible imports and exports in a given year.

BOP = Visible Exports — Visible Imports

Autonomous Transaction It refers to those international economic transaction which are taken with the motive of profit.

Accommodating Items All the items related to the monetary transfers correcting balance of payments dis equilibrium are accommodating items.

Foreign Exchange Market The market in which forei. cn currencies are bought and sold is called the foreign exchange market.

Foreign Institutional Investors (FII) are an investment fund or a gathering of investors. Such a fund is registered in a foreign country, i.e., not in the country it is investing in. Such institutional investors mostly involve hedge funds, mutual funds, pension funds, insurance bonds, high-value debentures, investment banks etc.

Foreign Exchange Rate The rate at which one currency i exchanged for other is known as the rate of exchanges n foreign exchange rate.

Fixed Exchanges Rate System It refers to the rate ni exchange fixed by the government. It has two important variants

(i) Gold standard system of exchanges rate.
(ii) Bretton woods system of exchanges rate.

Determination of Foreign Exchange Rate It i determined by the forces of supply and demand in the foreign exchanges market.

Devaluation It is the fall in the value of domestic currency in relation to foreign currency as planned by the government In a situation exchanges rate is fixed by government.

Depreciation It is the fall in the value of domestic currency in relation to foreign currency in a situation when exchange rate is determined by the forces of demand and supply in tin international money market.

Managed Floating It is a system that allows adjustments in exchanges rate according to set of rules and regulation which are officially declared in the foreign exchanges market.

Exercise

Frequently asked Questions (FAQ's)

1. What does balance of payment account show? Name the two parts of the balance of payments accounts.

2. What are the effects of disequilibrium in Balance of Payment?

3. What would a host economy(in terms of investment) prefer? FDI or FII? Explain.

4. What are some of the merits of a Fixed Exchange Rate System?

5. What are some of the sources of supply of foreign exchange?

Multiple Choice Questions (MCQ's)

1. Balance of payment is an accounting statement that records the economic transactions between:

   (a) Residents of a country and non- resident individuals

   (b) Residents of a country and rest of the world

   (c) Non- residents and rest of the world

   (d) None of the above

2. Economic transactions include which of the following:
   (a) visible items
   (b) Invisible items
   (c) Unilateral transfers
   (d) All of the above

3. Resident includes:
   (a) Individual
   (b) Firms
   (c) Government agencies
   (d) All of the above

4. Balance of payment is which of the following concepts?
   (a) Flow
   (b) Stock
   (c) Both (a) and (b)
   (d) None of the above

5. Balance of trade is:
   (a) Difference between export and import of goods.
   (b) Sum total of export and import of goods.
   (c) Difference between export and import of services.
   (d) Sum total of export and import of services

6. What are the components of balance of payment account?
   (a) current account
   (b) Capital account
   (c) Both (a) and (b)
   (d) None of the above

7. Which of the following is not a component of BOP?
   (a) Current account
   (b) Capital account
   (c) Real account
   (d) None of the above

8. Important export of goods is called:
   (a) Invisible trade   (b) Visible trade
   (c) Nominal trade   (d) None of the above

9. Import and export of services is called:
   (a) Invisible trade   (b) Visible trade
   (c) Nominal trade   (d) None of the above

10. Which of the following is not a component of capital account of BOP?
    (a) Borrowings
    (b) Investments
    (c) Foreign travel tour purchased by an individual resident
    (d) Change in foreign reserves

11. Which of the following is a type of investment?
    (a) Foreign direct investment
    (b) Portfolio investment
    (c) Foreign institutional investment
    (d) All of the above

12. Surplus in current account arises when:
    (a) Credit side is more than debit site
    (b) Debit side is more than credit side
    (c) Debit side equals the credit side
    (d) None of the above

13. Deficit in capital account arises when:
    (a) Credit side is more than debit side
    (b) Debit side is more than credit side
    (c) Debit side is equal to credit side
    (d) None of the above

14. Which account has a direct impact on income, output and employment?
    (a) Current account
    (b) Capital account
    (c) Real account
    (d) Nominal account

15. Which account does not have a direct impact on income, output and employment?
    (a) Current account
    (b) Capital account
    (c) Normal account
    (d) Real account

16. Capital account is which concept?
    (a) Stock   (b) Flow
    (c) Nominal   (d) None of the above

17. Which transactions are recorded in the balance of account with profit maximisation, motive?
    (a) Autonomous   (b) Accommodating
    (c) Compensatory   (d) None of the above

18. Which transactions are done to cover the surplus or deficit in BOP account?
    (a) Autonomous
    (b) Accommodating
    (c) Compensatory
    (d) None of the above

19. Which of the following transactions take place on both current and capital account?
    (a) Autonomous
    (b) Accommodating
    (c) Compensatory
    (d) None of the above

20. ________ is an accounting statement which records all economic transactions between non-resident and domestic territory.
    (a) Balance of payment
    (b) Balance of Trade
    (c) Final accounts
    (d) None of the above

21. "Current account is in surplus" because:
    (a) Receipts on current account or less than payment on current
    (b) Value of exports of goods and services is more than the value of import of goods and services
    (c) Receipts on capital account are more than payment on capital account
    (d) Receipts on current account are less than payment on capital account

22. "Interest on deposit from a foreign bank is recorded in the current account". Choose the correct reason:
    (a) It is a visible good
    (b) It is an invisible service
    (c) Income from abroad
    (d) It is a transfer receipt

23. The decrease in the value of domestic currency in relation to foreign currency due to fluctuations in foreign exchange rate is:
    (a) Devaluation   (b) Appreciation
    (c) Depreciation   (d) None of the above

24. The decrease in the value of foreign exchange rate which is done intentionally by the government is called:
    (a) Appreciation   (b) Depreciation
    (c) Devaluation   (d) Revaluation

25. In which system of exchange rate, the exchange rate does not change continuously?
    (a) Fixed exchange rate
    (b) Flexible exchange rate
    (c) Managed floating exchange rate
    (d) None of the above

🔑 Solutions

Frequently asked Questions (FAQ's)

1. Balance of payments(BOP) Account shows a countries inflow and outflows of foreign exchange. The two parts of the BOP are:
   i) The current account
   ii) The capital account

2. Effects of disequilibrium in Balance of Payments are:
   i) Economic credibility of a country obviously goes down.
   ii) It results in reduction of FOREX reserves.
   iii) It has an adverse effect on the economic growth and prosperity of the nation.
   iv) Foreign dependence may lead to political dependence and can hence result in bleeding of resources and exploitation of the country.

3. As far as the economy in which the money is being invested, they would generally prefer FDI. Since FDI causes long-term economic growth by increasing the GDP of the country. FII will increase the capital in an economy but may not have a significant effect on the economic growth of a country.

4. some of the benefits of a fixed exchange rate system are:
   - It provides stability to the exchange rate.
   - It encourages international trade and capital movement.
   - It also attracts foreign capital.
   - There is no speculation in a Fixed Exchange Rate system.
   - It puts pressure on the government to keep a check on inflation.

5. Some of the main sources of foreign exchange are:
   - When foreigners directly buy commodities in the domestic market.
   - When foreign companies or business invest directly in the domestic market.
   - When remittances are done by non-residents who are living out of their countries.
   - When non-residents make speculated purchases in the domestic market, it leads to the flow of foreign exchange.
   - By exporting goods and services.
   - Foreign direct investments.
   - Portfolio investment from rest of the world.

Multiple Choice Questions (MCQ's)

1. (b) Residents and rest of the world
2. (d) all of the above
3. (d) All of the above
4. (a) Flow
5. (a) Difference between export and import of goods.
6. (c) Both (a) and (b)
7. (c) Real account
8. (b) Visible trade
9. (a) Invisible trade
10. (c) Foreign travel tour purchased by an individual resident
11. (d) All of the above
12. (a) Credit side is more than debit side
13. (b) Debit side is more than credit side
14. (a) Current account
15. (b) Capital account
16. (a) Stock
17. (a) Autonomous
18. (b) Accommodating
19. (a) Autonomous
20. (a) Balance of payment
21. (b) Value of exports of goods and services is more than the value of import of goods and services
22. (c) Income from abroad
23. (c) Depreciation
24. (c) Devaluation
25. (a) Fixed exchange rate

Your Notes :

Indian Economic Development

CHAPTER 9

Indian Economy on The Eve of Independence

LEARNING OBJECTIVES
- ❖ What is Microeconomics?
- ❖ Central Problems

Chief concepts of this introductory chapter –

- A brief introduction of the state of Indian economy on the eve of independence
- Main features come up problems and policies of agriculture institutional aspects and new agricultural strategy
- Industry (IPR 1956 SSI- role &importance)
- Foreign trade

Overall Features of Indian Economy on The Eve of Independence

Indian economy in the ancient period was a vibrant and prosperous economy. On the agricultural front, it was self-contained rural economy where cultivators themselves were the owners of land. Industrial sector what's famous throughout the world for its handicraft products. Indian exports enjoyed global reputation. The silk and cotton textiles were famous for their fine quality and the metal and precious stonework were famous for excellent craftsmanship. Spices were of high quality.

The advent of British rule however marked the beginning of a systematic exploitation of the Indian economy. The agricultural sector was exploited as a source of revenue. The industrial sector was destroyed by exploiting the domestic market for the British products. Export of raw material was encouraged to promote supplies to the British industry. Import of British goods was encouraged to give impetuous to the industrial revolution which was then happening in Britain.

Due to the systematic exploitation of the agricultural and industrial sectors and restructuring of India's foreign trade in favour of the British economy, India changed from a vibrant economy to a stagnant in a backward economy.

9.1 Some of the features of the Indian economy on the eve of independence are:

1. **Stagnant economy** : most of the estimates done by notable individuals (Dadabhai Naoroji, Findlay Shirras, R.C.Desai and few others) who attempted to estimate India's national and Per Capita Income, revealed that the country's growth of aggregate real output during the first half of the 20th century was less than 2% and growth in per capita output per year was bigger 0.5%.

2. **Backward economy** : in 1947- 48, the per capita income in India was just Rs. 230. The bulk of the population was very poor, without sufficient food, clothing and shelter. Widespread unemployment caused by the destruction of handicraft industries was an important factor contributing to poverty.

3. **Dominance of agriculture:** Nearly 72% of the country's working population was engaged in agriculture However, the contribution of agriculture to GDP was only 50%, indicating the backwardness of this sector this sector suffered from low productivity, owing to which it had low contribution to GDP.

4. **Bleak industrialization:** By the time of independence, small- scale and cottage industries were almost ruined. Heavy industry showed a bleak growth, and for the bulk of capital goods requirements, we were dependent upon imports from Britain.

5. **Heavy dependence on imports:** India was heavily dependent upon imports, particularly for machinery and related equipment of production. Several consumer goods like sewing machines, medicines,

kerosene oil, bicycles, etc., were imported from abroad. Armed forces of the country were also dependent heavily on foreign imports for most of the defence equipment.

6. **Limited organisation:** When India got its independence, bulk of the population of India lived in villages. In 1948, only 14% of population lived in urban areas while 86% lived in rural areas. Rural population lacked opportunities outside agriculture. This compounded to their poverty.

7. **Semi- feudal economy:** Indian economy on the eve of independence, was neither wholly feudal nor a capitalist economy. It was a semi feudal economy. Such an economy has the mixture of feudalistic and capitalist modes of production. Feudalistic mode of production leads to low productivity. Low productivity leads to backwardness.

Thus, we can say that on the eve of independence, Indian economy was characterised with low level of economic development. It was developed only to the extent it could serve the colonial interest of the British government. Even though railways, ports came up, Post and Telegraph were developed to promote the process of colonial exploitation of the Indian economy. It was directed towards the protection and promotion of the economic interests of the British economy rather than the Indian economy.

9.2 Agricultural Sector on The Eve of Independence

India's agricultural sector (on the eve of independence) exhibited three principal characteristics; these characteristics pointed to backwardness of India's agriculture as well as its stagnationLow level of productivity

- Exploitive land settlement system: The British government in India set up a triangular relationship among the government, the owner of the soil and the tiller of the soil. This was popularly known as Zamindari system of Land settlement.

- Forced commercialization of agriculture: Farmers before to shift from subsistence cultivation (cultivation for self-consumption) to cultivation of cash crops for the market to cope with the needs of the British industry.

- Lack of investment in agriculture infrastructure: the colonial government or zamindars took no interest in promoting investment in agricultural infrastructure. Permanent means of irrigation were hardly available. Agriculture was heavily dependent on rainfall and therefore continued to be uncertain. Flood- control, drainage and de- salination of the soil which could have led to increased productivity

of the sector were totally neglected

- A wedge between owners of the soil and tillers of the soil.

- Small folding: most land holdings were uneconomic building low output at high cost. As Landholdings were both small as well as fragmented. Fragmented holding me up means a piece here and a piece there.

- Farming was taken mostly as a means of subsistence, to provide for the basic needs of the family. There is little surplus left for sale in the market. Implying a lack of commercial outlook. Accordingly, backwardness prevailed and poverty dominated.

9.3 Industrial Sector

"Systematic de-industrialisation" is the term that describes the status of industrial sector during the British rule. It implied two things

- Decay of world famous traditional handicraft industry owing to discriminatory policies of the British Government.

- Bleak growth of modern industry now to lack of investment opportunities.

Two-fold motive behind the systematic .(industrialisation during the British Rule in India.

- To exploit India's wealth of raw material and primary products. It was required to fulfil the emerging needs of industrial inputs in the wake of industrial revolution in Britain.

- To exploit India as a potential market for the industrial products of Britain.

9.4 Foreign Trade

Foreign Trade India had occupied a place of eminence in the area of Foreign trade, since ancient times. But the British rule in India ended this eminence.

India has been an important trading nation since ancient times.

But when the restrictive policies of commodity production, trade and tariff were imposed by the colonial government, it adversely affected the structure, composition and volume of India's foreign trade.

9.4.1 Following were the reasons behind the poor growth of foreign trade:

1. Exporter of Primary Products and Importer of Finished Goods

Under the colonial rule, India became an exporter of primary products such as raw silk, cotton, wool, sugar, indigo, jute, etc and an importer of finished consumer goods like cotton, silk and woollen clothes and capital goods like light machinery produced in the factories of Britain.

2. Britain's Monopoly Control

Britain maintained a monopoly control over India's exports and imports. Due to this, more than half of India's foreign trade was restricted to Britain while the rest was allowed with a few other countries like; China, Ceylon (Sri Lanka) and Persia (Iran). The opening of Suez Canal in 1869 further intensified British control over India's foreign trade.

3. Drain of India's Wealth

An important characteristic of foreign trade throughout the colonial period was the generation of a large export surplus. But this surplus came at a huge cost to the country's economy. Several essential commodities like food grains, kerosene, were scarcely available in the domestic market.

Also, this surplus was not used in any developmental activity of India.

Huge administrative expenses were incurred by the British Government to manage their colonial rule in India. Also, huge expenses were incurred by the British Government to fight wars in pursuit of their policy of imperialism.

All of this, led to the drain of Indian wealth.

9.5 Demographic Condition

Demographic conditions during the British rule exhibited all features of a stagnant and backward economy. Both birth rate and death rate were very high nearly 48 and 40 per thousand respectively.

Various details about the population of British India were first collected through a census in 1881. Before 1921, India was in the first stage of demographic transition. The second stage began after 1921. However, neither the total population of India nor the rate of population growth at this stage was very high. Though suffering from certain limitations, it revealed the Unevenness in India's population growth. The population grew at a rate of 1.2% up to the year 1951.

9.5.1 On the eve of independence, the demographic condition was as follows:

- The overall literacy level was less than 16%.

- The female literacy level was at a negligible low rate of about 7%.

- Public health facilities were either unavailable to large chunks of population or when available, were highly inadequate. Infant mortality rate was 218 per thousand in contrast to present infant mortality rate of 63 per thousand.

- Life expectancy was very low 44 years in contrast to the present 66 years.

- Both birth rate and death rate were very high at 48 and 40 per thousand of persons respectively.

9.6 Occupational Structure

Greater dependence on agriculture as suggested by occupational structure on the eve of independence implied lesser availability of land per head for the farming population. Accordingly, agriculture was taken largely as a means of subsistence and less as an occupation for profit.

During the colonial period, the occupational structure of India exhibited its backwardness. The agricultural sector accounted for the largest share of the work force which remained at a high of 70-75% of the work force and the manufacturing and services sectors accounted for only 10 and 15-20% respectively.

There existed a growing regional disparity with few states such as Orissa, Rajasthan and Punjab witnessing an increase in agricultural workforce while the states which were the parts of Madras presidency. Bombay and Bengal witnessed a decline in the percentage of work force dependent on agriculture.

9.7 Infrastructure

Infrastructure refer to the elements of economic change as well as elements of social change which serve as a foundation for growth and development of a country. Development of infrastructure is a precondition to the economic and social development of a country.

Infrastructure comprises of such industries which help in the growth of other industries. Under the colonial period, basic infrastructure such as railways, port per transport, posts and telegraphs developed.

However, the real motive behind this development was not to provide basic amenities to the people but to sub serve various colonial interests.

The state of infrastructure under the colonial rule can be understood with the help of following points

1. Roads

Roads constructed before independence were not fit for modern transport. It was very difficult to reach rural areas during rainy season.

The roads were built only to serve the purpose of mobilising the army within India and transporting raw materials from the countryside to the nearest railway station or the port for exporting it.

2. Railways

British rulers introduced railways in India in 1850 and it began its operation in 1853. It is considered as one of the important contribution of Britishers.

The railways affected the structure of the Indian economy in the following two ways

- It enabled people to undertake long distance travel and thereby break geographical and cultural barriers.

- It fostered commercialisation of Indian agriculture which adversely affected the self-sufficiency of the village economies in India.

So, the social .benefits provided by the Railways was outweighed by the country's huge economic loss.

3. Water and Air Transport

The colonial rulers took measures for the development of water transport. The inland waterways, at times, also proved uneconomical as in the case of the coast canal on the Orissa coast. The main purpose behind their development was to serve Britain's colonial interest.

The colonial government also showed way to the air transport in 1932 by establishing Tata Airlines. Thus, in this way it inaugurated the aviation sector in India.

4. Communication

Modern postal system started in India in 1837. The first telegraphy line was opened in 1857. The introduction of the expensive system of electric telegraph in India served the purpose of maintaining law and order.

9.8 Conclusion

Prevalence of rampant poverty and unemployment after independence required welfare orientation of public economic policies. The social and economic challenges before the country were enormous.

Key Statements

Zamindari System: The three major components of the Zamindari System were – British Government, Zamindar (Landlord) and peasants. Known as one of the major land revenue systems.

Demographic Transition: Demographic transition is a model used to represent the movement of high birth and death rates to low birth and death rates as a country develops from a pre-industrial to an industrialized economic system. It works on the premise that birth and death rates are connected to and correlate with stages of industrial development.

Infant Mortality Rate: The infant mortality rate is, by definition, the number of children dying under a year of age divided by the number of live births that year. The infant mortality rate is also called the infant death rate.

Life Expectancy: The term "life expectancy" refers to the number of years a person can expect to live. By definition, life expectancy is based on an estimate of the average age that members of a particular population group will be when they die.

Colonial Regime: A rule by the wealthy or powerful nation over a weaker country is the colonial rule. For the more powerful nation, the smaller ruled nation is a colony. There is no justice in it and the weaker nation would be exploited of its resources. India was under the colonial regime of the Britishers till Independence on 15th of August,1947.

Natural Calamities: Earthquakes, floods, volcanic eruptions, landslides, fires, spontaneous tree limbs falling, winds, hurricanes, tornadoes, ice storms. Natural calamities are occurrences, events or phenomenon that happen in nature of their own accord or because of certain acts of man (vehicles also cause damage to air by pollution)

Exercise

Frequently asked Questions (FAQ's)

1. Where there any positive side effects of the British rule in India ?
2. What do you mean by Population census?
3. What is meant by subsistence agriculture?
4. Legally Zamindari system off land revenue has been abolished in independent India. Yet Indian agriculture continues to be in a state of backwardness. Why?
5. How did discriminatory trade policy contribute to the success of industrial revolution in Great Britain?

Multiple Choice Questions (MCQ's)

1. Indian economy under British rule was:
   - (*a*) Developed economy
   - (*b*) Developing economy
   - (*d*) Growing economy

2. Most of India's population during British rule was dependent on which sector for a living?
   - (*a*) Primary sector
   - (*b*) Secondary sector
   - (*c*) Tertiary sector
   - (*d*) Equally in all the above sectors

3. Which factor caused low productivity in agriculture ?
   - (*a*) system of land settlement
   - (*b*) Low level of technology
   - (*c*) Lack of investment
   - (*d*) All of the above

4. British rulers' policy towards industrialization in India was to make India mainly:
   - (*a*) Importer of primary products from Britain and exporter of finished products to Britain
   - (*b*) Importer of finished products from Britain and exporter of primary products to Britain

(c) Exporter of both primary products and finished products

(d) Importer of both primary products and finished products

5. One of the following what is high during the British rule over India:
   (a) Literacy rate
   (b) Female literacy rate
   (c) Infant mortality rate
   (d) Life expectancy

6. The occupational structure of India during the British rule revealed that the Indian economy was:
   (a) Underdeveloped
   (b) Developed
   (c) Stagnant
   (d) Underdeveloped and Stagnant

7. The opening of the _________ Canal significantly reduce the cost of transportation of goods between Britain and India.
   (a) Agra
   (b) Ainsley
   (c) Suez
   (d) Canoly

8. The main interest of the Zamindar was:
   (a) To collect rent
   (b) To improve the condition of agriculture
   (c) To produce food crops
   (d) To produce cash crops

9. India enter the _________ stage of Demographic Transition after the year 1921.
   (a) Fourth
   (b) Second
   (c) Third
   (d) First

10. Decay of handicrafts was caused by:
    (a) British tariff policy
    (b) Competition from man-made machines
    (c) New patterns of demand
    (d) All of the above

11. On the eve of independence, India was a net exporter of :
    (a) Primary products
    (b) Industrial products
    (c) Capital goods
    (d) Agricultural goods

12. In the history of demographic Transition, which year is regarded as the 'year of great divide'?
    (a) 1901
    (b) 1912
    (c) 1921
    (d) 1925

13. Which up the following industries were in operation in our country at the time of independence?
    (a) Cotton and Jute textile industries
    (b) Iron and steel industries
    (c) Sugar, cement and paper industries
    (d) All of the above

14. Which of the following 'Land Tenure Systems'?
    (a) Zamindari system
    (b) Mahalwari system
    (c) Rotwari system
    (d) All of the above

15. What percentage India's population was dependent on agriculture on the eve of independence?
    (a) 75%
    (b) 50%
    (c) 85%
    (d) 65%

16. Commercialization agriculture during British rule led to:
    (a) more production of food crops
    (b) Improvement in the economic condition of farmers
    (c) More production of cash crops used by Britishers as raw material
    (d) The aggregate area under cultivation expanded

17. The occupational structure of India was biased towards:
    (a) Agriculture
    (b) Industry
    (c) Foreign trade
    (d) None of the above

18. The First official census was conducted in the year:
    (a) 1891
    (b) 1921
    (c) 1781
    (d) 1881

19. The British government used Indian foreign exchange surplus in which of the following ways?
    (a) Pay for war expenses
    (b) Pay for the deficit of the British government
    (c) Payment of salaries
    (d) All of the above

20. Which Industry was adversely affected due to partition?
    (a) silk
    (b) Cotton
    (c) Jute
    (d) Nylon

21. Land holdings At the time of independence were:
    (a) fragmented
    (b) Large
    (c) Small
    (d) Both (a) and (c)

22. Railways were introduced in India in the year:
    (a) 1850　　　　　(b) 1853
    (c) 1854　　　　　(d) 1855

23. Which industry of India got severely affected under the colonial rule?
    (a) Sugar industry
    (b) Iron and steel industry
    (c) Handicraft industry
    (d) Paper industry

24. Stagnant economy is the one which shows:
    (a) Little growth in income
    (b) High growth and income
    (c) Low level of productivity
    (d) Both (a) and (c)

Solutions

Frequently asked Questions (FAQ's)

1. Yes, with a view to enlarging size of the market for British goods in India, the British government needed to provide some infrastructure and facilities in India. These included:
   (a) transport facilities, largely in terms of railways
   (b) Development of ports
   (c) Provision of post and Telegraph services.

   The British government has left a legacy of a strong and efficient administrative set up in India.

2. Population census is a detailed estimation of population size, along with a complete demographic profile of the country.

3. Subsistence agriculture is a form of farming in which only subsistence crops are grown to provide for the basic needs of the family.

4. Despite abolition of the Zamindari system, poverty continues to be pervasive in Indian agriculture owing to two reasons:
   i. The bulk of the Indian farmers are small and marginal holders. Small and marginal holdings are not conducive to the adoption of innovative techniques of farming, and
   ii. The delivery mechanism related to financial help by the state is grossly inefficient and ineffective.

5. Discriminatory trade policy contributed to the success of industrial revolution in Great Britain in two ways:
   (a) Low duty on the import of British industrial goods into India led to the growth of domestic demand of these goods, and
   (b) Low duty on the export of raw material from India ensured availability of low-cost inputs for the British industry.

Multiple Choice Questions (MCQ's)

1. (c) Underdeveloped economy
2. (a) Primary sector
3. (d) All of the above
4. (b) Importer of finished products from Britain and exporter of primary products to Britain
5. (c) Infant mortality rate
6. (d) Underdeveloped and Stagnant
7. (c) Suez
8. (a) To collect rent
9. (b) Second
10. (d) All of the above
11. (a) Primary products
12. (c) 1921
13. (d) All of the above
14. (d) All of the above
15. (c) 85%
16. (c) More production of cash crops used by Britishers as raw material
17. (a) Agriculture
18. (d) 1881
19. (d) All of the above
20. (c) Jute
21. (d) Both (a) and (c)
22. (a) 1850
23. (c) Handicraft industry
24. (d) Both (a) and (c)

CHAPTER 10

Indian Economy 1950 -1990 Five Year Plans In India Agriculture, Industry and Trade 1950-1990

LEARNING OBJECTIVES

- ❖ Goals of India's five year plans
- ❖ Development policies in different sectors such as agriculture and industry from 1950 – 1990
- ❖ Merits and limitations of a regulated economy
- ❖ Development policies in different sectors such as agriculture and industry from 1950 – 1990
- ❖ Trade Strategy of Import substitution

Chief concepts of this chapter –

- What is Economic Planning?
- Five Year Plans in India
- Need for Planning in India
- Economic System and Planning in India
- Goals and Achievements of the Goals
- Agriculture reforms
- Industrial reforms
- Inward looking strategies off Trade

Economic Planning

It is a process under which a central authority defines a set of targets to be achieved within a specified period of time.

"Economic planning means utilisation of countries resources in different development activities in accordance with the national priorities."

- Planning Commission

The central objective of planning in India, is to initiate a process of development which will raise the living standards and open out to the people new opportunities for richer and more varied life.

- First Five Year Plans

10.1 Five Year Plans in India

Plan was introduced in 1951 and the last in 2012. In between these years, some annual plans were also introduced as these: three annual plans from April 1st 1966 to March 31st 1969; one annual plan from April 1st 1979 to March 31st 1980; two annual plans from April 1st 1990 to March 31st 1992. Different Five Year Plans had different goals. It is important to note that the Plan documents not only specify the objectives to be achieved in the five years of a plan, but also what is to be achieved in the long run. Long- term plan is called a 'perspective plan'.

10.2 Need for planning in India

India inherited from the British a backward and stagnant economy. It was backward as the level of output and productivity were low. Indian economy was stagnant as the GDP growth was extremely low (dismal). Such an economy cannot be left to the market forces of supply and demand for its path of growth and development. It needed a big push of investment, which needed the support by the government. In 1950, the Planning Commission was set up with the Prime Minister as its Chairperson, to take care of the Indian economic planning

10.3 Economic System and Planning

10.3.1 Economic System

Economic system is defined as an arrangement by which the central problems of an economy are solved.

The three basic central problems of an economic system are

- Choice of Production What goods and services should be produced in the country?

- Choice of Technology How should the goods and services be produced? Should producers use more human labour or more capital for producing things,

- Distribution of Goods and Services How should goods and services be distributed among people?

On the basis of government intervention, economic system can be classified as

10.3.1.1 Socialist Economy

It is an economic system in which all economic decisions are taken by the government. In this system, the government decides what goods are to be produced in accordance with the needs of society, how goods are to be produced and how they should be distributed.

Socialist economy promotes equitable distribution of income. However, it also suffers from the drawbacks of a bureaucratic set up in the form of red-tapism and corruption.

In Cuba and China, most of the economic activities are governed by the socialistic principles.

10.3.1.2 Capitalist Economy

It is an economic system in which major economic decisions like

- What goods and services are to be produced.

- How goods and services are to be distributed are left to the free play of the market forces or the forces of supply and demand.

Capitalist economies depend upon the market forces of demand and supply. In this type of economy, only those consumer goods will be produced that have good demand in the market and yield profit to the producers.

For example, cars will be produced if they are in demand and also if they can earn profits for the producer.

In this economy, the goods and services produced are distributed among people not on the basis of what people need but on the basis of purchasing power.

- Capitalist economy generally manifests unequal distribution of income, but it also generates fastest growth in output and national income

- Capitalist economy is also called laissez faire or free market economy, it exists in North America, Japan, Australia, Western Europe, etc.

10.3.1.3 Mixed Economy

It is an economic system in which public sector and private sector exist side by side.

In this economy, the market will provide whatever goods and services it can produce well and the government will provide essential goods and services which the market fails to provide.

It is an economic system in which major economic decisions are taken by the Central Government authority as well as are left to the free play of the market forces.

Merits of Mixed Economy

- Mixed economy gives proper scope to private individuals to co-exist and contribute towards economic development.

- In this, planned economic development ensures stability . and balanced development.

- In this, competition between the private sector and public sector industries is there. It leads to enhanced productivity.

Demerits of Mixed Economy

- Mixed economy cannot effectively control the private sector industries which are outside the government purview.

- It is characterised by red-tapism and high degree of corruption.

- In it, there is concentration of economic power in the hands of private sector, politicians and bureaucrats.

10.4 Economic Planning

Economic planning is a process in which a central authority of a country defines a set of goals to be achieved within a specified period, sets out a plan to achieve those goals, keeping in view the country's resources.

Planning commission defines economic planning as, 'Economic planning means utilisation of country's resources in different development activities in accordance with national priorities. Now, let us understand what a 'plan' is?

- A plan spells out how the resources of nation should be efficiency utilised.

- It should have some general goals which are achieved through specific objectives within a specified period of time.

To formulate plans, Planning Commission was set up in 1950 under the chairmanship of Jawaharlal Nehru, the first Prime Minister of independent India.

Its aim was to promote rapid rise in standard of living of the people, increase production and offer employment opportunities in India. To facilitate economic planning Five Year Plans were formulated. The first Five Year Plan was introduced in April 1951.

10.5 Goals of Five Year Plans

A plan should have some clearly specified goals. The goals of five year plans are

- Growth Economic growth implies a consistent increase in GDP or a consistent increase in the level of output or a consistent increase in the flow of goods and services in the economy over a long period of time.

- Modernisation To increase the production of goods and services to producers with the adoption of new technology.

- Self-reliance It means avoiding imports of those goods which could be produced in India itself. This policy was considered a necessity in order to reduce our dependence on Foreign countries, especially for food.

- Equity It implies equitable distribution of income so that the ^benefits of growth are shared by all sections of the society.

10.5.1 All the Five Year Plans are formulated keeping the below objectives in mind

10.5.1.1 Growth

It refers to increase in the country's capacity to produce the output of goods and services within the country. It implies either a larger stock of productive capital or a large size of supporting services like transport and banking.

Increase is GDP is a good indicator of economic growth. Gross Domestic Product (GDP) is the market value of all final goods and services produced in the different sectors of an economy, viz the primary sector, the secondary sector and the tertiary sector during an year within the domestic territory of a country.

10.5.1.2 Modernisation

Adoption of new technology is called modernisation. It is done with an aim to increase the production of goods and services. For example, a farmer can increase the output on the farm by using new seed varieties instead of using old ones.

Modernisation refers to not only change in production methods, but also change in the social outlook of a society by granting equal status to women and making use of their talent in the productive process.

10.5.1.3 Self-Reliance

A nation can promote economic growth and modernisation by using its own resources or by using resources imported from other nations. The first seven Five Year Plans gave importance to self-reliance by avoiding imports. This policy was considered a necessity in order to reduce our dependence on foreign countries especially for food.

10.5.1.4 Equity

It refers to reduction in disparity of income or wealth, by uplifting weaker sections of the society. It also refers to distribution of economic power equally or in such way that every Indian should be able to meet his or her basic needs such as food, a decent house, education, healthcare, etc.

10.6 Achievements of the Goals

Following are the observations of the achievements of the goals of the Five Year Plans:

1) **Increase in national income :** even though, for most of the plans, India failed to achieve the targeted rate of growth, it was successful in breaking the deadlock of economic stagnation that it had experienced at the time of independence. Prior to planning, national income in India increased at the rate of 0.5% per annum. By the end of 7th Plan, it was recorded to be 5.8%.

2) **Reforms in agriculture :** Five year plans contributed to the development of agriculture in two ways:
   (a) through land reforms
   (b) through improvement in technology

   Green Revolution and self- sufficiency in food grain was the hallmark of this change.

3) **Growth and diversification of industry :** Five year plans gave a big push to the basic and capital good industries (Iron and steel, machinery, chemical fertilisers, etc.). Along with, consumer goods industries have substantially grown to achieve the level of self-sufficiency.

   By the end of 1990, Indian economy had achieved the recognition of an emerging industrial economy.

4) **Economic infrastructure:** Means of transport and communication, irrigation facilities and power generation capacity, banking and insurance facilities are the key elements of economic infrastructure. During the period 1950- 90, economic infrastructure had recorded a significant growth. Indian Railways had achieved the distinction of the largest network in the country generating opportunities of employment.

5) **Social infrastructure:** Health and educational facilities(the key parametres of social infrastructure) were also boosted under these plans. It was owing to expansion of health facilities that there was a significant fall in the death rate and a significant rise in average life- expectancy.

6) *International trade:* During the period 1950- 91, there was a considerable change in the volume, value and composition of India's exports and imports. Before the planning started, India wasn't exporter of primary products an importer of finished products. The period 1950- 90 so a gradual shift in this trend: India started exporting engineering goods, a sign of India emerging as an industrial nation.

Indian economy during the period 1950- 9090 recorded a noticeable growth in national income along with a significant structural change across all sectors of the economy.

There are certain dark spots and stock failures which still need to be taken care of:

(a) We failed to eradicate poverty

(b) We failed to curb the high rate of inflation

(c) We fail to contain crisis of unemployment

(d) We failed to generate economic and social infrastructure needed to bring momentum in the process of the growth

There has been a substantial shift in the strategy of growth in the year 1991. NEP (new economic policy) was designed and implemented to foster the process of growth.

10.7 The Architect of Indian Planning

Prasanta Chandra Mahalanobis was born in 1893 in Calcutta. He was educated at the Presidency College in Calcutta and at Cambridge University in England. His contributions to the subject of statistics brought him international fame. In 1946, he was made a Fellow (member) of Britain's Royal Society, one of the most prestigious organisations of scientists.

Mahalanobis established the Indian Statistical Institute (ISI) in Calcutta and started a journal, Sankhya. Mahalanobis had contributed a lot in the formulation of our Five Year Plans. The Second Plan became the landmark of his contribution.

During the Second Plan period, Mahalanobis invited many distinguished economists from India and abroad to advise him on India's economic development. Some of these economists became Nobel Prize winners later

Many economists today reject the approach to planning formulated by Mahalanobis but he will always be remembered for playing a vital role in putting India on the road to economic progress and statisticians continue to profit from his contribution to statistical theory.

10.8 Let us now see these goals and the extent to which they succeeded in doing so, with regards to agriculture, industry and trade:

10.8.1 Agriculture

It refers to all those activities which are related to the cultivation of land for the production of crops; food crops and non-food crops.

(i) Importance of Agriculture in the Indian Economy
- Contribution to GDP
- Supply of wage goods
- Employment
- Industrial raw material
- Contribution to international trade
- Contribution to domestic trade
- Wealth of the nation

(ii) Problems of Indian Agriculture
- Lack of permanent means of irrigation
- Deficiency of finance
- Conventional outlook
- Small and scattered holding
- Lack of organised marketing system

10.8.1.1 Reforms in Indian Agriculture

(i) Technical Reforms
- Use of HYV seeds
- Use of chemical fertilisers
- Scientific farm management practices
- Mechanised means of cultivation

(ii) Land Reforms
- Abolition of intermediaries
- Regulation of rent
- Consolidation of holding
- Ceiling on land holding
- Co-operative farming

(iii) General Reforms
- Expansion of irrigation facilities
- Provision of credit
- Regulated market
- Price support policy

Marketable Surplus

It refers to surplus of farmer's output over and above his own farm consumption.

Thus, Marketable surplus of wheat = Output of wheat – On farm consumption of wheat

Green Revolution

It started in India in year 1967-68. In the year, 1967-68 itself, food grain production increased by nearly 25%. So, much increase in food grain production in a country which earlier used to import food grains.

10.8.2 Industry and Trade

Industry provides employment in agriculture; it promotes modernisation and overall prosperity.

Importance of industry are as follows

- Structural transformation
- Source of employment

- Source of mechanised means of farming
- Imparts dynamism to growth process
- Growth of civilisation
- Infrastructural growth

10.8.2.1 Industrial Policy Resolution 1956 (IPR-1956)

- Three-fold classification of industries
- Industrial licensing
- Industrial Concessions- tax holiday and subsidised power supply.

Private Sector

It was assigned only a secondary role in the process of industrialisation. Industries in the private sector could be established only through a license from the government.

Small Scale Industries (SSI)

These were accorded a high priority with a view to promoting the goals of 'employment and equity'.

10.8.2.2 Trade: Strategy of Import Substitution

Inward looking trade strategy is called import substitution:

i. Import substitution implies domestic production of those goods which the economy has been importing from rest of the world. This is a strategy to save foreign exchange by restricting the volume of imports.

ii. Foreign exchange was to be utilised for developmental imports for example import of plant and machinery which is essential for growth and development but cannot be produced domestically, owing to the lack of technology or the lack of investment funds.

iii. By adopting inward looking trade strategy, the government preferred to economise the use of foreign exchange through import substitution rather than maximise the generation of foreign exchange through export promotion.

iv. The government also wanted to protect the domestic industry from international competition.

On 15th August 1947, India attained its freedom. After independence, Nehru and many other leaders decided the type of economic system that will prove beneficial for India. In order to achieve the objectives of 'growth with equity', mixed economy was introduced as the economic system of India.

10.8.3 Conclusion

As a result of this strategy of growth under five year plans, Indian economy broke the barrier of economic stagnation. India became self- sufficient in food grain production. Land

reforms and HYV technology turn Indian agriculture from a stagnant in backward sector into a vibrant and growing sector of the economy. The industrial sector also diversified. A structural shift in terms of the relative contribution of agriculture and industrial sector to GDP , but unfortunately, even as the industrial sector grew and the contribution of agriculture sector to GDP declined, almost 65% of the population still continued to be employed in the agriculture sector till 1990. Implying that the growth in industrial and service sector was not sufficient to absorb the surplus labour force of the agriculture sector.

With the passage of time, bad effects of the strategy of industrialization started overshadowing the good effects. So much so, that the government was compelled to revisit the entire strategy of the economic growth. This led to the emergence of any NEP (New Economic Policy).

Key Statements

Structural Change: as the country develops, the contribution of each economic sector to GDP changes, this is referred to as 'structural change'.

Import Substitution Policy: It refers to fixing the maximum limit on the imports of a commodity by a domestic producer. They specify the number of goods that can be imported.

Industrial Policy Resolution 1956 (IPR 1956): this resolution from the basis of the second five year plan, the plan which tried to build the basis for a socialist pattern of society. This resolution classified industries into three categories. The first category comprised industries which would exclusively be owned by the government. The second category consisted of industries in which the private sector could supplement the efforts of the public sector, with the government taking the sole responsibility for starting new units and, the third category consisted of the remaining industries which were to be in the private sector. No new industry was allowed unless a licence was obtained from the government. This policy was used for promoting industry in the backward regions. In addition, such units were given certain concessions such as tax benefit and electricity at lower tariff. The purpose of this policy was to promote regional equality.

Marketed Surplus: the portion of agricultural produce which is sold in the market by the farmer is called marketed surplus.

Land Ceiling: was another policy to promote equity in the agriculture sector. This means fixing the maximum size of land which could be owned by an individual. The purpose of land ceiling was to reduce the concentration of land ownership in a few hands.

Exercise

Frequently asked Questions (FAQ's)

1. Why should Plans have Goals?
2. What can be the ways in a country to increase its GDP?
3. What is social justice?
4. What is 'Free Play of Market Forces?
5. What is Green Revolution and when did the Green Revolution start in India?

Multiple Choice Questions (MCQ's)

1. An economy in which economic decisions are taken by some central authority of the government with a view to maximising social welfare is called:
   (*a*) Capitalist economy
   (*b*) Socialist economy
   (*c*) Market economy
   (*d*) Mixed economy

2. In Which year was India's First Five Fear Plan launched ?
   (*a*) 1951   (*b*) 1947
   (*c*) 1940   (*d*) 1955

3. Which of the following bodies/institutions were engaged in the formulation of Five Fear Plans in India?
   (*a*) Planning Commission
   (*b*) National development council
   (*c*) Finance ministry
   (*d*) Home ministry

4. when was the Planning Commission established in India?
   (*a*) 1947   (*b*) 1948
   (*c*) 1950   (*d*) 1951

5. Planning Commission in India was established under the Chairmanship of:
   (*a*) B.R. Ambedkar
   (*b*) P.C.Mahalanobis
   (*c*) Jawahar Lal Nehru
   (*d*) V.K.R.V.Rao

6. An economy in which means of production are used in a manner such that social welfare is maximised is called:
   (*a*) Market economy
   (*b*) Capitalist economy
   (*c*) Socialist economy
   (*d*) Mixed economy

7. Three consecutive were launched during the period:
   (*a*) April 1st, 1966, to March 31st, 1969
   (*b*) April 1st, 1969, to March 31st, 1972
   (*c*) April 1st, 1963, to March 31st, 1966
   (*d*) None of the above

8. Planning Commission, the erstwhile central planning authority in India, has been replaced by:
   (*a*) Finance Commission
   (*b*) Central Statistical Commission
   (*c*) National institution for Transforming India (NITI) Ayog
   (*d*) Indian Statistical Institute (ISI)

9. Which of the following is correct about the Planning in India?
   (*a*) Mixed economy has been the framework of planning in India
   (*b*) The duration of the Twelfth Five Year Plan was 2012-17
   (*c*) Planning in India started with a heavy reliance on the public sector
   (*d*) All of the above

10. the industrial policy resolution was introduced in India in the year:
    (*a*) 1948
    (*b*) 1951
    (*c*) 1991
    (*d*) 1995

11. Which of the following is not a long period objective of Planning in India?
    (*a*) GDP Growth
    (*b*) Modernization
    (*c*) Better quality of life
    (*d*) Equitable distribution

12. Which was the last Five Year Plan in India?
    (*a*) Tenth Plan
    (*b*) Eleventh Plan
    (*c*) Twelfth Plan
    (*d*) Thirteenth Plan

13. The final approval to the Five Year Plans of India is given by:
    (*a*) NITI Aayog
    (*b*) President of India
    (*c*) National Development Council
    (*d*) Ministry of Finance

14. The main objective of the First Five Year Plan of India was?
    (a) Development of infrastructure
    (b) Development of ports
    (c) Development of the industries
    (d) Development of agriculture

15. Who is the President of the National Development Council?
    (a) Vice-President   (b) RBI Governor
    (c) Home Minister   (d) Prime Minister

16. National Development Council was established in:
    (a) 1952   (b) 1971
    (c) 1958   (d) 1964

17. NITI Aayog or the National Institution for Transforming India replaced which of the following commission?
    (a) Public Service Commission
    (b) Civil Service Commission
    (c) The Election Commission
    (d) The Planning Commission

18. Who is the chairman of NITI Aayog?
    (a) Prime Minister
    (b) Home Minister
    (c) President of India
    (d) Finance Minister

19. The main aim of the Eleventh Five Year Plan was:
    (a) Eradication of regional imbalances
    (b) Food, Work and Productivity
    (c) Inclusive Growth in all sectors
    (d) Eradication of Poverty

20. Which of the following steps promoted the growth of the economy as a whole by stimulating the development of industrial and tertiary sectors?
    (a) Independence   (b) Planning
    (c) Colonial rule   (d) Green revolution

21. Which of the following is the main objective of carrying out various economic activities?
    (a) Profit   (b) Public welfare
    (c) Competition   (d) Equality

22. What was the prime target of the First Five Year Plan of India?
    (a) Development of the Industries
    (b) Development of agriculture
    (c) Development of infrastructure
    (d) Development of ports

23. In which Five Year Plan India opted for Mixed Economy?
    (a) First   (b) Second
    (c) Third   (d) Fourth

24. Which of the following five year plan gave the slogan of 'Garibi Hatao'?
    (a) Fourth Five Year Plan
    (b) Fifth Five Year Plan
    (c) Sixth Year Plan
    (d) Seventh Year Plan

25. Economic planning is in:
    (a) Union list
    (b) State list
    (c) Concurrent list
    (d) Not in any specified list

Solutions

Frequently asked Questions (FAQ's)

1. Without Goals, there is no planning. In fact, planning is defined as a strategy that defines how to allocate the country's scarce resources to different uses with a view to achieving a given set of goals. These Goals often relate to growth and social justice.

2. In a country the ways of increasing the GDP are:

   (*a*) Discovery of more and more resources in the country that increases resource-base of the country.

   (*b*) Innovative technology, that enhances productivity or output per unit of input.

3. Social justice is achieved when the process of economic growth leads to equitable distribution of income and wealth.

4. It refers to a situation when the government of a country does not interfere with the market forces of supply and demand.

   i)   Producers are free to allocate resources to the production of different goods and services with a view to maximising their profit.

   ii)   Producers will simply produce those goods which fetch them high price and high profits, no matter whether the poor get even the minimum of food, shelter and clothing.

   iii) 'Maximisation of profit' dominates the process of decision- making.

5. The Green Revolution was a period that began in the 1960s during which agriculture in India was converted into a modern industrial system by the adoption of technology, along with the introduction of many modern methods of farming like tractors, pesticides, fertilizers, irrigation facilities, such as the use of high yielding variety (HYV) seeds, mechanised farm tools, irrigation facilities, pesticides and fertilizers. The Green revolution started in India started with its introduction in Punjab in 1966.

Multiple Choice Questions (MCQ's)

1. (b) Socialist economy
2. (a) 1951
3. (a) Planning Commission
4. (c) 1950
5. (c) Jawahar Lal Nehru
6. (c) Socialist economy
7. (a) April 1st, 1966, to March 31st, 1969
8. (c) National Institution for Transforming India (NITI) Ayog
9. (d) All of the above
10. (a) 1948
11. (c) Better quality of life
12. (b) Twelfth Plan
13. (c) National Development Council
14. (d) Development of agriculture
15. (d) Prime Minister
16. (a) 1952
17. (d) The Planning Commission
18. (a) Prime Minister
19. (c) Inclusive Growth in all sectors
20. (b) Planning
21. (b) Public Welfare
22. (b) Development of Agriculture
23. (b) Second
24. (b) Fifth Five Year Plan
25. (c) Concurrent list

Economic Reforms Since 1991

Chief concepts of this chapter –

- Features and appraisals of liberalisation
- Globalisation and privatisation (LPG policy)
- Concepts of demonetization and GST

Economic Reforms

These were based on the assumption that market forces would steer the economy into the path of growth and development. Economic reforms started in 1991 in India.

Need for Economic Reforms:

- Mounting fiscal deficit
- Adverse balance of payment
- Gulf crisis
- Fall in foreign exchange reserves
- Rise in prices

11.1 Liberalisation

Liberalisation of the economy means its freedom from direct or physical controls imposed by the government.

Liberalisation was introduced with an aim to put an end to those restrictions which became major hindrances in growth and development of various sectors. It is generally defined as the loosening of government regulations in a country to allow for private sector companies to operate business transactions with fewer restrictions. In relation to developing countries, this term refers to opening of economic border for multinationals and foreign investment.

Objectives of Liberalisation

The main objectives of liberalisation policy are

- To increase competition among domestic industries.
- To increase foreign capital formation and technology.
- To decrease the debt burden of the country.
- To encourage export and import of goods and services.
- To expand the size of the market.

Economic Reforms Under Liberalisation

Reforms under liberalisation were introduced in many areas. Let us discuss these now

Industrial Sector Reforms

The following steps were taken to deregulate the industrial sector

(i) Abolition of Industrial Licensing Government abolished the licensing requirement of all industries, except for the five industries, which are
  - Liquor
  - Cigarettes
  - Defence equipment
  - Industrial explosives
  - Dangerous chemicals, chugs and pharmaceuticals.

(ii) Contraction of Public Sector The number of industries reserved for the public sector was reduced from 17 to 8. Presently, only three industries are ' reserved for public sector. They are
  - Railways
  - Atomic energy
  - Defence

(iii) **De-reservation of Production Areas** The production areas which were earlier reserved for SSI were de-reserved.

(iv) **Expansion of Production Capacity** The producers were allowed to expand their production capacity according to market demand. The need for licensing was abolished.

(v) **Freedom to Import Capital Goods** The business and production units were given freedom to import capital goods to upgrade their technology.

Financial Sector Reforms

Financial sector includes financial institutions such as commercial banks, investment banks, stock exchange operations and foreign exchange market.

The following reforms were initiated in this sector

- **Reducing Various Ratio** Statutory Liquidity Ratio (SLR) was lowered from 38.5% to 25%.
  Cash Reserve Ratio (CRR) was lowered from 15% to 4.1%.

- **Competition from New Private Sector Banks** The banking sector was opened for the private sector. This led to an increase in competition and expansion of services for consumers.

- **Change in the Role of RBI** RBI's role underwent a change from a 'regulator' to a 'facilitator'.

- **De-regulation of Interest Rates** Except for savings accounts, banks were able to decide their own interest rates.

Tax Reforms/Fiscal Reforms

Tax reforms are concerned with the reforms in government's taxation and public expenditure policies which are collectively known as its fiscal policy.

Moderate and Simplified Tax Structure Prior to 1991, the tax rates in the country were quite high, which led to tax evasion. The fiscal reforms simplified the tax structure and lowered the rates of taxation. This reduced tax-evasion and increased government's revenues.

Foreign Exchange Reforms/External Sector Reforms

External sector reforms include reforms relating to foreign exchange and foreign trade. The following reforms were initiated in this sector

(i) **Devaluation of Rupee** Devaluation implies a fall in the value of rupee against some foreign currency. In 1991, the rupee was devalued to increase our country's exports and to discourage imports.

(ii) Other Measures
- Import quotas were abolished.
- Policy of import licensing was almost scrapped.
- Import duty was reduced.
- Export duty was completely withdrawn.

11.2 World Trade Organisation (WTO)

The WTO was founded in 1995 as the successor organisation to the General Agreement on Trade and Tariff (GATT). GATT was established in 1948 with 23 countries as the global trade organisation to administer all multinational trade agreements by providing equal opportunities to all countries in international market for trading purpose. However, this had certain problems hence.

WTO was expected to establish a rule based trading regime in which nations cannot place arbitrary restrictions on trade. Its purpose was mainly to expand production and trade in order to have optimum utilisation of world resources.

The WTO agreements cover trade in goods as well as services to facilitate international trade through removal of tariff as well as non-tariff barriers and provide better market access to all countries. Being an important member of WTO. India has been in front to frame rule and regulations and safeguards interest of developing world.

India has kept commitments towards liberalisation of trade in WTO by removing quantitative restrictions on imports and reducing tariff rates.

11.2.1 Functions of WTO

- It facilitates the implementation, administration and operation of the objectives of multilateral trade agreements.

- It administers the 'trade review mechanism'.

- It administers the 'understanding rules and procedures , governing the settlement disputes'.

- It is a watchdog of international trade; it examines the trade regimes of individual members.

- Trade disputes that cannot be solved through bilateral talks are forwarded to the WTO dispute settlement 'court'.

- It is a management consultant for world trade. Its economist keep a close watch on the activities of the global economy and provide studies on the main issues of the day.

11.3 Privatisation

It refers to giving greater role to private sector thereby reducing the role of public sector. In other words, it means shedding of the ownership or management of a government owned enterprise.

It may also mean de-reservation of industries previously reserved for public sector.

Government companies (public companies) are converted into private companies in two ways

- By withdrawal of the government from ownership and management of the public sector companies.
- By the method of disinvestment.

Forms of Privatisation

Different forms of privatisation are

- Denationalisation When 100% overnment ownership of productive assets is transferred to the private sector, it is called denationalisation. It is also known as strategic sale.

- Partial Privatisation When less than 100% or more than 50% ownership is transferred, it is a case of partial privatisation with private sector owning majority of shares. In this situation, the private sector can claim to possess substantial autonomy in its functioning. It is also known as partial sale.

- Deficit Privatisation/Token Privatisation :When the government disinvests its shares to the extent of 5 to 10% to meet the deficit in the budget, this is termed as deficit privatisation or token privatisation.

11.3.1 Objectives of Privatisation

The most common and important objectives of privatisation are

- Improving the financial condition of the government.
- Raising funds through disinvestment.
- Reducing the workload of public sector.
- Increasing the efficiency of the government undertakings.
- Providing better goods and services to consumers.
- Bringing healthy competition within an economy.
- Making way for Foreign Direct Investment (FDI).

11.4 Navratnas and Public Enterprise Policies

In order to improve efficiency, infuse professionalism and enable them to compete more effectively in the liberalised global environment, the government identifies PSUs and declare them as maharatnas, navratnas and mininavratnas. They were given greater managerial and operational autonomy, in taking various decisions to run the company efficiently and thus increase their profits. Greater operational, financial and managerial autonomy has also been granted to profit-making enterprises referred to as mininavratnas.

In 2011, about 90 public enterprises were designated with different status.

A few examples of public enterprises with their status are as follows

- Maharatnas
    - Indian Oil Corporation Limited
    - Steel Authority of India Limited
- Navratnas
    - Bharat Heavy Electricals Limited
    - Mahanagar Telephone Nigam Limited
- Mininavratnas
    - Bharat Sanchar Nigam Limited
    - Airport Authority of India

11.5 Privatisation

Privatisation is the general process of involving the private sector in the ownership or operation of a state owned enterprise.

11.6 Disinvestment

It refers to a situation when government sell off a part of its share capital of PSUs to the private investors.

11.7 Globalisation

It may be defined as a process associated with increasing openness, growing economic interdependence and deepening economic integration in the world economy. It means integration of the economy of the country with the world economy. Globalisation encourages foreign trade and private and institutional foreign investment.

Globalisation is a complex phenomenon and an outcome of the set of various policies that are aimed at transforming the world towards greater interdependence and integration. Globalisation attempts to establish links in such a way that the happenings in India can be in need by events happening miles away. It is turning them into one whole or creating a borderless world.

11.7.1 Outsourcing

An Outcome of Globalisation

This is one of the important outcome of the globalisation process. In outsourcing, a company hires regular service from external sources, mostly from other countries, which were previously provided internally or from within the country like legal advice, computer service, advertisement, etc. In other words, outsourcing means getting a work done on contract from Someone outside.

- As a form of economic activity, outsourcing has intensified, in recent times, because of the growth of fast modes of communication particularly the growth of Information Technology (IT).

- Many of the services such as voice-based business processes (popularly known as BPO or call centres), record keeping, accountancy, banking services, music recording, film editing, book transcription, clinical advice or even teaching are being outsourced by companies in developed countries to India.

- Most multinational corporations and even small companies are outsourcing their services to India where they can be availed at a cheaper cost with reasonable degree of skill and accuracy. The low wage rates and availability of skilled manpower in India have made it a destination for global outsourcing in the post reform period.

11.7.2 Policy Strategies Promoting Globalisation of the Indian Economy

- Increase in equity limit of foreign investment
- Partial convertibility
- Long term trade policy
- Reduction in tariffs
- Withdrawal of quantitative restriction

11.8 An appraisal of LPG Policies

Positive Impact of the LPG (Liberalisation, Privatisation and Globalisation) Policies

- A vibrant economy
- A stimulant to industrial production
- A cheek on fiscal deficit
- A cheek on inflation
- Consumer's sovereignty
- Flow of private foreign investment

Negative Impact of LPG (Liberalisation, Privatisation and Globalisation) Policies

- Neglection of agriculture
- Urban concentration of growth process
- Economic colonialism
- Spread of consumerism
- Lopsided growth process
- Cultural erosion

During the tenure of Narasimha Rao Government (1991), India met with an economic crisis relating to its external debt. The government was unable to make repayments on its borrowings from abroad; foreign exchange reserves were not sufficient to repay the debts. The prices of essential goods were rising and the imports were growing at a very high rate.

As a result, the government initiated a new set of policy measures to reform the conditions of an economy and several economic reform programme were also introduced in this respect to promote privatisation, liberalisation and globalisation.

11.9 Economic Crisis of 1991 and Indian Economy Reforms

Crisis in India is figured out because of the inefficient management of Indian Economy in 1980s.

The revenues generated by the government were not adequate to meet the growing expenses. So, the government resorted to borrowing to pay for its debts and was caught is a debt-trap.

Deficit it refers to the excess of government expenditure over its revenue.

11.9.1 Causes of Economic Crisis

Different causes of economic crisis are given as under

- The continued spending on development programmes of the government did not generate additional revenue.

- The government was not able to generate sufficient funds from internal sources such as taxation.

- Expenditure on areas like social sector and defence do not provide immediate returns, so there was a need to utilise the rest of its revenue in a highly effective manner, which the government failed to do.

- The income from public sector undertakings was also not very high to meet the growing expenditures.

- Foreign exchange borrowed from other countries and international financial institutions was spent on meeting consumption needs and to make repayments on other loans.

- No effort was made to reduce such increased spending and sufficient attention was not given to boost exports to pay for die growing needs.

Due to above stated reasons, in the late 1980s, government expenditure began to exceed its revenue by such large margins that meeting the expenditure through borrowings became unsustainable.

11.10 Need for Economic Reforms

The economic policy followed by the government up to 1990 failed in many aspects and landed the country in an unprecedented economic crisis. The situation was so alarming that India's reserves of foreign exchange were barely enough to pay for two weeks of imports. New loans were not available and NRIs were withdrawing large amounts. There was an erosion of confidence of international investors in the Indian economy.

The following points highlight the need for economic reforms in the country

- Increasing fiscal deficit
- Adverse Balance of Payments
- Gulf crisis
- Rise in prices
- Poor performance of Public Sector Units (PSUs).
- High rate of deficit financing.

11.11 Emergence of New Economic Policy (NEP)

Finally, India approached International Bank for Reconstitution and Development, popularly known as World Bank and International Monetary Fund (IMF) and received $ 7 million as loan to manage the crisis. International agencies expected India to liberalise and open up economy by removing restrictions on private sector and remove trade restrictions between India and other countries.

India agreed to conditions of World Bank and IMF and had announced New Economic Polity (NEP) which consist of wide range of economic reforms.

The measures adopted in the New Economic Policy can be broadly classified into two groups i.e.,

- Stabilisation Measures They are short-term measures which were intended to correct some weakness that have developed in the Balance of Payments and to bring Inflation under control.

- Structural Reforms They are long-term measures, aimed at improving the efficiency of the economy and increasing its international competitiveness by removing the rigidities in various segments of the Indian economy.

11.12 Economic Growth During Reforms

Growth of an economy is measured by the Gross Domestic Product (GDP). The growth of GDP increased from 5.6% during 1980-91 to 8.2% during 2007-2012.

Main highlights of economic growth during reforms are given below

- During the reform period, the growth of agriculture has declined. While the industrial sector reported fluctuation, the growth of service sector has gone up. This indicates that the growth is mainly driven by the growth in the service sector.

- The opening up of the economy has led to rapid increase in foreign direct investment and foreign exchange reserves.

The foreign investment, which includes Foreign – Direct Investment (FDI) and Foreign Institutional Investment(FII), has increased from about US $ 100 million in 1990-91 to US $ 400 billion in 2010-11.

- There has been an increase in the foreign exchange Reserves from about US $ 6 billion in 1990-91 to US $ 300 billion in 2011-12. In 2011, India is the seventh largest foreign exchange reserve holder in the world.

- India is seen as a successful exporter of auto parts, engineering goods, IT software and textiles in the reform period. Rising prices have also been kept under control.

11.13 Failures of Economic Reforms

I. Neglect of Agriculture

There has been deterioration in agricultural growth rate. This deterioration is the root cause of the problem of rural distress that reached crisis in some parts of the country. Economic reforms have not been able to benefit the agricultural sector because

- Public investment in agriculture sector especially in infrastructure which includes irrigation, power, roads, market linkages and research and extension has been reduced in the reform period.

- The removal of fertiliser subsidy has led to increase in the cost of production which has severely affected the small and marginal formers.

- Various policy changes like reduction in import duties on agricultural products, removal of minimum support price and lifting of quantitative restrictions have increased the threat of* international competition to the Indian formers.

- Export-oriented policy strategies in agriculture has been a shift from production for the domestic market towards production for the export market focusing on cash crops in lieu of production of food grains.

II. Uneven Growth in Industrial Sector

Industrial sector registered uneven growth during this period.

This is because of decreasing demand of industrial products due to various reasons

- Cheaper imports have decreased the demand for domestic industrial goods.

- Globalisation created conditions for the free movement of goods and services from foreign countries that adversely affected the local industries and employment opportunities in developing countries.

- There was inadequate investment in infrastructural facilities such as power supply.

- A developing country like India still does not have the access to developed countries markets because of high non-tariff barriers.

11.14 Siricilla Tragedy

Privatisation of power supply in Andhra Pradesh resulted in substantial increase in power-rates, causing many power looms to shut down in a small town, Siricilla (a small town in Andhra Pradesh).

50 workers committed suicide because of loss in means of livelihood.

Other Failures

In addition to the above mentioned failures, the other drawbacks of LPG policy were:

- It led to urban concentration of growth process.

- It encouraged economic colonialism.

- It resulted in the spread of consumerism.

- It led to cultural erosion.

11.15 Goods and Services Tax (GST) and Demonetization In India:

Goods and Services Tax (GST) has been introduced in India with a view to providing a uniform tax structure across all parts of the country. Best, GST carries the slogan of 'one tax, one nation, one market'. GST is expected to generate additional tax revenue for the government, increase tax compliance and reduce tax evasion.

Goods and services have been classified into different categories will stop each category or goods carry a specific rate of taxation. Few category of goods have been kept under the tax exempt, considering the needs and means of quarter section of the society.

11.15.1 Structure of GST:

Category of Goods	Tax Rate
Sanitary napkins, fortified milk, fresh fruits and vegetables	0%
Coffee, tea, spices and electric vehicles	5%
Butter, frozen meat products, Ayurvedic medicines and spectacles	12%
Pasta, pastries and cakes and detergents	18%
Automobiles, dishwasher and vending machines	28%

11.15.2 Characteristics

There are three typical characteristics of GST:

i. GST is levied at each stage of value edition

ii. GST focuses on the supply of goods rather than their production. Tax is levied as and when goods are supplied (or when goods leave their destination for their buyers).

iii. GST paid by the producers on the purchase of inputs is allowed to be adjusted by the producers in their payment of GST proceeds to the government.

11.15.3 Merits of GST

i. it is simplified tax structure, as it is one tax instead of all the indirect taxes, and it is a uniform tax across all parts of the country.

ii. Since refund of GST on inputs is available to the producers only when they buy inputs from the registered suppliers, it ensures higher degree of transparency in business: black money transactions are reduced.

iii. Being a uniform tax across all parts of the country, GST has enhanced size of the market for the domestic producers.

iv. GST has raised government revenue as there is a higher degree of transparency in business.

11.15.4 Teething problems and Demerits of GST

Any new concept always suffers from some teething problems when it comes to its implementation. the teething problems of GST are often highlighted as its demerits. Two observations are notable in this context:

i. GST is yet to cover all goods produced in the country. Electricity generation, alcohol, petrol and diesel are some notable products out of the ambit of GST.

ii. GST rates across different goods and services are still not finally settled, and to that extent uncertainty looms in the economy. This uncertainty hampers decision- making and therefore investment in production activity.

11.15.5 Demonetisation in India

Demonetisation is referred to as the process of stripping a currency unit of its status to be used as a legal tender. In simple words, demonetisation is the process by which the demonetised notes cease to be accepted as legal currency for any kind of transaction.

After demonetisation is done, the old currency is replaced by a new currency, which may be of the same denomination or may be of a higher denomination.

The impact of changing the legal tender status of a currency unit has a huge impact on the economic transactions that take place in an economy.

Demonetisation can cause unrest in an economy or it can help in stabilizing the economy from existing problems. Demonetisation is usually taken by a country for various reasons.

Demonetisation in India has taken place three times till now, namely in the years of 1946, 1978 and 2016. Let us have a look at all the three events.

11.15.5.1 Demonetisation 1946

The first demonetisation event happened in 1946, at that time the denominations of Rs.1000 and Rs.10000 were removed from circulation.

There was a visibly low impact of the demonetisation as the higher denomination currencies were not available to the common people.

In 1954, these notes were again introduced with an additional denomination of 5000.

11.15.5.2 Demonetisation in 1978

The second demonetisation in India took place in 1978, at that time the Prime Minister was Morarji Desai. During the second demonetisation the denominations of 1000, 5000 and 10000 were taken out of circulation.

The whole purpose of demonetisation was to reduce the circulation of black money in the country. The announcement was made by Morarji Desai over the radio.

11.15.5.3 Demonetisation in 2016

The latest demonetisation was announced on 8th November, 2016 by the Prime Minister Narendra Modi.

During this demonetisation the notes that were taken out of circulation were the denominations of 500 and 1000.

PM Modi also introduced new currency of denominations 500 and 2000 after demonetisation.

11.15.5.4 Objectives of Demonetisation

The objectives of demonetisation are as follows:

1. To stop the circulation of black money in the market.

2. To help in reducing the interest rates of the prevalent banking system

3. To help in creation of cashless economy

4. To formalise the informal Indian Economy.

5. To remove counterfeit notes from the market.

6. To help reduce anti-social activities and their finances.

Key Statements

Foreign Exchange Reserves: Foreign exchange reserves are assets held on reserve by a central bank in foreign currencies. Foreign exchange reserves are used to back liabilities and influence monetary policy.

Financial Institutions: Any institution that collects money and puts it into assets such as stocks, bonds, bank deposits, or loans is considered a financial institution. There are two types of financial institutions: depository institutions and non-depository institutions.

Stock Exchange: is a place where security trading is conducted on an organized system. It is an association or group of people organized to provide an auction market among themselves for the purchase and sale of securities.

Inflation: is a situation of rising prices in the economy. A more exact definition of inflation is a sustained increase in the general price level in an economy. Inflation means an increase in the cost of living as the price of goods and services rise. The rate of inflation measures the annual percentage change in the general price level.

Foreign Institutional Investors (FII): A foreign institutional investor (FII) is an **investor or investment fund investing in a country outside of the one in which it is registered or headquartered.**

Foreign Direct Investment (FDI): Foreign direct investment (FDI) is an investment made by a firm or individual in one country into business interests located in another country.

Export: Exports are goods and services that are produced in one country and sold to buyers in another. Example : Clothes made in India and sold to European countries.

Import: An import is a good or service brought into one country from another. The word "import" derives from the word "port" since goods are often shipped via boat to foreign countries. Example cars imported from European countries by India.

Exercise

Frequently asked Questions (FAQ's)

1. Why is it necessary to become a member of WTO?
2. Why are tariffs imposed?
3. Why were reforms introduced in India ?
4. What is Outsourcing?
5. What is disinvestment?

Multiple Choice Questions (MCQ's)

1. Stabilisation measures and structural reform measures are the two groups of which policy?
   (a) New Industrial Policy
   (b) New Economic Policy
   (c) Trade policy
   (d) Monetary policy

2. How many industries were reserved for the public sector at the time of deregulation of industrial sector in 1991?
   (a) 17   (b) 18
   (c) 19   (d) 20

3. Which institution regulates the financial sector in India?
   (a) SEBI   (b) NABARD
   (c) SBI   (d) RBI

4. What is the name of the tax introduced by Indian parliament in 2016 to unify the indirect tax systems in India?
   (a) sales tax
   (b) VAT Value Added Taxes
   (c) GST Goods and Services Tax
   (d) Custom duty

5. Which policy involves integrating Domestic economy with the World economy?
   (a) Globalisation   (b) Privatisation
   (c) Liberalisation (d) None of the above

6. Name the successor organisation of General Agreement on Trade and Tariff (GATT)?
   (a) World Bank
   (b) International Monetary Fund (IMF)
   (c) Food and Agriculture organisation (FAO)
   (d) World Trade Organisation (WTO)

7. Following the New Economic Policy, which sector mainly drives the growth of the Indian economy?
   (a) Agriculture
   (b) Service
   (c) Industry
   (d) Construction

8. The process through which a company hire services from external sources, mainly foreign countries is known as:
   (a) Incoming   (b) Outsourcing
   (c) Deregulation   (d) Devaluation

9. In which sector was a spectacular growth visible after 2000?
   (a) Service   (b) Industry
   (c) Social   (d) All of the above

10. What are short term measures, intended to correct the weaknesses of balance of payment and to bring inflation under control?
    (a) Stabilisation
    (b) Structural Reforms
    (c) Federal Reforms
    (d) None of the above

11. One of the main aims of the financial sector reforms is to reduce the role of RBI from that of a _________ to a facilitator of financial sector.
    (a) Coordinator
    (b) Regulator
    (c) Administrator
    (d) None of the above

12. Tax reforms are concerned with reforms in the Government's __________ and ________ Policies, which are collectively known as Fiscal Policy.
    (a) Taxation; Public Expenditure
    (b) Taxation; Non-taxation
    (c) Taxation; Private Expenditure
    (d) Private expenditure; Taxation

13. The goods and service Tax Act (GST) came into effect from:
    (a) April 2017   (b) May 2017
    (c) June 2017   (d) July 2017

14. In 1991, as an immediate measure to resolve the balance of payment crisis, the rupee was _________ against foreign currencies.
    (a) Revalued   (b) Devalued
    (c) Appreciated   (d) Depreciated

15. Financial sectors includes:
    (a) Banking and non-banking financial institutions
    (b) Stock Exchange market
    (c) Foreign exchange market
    (d) All of the above

16. Under 1991 reforms, the industrial licence was abolished for:
    (*a*) Liquor
    (*b*) Health, security and environment
    (*c*) Defence equipment
    (*d*) All of the above

17. What refers to the process of transferring/involving the private sector in the ownership, management and control of public sector enterprises?
    (*a*) Liberalisation   (*b*) Privatisation
    (*c*) Globalisation   (*d*) None of the above

18. Which of the following industries were exclusively reserved for public sector?
    (*a*) Railway transport
    (*b*) Communication
    (*c*) Metro transport
    (*d*) All of the above

19. Which of the following is not an element of fiscal reforms?
    (*a*) Taxation Reforms
    (*b*) Control on Public Debt
    (*c*) Change in interest rate
    (*d*) Public Expenditure Reforms

20. Which of the following is an example of indirect tax?
    (*a*) Income tax
    (*b*) Wealth tax
    (*c*) Goods and Services tax
    (*d*) None of the above

21. Which off the following is the strategy to promote globalisation of the Indian economy?
    (*a*) Partially convertibility
    (*b*) Reduction in tariffs

(*c*) Increase in equity limit of foreign investment
(*d*) All of the above

22. in the context of Indian experience, controls were imposed by the government with a view to:
    (*a*) checking the growth of private monopolies
    (*b*) minimising the hold of large industrial houses on the financial resources of the country
    (*c*) both (*a*) and (*b*)
    (*d*) None of the above

23. Which of the following is not a consequence of the policy of privatisation?
    (*a*) Contraction of Public Sector
    (*b*) Disinvestment in Public Sector enterprises
    (*c*) Sale of Public Sectors shares
    (*d*) Purchase of industrial shares by the government

24. External sector reforms under New Economic Policy (NEP) included:
    (*a*) foreign exchange reforms
    (*b*) Foreign trade policy reforms
    (*c*) Both (*a*) and (*b*)
    (*d*) None of the above

25. The WTO was founded as the successor organisation to:
    (*a*) International Monetary Fund
    (*b*) International bank for reconstruction and development (IBRD)
    (*c*) General Agreement on Tariffs and Trade (GATT)
    (*d*) National Bank for agriculture and rural development (NABARD)

🔑 Solutions

Frequently asked Questions (FAQ's)

1. It is necessary for a country to become a member of WTO due to the following reasons:

   i. WTO is supposed to promote free trade in the international market by reducing tariff barriers and by removing non-tariff barriers. It benefits all member countries.

   ii. By promoting World Trade, WTO ensures optimum utilisation of resources of the member countries.

   iii. WTO promotes competition in the international market and free access to markets for member countries.

   iv. WTO facilitates bilateral as well as multilateral trade agreements among the member countries.

2. Direct imposed to protect domestic industry and to restrict imports. It is also imposed to generate revenue for the government.

3. Because foreign exchange reserves were dwindling and fiscal deficit was mounting. Also, the rate of inflation was rising too alarming limits. Further, public sector undertakings were facing bloating inefficiency.

4. How to sing refers to a system of hiring business services (like call centres, transcription, clinical advice, teaching/coaching, etc.) from the outside world.

5. Disinvestment refers to selling of share capital of PSU's (public sector undertakings) to the private entrepreneurs.

Multiple Choice Questions (MCQ's)

1. (b) New Economic Policy
2. (a) 17
3. (d) RBI
4. (c) GST Goods and Service Tax
5. (a) Globalisation
6. (d) World Trade Organisation (WTO)
7. (b) Service
8. (b) Outsourcing
9. (a) Service
10. (a) Stabilisation
11. (b) Regulator
12. (a) Taxation; Public Expenditure
13. (d) July 2017
14. (b) Devalued
15. (d) All of the above
16. (d) All of the above
17. (b) Privatisation
18. (a) Railway transport
19. (c) Change in interest rate
20. (c) Goods and Services tax
21. (d) All of the above
22. (b) both (a) and (b)
23. (d) Purchase of industrial shares by the government
24. (c) Both (a) and (b)
25. (c) General Agreement On Tariffs And Trade (GATT)

CHAPTER 12

Current Challenges Facing Indian Economy Poverty

LEARNING OBJECTIVES

❖ Poverty

❖ Poverty Line and measurement of Absolute Poverty

❖ Extent of Poverty in India

❖ Causes of Poverty

❖ Policies and Programmes to combat Poverty in India (Poverty Alleviation Programmes)

❖ Critical Assessment of Policies and Programmes

Chief concepts of this chapter

- Understand the various attributes of poverty - absolute and relative

- Comprehend the diverse dimensions relating to the concept of poverty

- Critically appreciate the way poverty is estimated

- Appreciate and be able to assess existing poverty elevation programmes

Poverty

It is inability to fulfil the minimum requirements of life. Relative Poverty It refers to poverty in relation to different classes, regions or countries.

- Absolute Poverty In India, concept of poverty line is used as a measure of absolute poverty.

12.1 Poverty Line

It is that line which expresses per capita average monthly expenditure by which people can satisfy their minimum needs.

Relative poverty and absolute poverty are the two variants of poverty.

Poverty line is fixed in India

- in the estimation of consumption cut off.

- in private consumption expenditure.

- frequencies are recorded against each class-interval. Each frequency counts the number of heads belonging to a particular consumption class.

Due to various limitations in the official estimation of poverty, scholars have attempted to find alternative methods. For instance, Amartya Sen, noted noble laureate, has developed an index known as Sen index. There are other tools such as Poverty Gap Index and Squared Poverty Gap.

12.2 Categorising Poverty

- Category 1 Chronic poor Those who are always poor and those who are usually poor e.g., Landless workers.

- Category 2 Transient Poor Those who are moving in and out of poverty and occasionally poor.

- Category 3 Never Poor These are categorised as non-poor people.

Rural Poor

These include landless agricultural work marginal holders and tenants-at-will.

Urban Poor

These include migrants from the rural areas in search of employment, casual factory workers and self-employed serving largely as street vendors.

Urban poor are largely the spill over of the rural poor who are forced to migrate in search of jobs.

Rural and Urban Poverty

The difference between rural and urban poverty is mainly of the nature of poverty.' The poor are identified on the basis of their occupation and ownership of assets. The rural poor work mainly as landless agricultural labourers, cultivators with very small landholdings, landless labourers who are engaged in a variety of non-agricultural jobs and tenant cultivators with small landholdings.

On the other hand, the urban poor are largely the overflow of the rural poor who had migrated to urban areas in search of alternative employment and livelihood, labourers who do a variety of casual jobs and the self-employed who sell a variety of things on roadsides and are engaged in various activities.

It can be seen from the following table showing the trends in poverty ratio that poverty has shifted from rural to urban areas.

YEAR WISE POVERTY RATIO

Year	Poverty Ratio		
	Rural (%)	Urban (%)	Total (%)
1973-74	56.4	49.0	54.9
1977-78	53.1	45.2	51.3
1983	45.6	40.8	44.5
1987-88	39.1	38.2	38.9
1993-94	37.3	32.4	36.0
1999-2000	27.1	23.6	26.1
2004-05	28.3	25.7	27.5

Source: Planning Commission Estimates (Uniform Reference Period).

It is evident from the above table that rural poverty has declined significantly from 56.4% in 1973-74 to 28.3% in 2004-05 whereas decline in urban poverty (from 49% to 25.7%) is not that significant. Moreover, the gap between the rural and urban poverty ratios which was around 7% in 1973-74 fell to just around 2% in 2004-05 again signifying the shift in poverty from rural to urban areas.

12.3 Causes of Poverty

- Low level of national product
- Low rate of growth
- Heavy pressure of population
- Inflationary pressures
- Chronic unemployment and under employment
- Capital deficiency
- Outdated social institutions
- Lack of infrastructure

12.4 Measures to Remove Poverty

- Combating poverty by accelerating the place of economic growth.
- Combating inequality of income through fiscal and legislative measures.
- Combating poverty through population control.
- Other measures enhancing quality of life of the poor.

12.5 Poverty Alleviation Programmes

Some of the principle measures adopted by the government to remove poverty are given below

- Samaranjayanti Gram Swarozgar Yojana (SGSY)
- Sampoorna Gramin Rozgar Yojana (SGRY)
- Pradanmantri Gramoday Yojana (PGY)
- Jai Prakash Rozgar Guarantee Yojana (JPRGY)
- The Swaran Jayanti Shahri Rozgar Yojana (SJSRY)
- Prime Minister's Rozgar Yojana
- Development of Small and Cottage Industries (viii) Minimum Needs Programme
- Twenty Point Programme
- Mahatma Gandhi National Rural Employment Guarantee

12.6 Calorie-Based Norm to identify the Poor

The government uses Monthly Per Capita Expenditure (MPCE) as proxy for income of households to identify the poor. Poverty line is estimated by the monetary value (per capita expenditure) of the minimum calorie intake that was estimated at 2400 calories for a rural person and 2100 for a person in the urban area. But this calorie-based norm is not adequate to identify the poor due to following reasons

- This mechanism groups all the poor together and does not differentiate between the very poor and the other poor which makes it difficult to identify who amongst them needs help the most.
- Economists question, the basis of taking expenditure on food and a few select items as proxy for income.
- This norm does not take into account the other factors associated with poverty such as accessibility to basic education, health care, drinking water and sanitation.
- This norm does not take social factors such as illiteracy, lack of access to resources, discrimination or lack of civil and political freedoms into consideration.

12.7 'Food for Work' Programme

The National Food for Work Programme was launched in November 2004 in 150 most backward districts of the country, identified by the Planning Commission in consultation with the Ministry of Rural Development and the State Governments. The objective of the programme was to provide additional resources apart from the resources available under the Sampoorna Grameen Rozgar Yojana to 150 most backward districts of the country so that generation of supplementary wage employment and providing of food security through creation of need based economic, social and community assets in these districts are further intensified.

The scheme was 100 per cent centrally sponsored and was open to all rural poor who were in need of wage employment and wanted to do manual and unskilled work.

The focus of the programme was on work relating to water conservation, drought proofing and land development. Flood control protection, rural connectivity in terms of all-weather roads and any other similar activity for economic sustainability could be included.

Food grains were given as part of wages under the NFFWP to the rural poor at the rate of 5 kg per man day and the remaining portion may be given in cash. More than 5 kg food grains can be given to the labourers under this programme in exceptional cases subject to a minimum of 25% of wages to be paid in cash. The programme has now been subsumed in National Rural Employment Guarantee Act, which has come in force in 200 identified districts of the country including 150 NFFWP districts.

12.8 Employment Generation Programmes and Poverty Alleviation in India

In India, twin problems exist i.e., poverty and unemployment. Poverty alleviation has been one of the guiding principles of the planning process in India. Poverty can effectively be eradicated only when the poor start contributing to growth by their active involvement in the growth process. This can only be achieved by launching various employment schemes.

Following points discussed the importance of Employment Generation Programmes to eradicate poverty.

- Nexus between Unemployment and Poverty There exists a deep nexus between unemployment and poverty. If employment opportunities are generated, then more people will be employed leading to rise in their income which in turn will reduce poverty.

- Availability of Basic Facilities With the rise in employment opportunities, income increases and poor people are able to get access to education, health facilities, proper sanitation etc.

- Creation of Assets The Employment Generation Programmes aim at creation of assets like water harvesting, irrigation facilities, construction of roads, construction of dams etc. All these assets help in the social and economic development of the rural areas and hence eradication of poverty.

- Creation of Skills An essential element of employment generation programmes is the formation of human capital by imparting skills to the unskilled labourers through training. This skill formation enhances income earning capability of poor people.

Thus, such poverty alleviation programmes like Prime Minister's Rozgar Yojana, Swarna Jayanti Shahari Rogzar Yojana, National Food for Work Programme, Annapurna are came into an existence.

12.9 Creation of Income Earning Assets address the Problem of Poverty

The problem of poverty cannot be solved by giving food grains to the poor or distributing clothes to them as no government can keep doing these activities for long due to lack of resources. Poverty can effectively be eradicated only when the poor start earning for themselves and in turn contribute to growth by their active involvement in the growth process. This is possible by providing income generating assets to the poor in the form of land for agriculture, tools and instruments to set up self-employment units and giving them proper training, which will enhance their income earning capacity.

This can help poor people to participate in economic activities and make them empowered. This will also help create employment opportunities which may lead to increase in levels of income, skill development, health and literacy and thus poor can be assured of income per month which will help him to come above the poverty line.

12.10 Struggles and deficiencies of Poverty Alleviation Programmes

The three dimensional attack on poverty adopted by the government has not succeeded in poverty alleviation in India.

Poverty alleviation has always been accepted as one of the major objectives of planned development process in India but even after vast spending on poverty alleviation programmes, the government has not succeeded in poverty alleviation in India.

Despite various strategies to alleviate poverty, problems like hunger, malnourishment, illiteracy and lack of basic amenities are prevalent in India. None of the poverty alleviation strategies resulted in any radical change in the ownership of assets, process of production and improvement of basic amenities to the needy.

Due to unequal distribution of assets, the benefits from poverty alleviation programmes have not actually reached the poor. The amount of resources allocated for the poverty alleviation programmes is not sufficient when we take the magnitude of poverty into consideration.

The implementation of the poverty alleviation programmes is the responsibility of government and bank officials who are ill motivated, inadequately trained, corruption prone and vulnerable to pressure from local elites. The resources are thus used inefficiently.

Government policies have also failed to address the various issues related to poverty due to non-participation of local level institutions in programme implementation. It is evident that high growth alone is not sufficient to reduce poverty without the active participation of the people.

Further, it is necessary to identify poverty stricken areas and provide infrastructure such as schools, roads, power, telecom, IT services, training institutions etc. Institutional weaknesses abound and implementation failure are the biggest reasons that these programmes not succeeded.

12.11 Programmes adopted by the government to help the elderly people, poor and destitute women:

In accordance with the Directive Principles of State Policy, the Government of India introduced National Social Assistance Programme (NSAP) in 1995 to help the elderly people and poor and destitute women.

The NSAP aims at ensuring minimum national standard for social assistance in addition to the benefits that states are currently providing or would provide in future. At present, NSAP comprises of the following five schemes for BPL persons

- Indira Gandhi National Old Age Pension Scheme (IGNOAPS)

- Indira Gandhi National Widow Pension Scheme (IGNWPS)

- Indira Gandhi National Disability Pension Scheme (IGNDPS)

- National Family Benefit Scheme (NFBS)

- Annapurna

Under Indira Gandhi National Old Age Pension Scheme (IGNOAPS), ₹ 200 per month provided to the beneficiary of age 65 or more and belonging to a BPL family according to criteria prescribed by Government of India.

Widow pension is provided under IGNWPS to the BPL widows of age group of 40-64 years. Disability pension is provided to the multiple or severely disabled persons of age group of 18-64 years under IGNDPS. Central assistance of Rs. 200 per month per beneficiary is provided under Indira Gandhi National Disability Pension Scheme (IGNDPS) and Indira Gandhi , National Widow Pension Scheme (IGNWPS).

The states are urged to contribute another Rs. 200 from their own resources so that a pensioner could get at least Rs. 400 per month in the above programmes.

12.12 Unemployment And Poverty

There exists a deep nexus between unemployment and poverty. Unemployment or under employment and the casual and intermittent nature of work in both rural and urban areas drives unemployed people who do not have resources to make their ends meet into indebtedness and poverty.

If employment opportunities are generated, then more people will be employed leading to rise in their income which in turn will reduce poverty.

Due to unemployment, income of the people is reduced to a large extent and they are unable to get access to education, health facilities, proper sanitation, etc. This causes poor quality of living and hence poor human capital and skills which in turn lead to poverty making a vicious circle of poverty.

12.13 Conclusion

Poverty elevation has always been accepted as one of India's main challenges by the policymakers, regardless of which government was in power. The absolute number of poor in the country has gone down and some states have less proportion of poor than even the national average. Yet, critics point out that even though vast resources have been allocated and spent, we are still far from reaching the goal. There is improvement in terms of per capita income and average standard of living. Some sectors of the economy, section of people, regions of the country have considerably developed in terms of social and economic development though there are many others who are still stuck in the vicious circle of poverty.

Key Statements

Exercise

Frequently asked Questions (FAQ's)

1. Who are poor?
2. What are the different categories of poverty?
3. Does population growth always compound the problem of poverty?
4. When is Growth converted into Development?
5. How is sickness and inefficiency related to poverty?
6. What is meant by MGNREGA?

Multiple Choice Questions (MCQ's)

1. What was the percentage of the population below the poverty line in India in 2011-12?
   (a) 26.1%   (b) 19.3%
   (c) 22%   (d) 32%

2. Which of the following is the poverty determination measure?
   (a) Head Count Ratio
   (b) Sen Index
   (c) Poverty Gap Index
   (d) All of these

3. Those who regularly move in and out of poverty are called:
   (a) Chronically poor
   (b) Churning poor
   (c) Occasionally poor
   (d) Transient poor

4. In 2011-12, poverty line was defined worth _______ as consumption per person a month for rural areas and _______ for urban areas.
   (a) Rs. 816 and Rs. 1,000
   (b) Rs. 1,012 and Rs. 1,210
   (c) Rs. 550 and Rs. 860
   (d) Rs. 860 and Rs. 673

5. Which of the following is an action adopted under the provision of minimum basic amenities to the people?
   (a) Prime Minister's Rozgar Yojana
   (b) Swarna Jayanti Shahari RozgarYojana
   (c) Pradhan Mantri Gramodaya Yojana
   (d) National Rural Livelihood Mission

6. In 2011-12, which state had the highest poverty rate in India?
   (a) Odisha
   (b) Bihar
   (c) Madhya Pradesh
   (d) West Bengal

7. NFWP was launched in:
   (a) November 2004
   (b) December 2003
   (c) November 2002
   (d) December 2005

8. Which of the following programmes provide assistance to elderly people are given under?
   (a) VAMBAY   (b) NSAP
   (c) PMGY   (d) PMRY

9. Which was the programme which had the objective to provide self- employment or wage employment to urban unemployed or under employed persons?
   (a) Swarna Jayanti Shahri Rozgar Yojana
   (b) Shahri Jeewan Sudhar Rashtriya Yojana
   (c) Sampoorna Jeewn Shahri Rozgar Yojana
   (d) None of the above

10. The earlier 'Food for work Programme' has now been converted into:
    (a) Intensive Area Development Programme
    (b) Integrated Rural Development Programme
    (c) Mahatma Gandhi National Rural Employment Programme
    (d) Minimum Needs Programme

11. Which of the following is a characteristic of poor people?
    (a) Poor Health   (b) Debt Trap
    (c) Smaller Families (d) Gender Inequality

12. ____________ refers to poverty of people, in comparison to other people, regions or nations.
    (a) Absolute Poverty
    (b) Relative Poverty
    (c) Both (a) and (b)
    (d) Neither (a) nor (b)

13. The Programme initiated by the Government to improve food and nutritional level of poor was:
    (a) Public Distribution System
    (b) Integrated Child Development Scheme
    (c) Midday Meal Scheme
    (d) All of the above

14. Why poor have very limited economic opportunities?
    (a) As they live in a rural area
    (b) Scarcity of funds
    (c) Lack of basic literacy and skills
    (d) All of the above

15. Amartya Se, noted Noble Laureate, has developed an index known as:
    (*a*) Poverty Gap Index
    (*b*) Sen Index
    (*c*) Squared Poverty Gap
    (*d*) Income Disparity Gap Index

16. Which of these is not a poverty alleviation programmes?
    (*a*) Rural employment generation programme REGP
    (*b*) Prime Minister's Rozgar Yojana
    (*c*) Swarna Jayanti Shahri Rozgar Yojana
    (*d*) National Social Assistance Programme

17. In August 2005, the Parliament passed a new act to provide guaranteed wage employment to every rural household whose adult volunteer is to do unskilled manual work for a minimum of 100 days in a year. This act is known as:
    (*a*) Mahatma Gandhi National Rural Employment Guarantee Act
    (*b*) Minimum Wages Act
    (*c*) Minimum Wage Is Guarantee Act
    (*d*) Rural Employment Guarantee Act

18. Estimation of Poverty in rural economies is at per day consumption of calories:
    (*a*) Less than 2200   (*b*) Less than 2100
    (*c*) Less than 2400   (*d*) Less than 2000

19. Which of the following statement is true regarding the failure of poverty alleviation programs in India:
    (*a*) The poor still lack the basic amenity
    (*b*) The improper implementation of various schemes
    (*c*) Success of the land reform policies
    (*d*) None of the above

20. Poverty continues to persist in India, because of:
    (*a*) Rising prices
    (*b*) Rising population
    (*c*) Lack of opportunities for employment
    (*d*) All of the above

21. The first poverty line was based on:
    (*a*) Adult cost of living
    (*b*) Adult jail cost of living
    (*c*) Inadequacy of capital
    (*d*) All of the above

22. Current poverty line in India is based on the recommendations of:
    (*a*) Tendulkar Committee
    (*b*) Rangarajan Committee
    (*c*) Planning Commission
    (*d*) NITI Aayog

23. Which of the following is a reason of poverty in India?
    (*a*) Low rate of growth
    (*b*) Inflation
    (*c*) Inadequacy of capital
    (*d*) All of these

24. Rural poor mainly includes:
    (*a*) Landless labourers
    (*b*) Street vendors
    (*c*) Ragpickers
    (*d*) Pushcart vendors

25. The scheme aimed at providing financial security to the poor is:
    (*a*) Public Distribution System
    (*b*) Pradhan Mantri Jan Dhan Yojna
    (*c*) National Social Assistance Programme
    (*d*) National Urban Livelihood Mission

🔑 Solutions

Frequently asked Questions (FAQ's)

1. Poor are identified on the basis of the occupation and ownership of assets. In urban areas, poor other labourers engaged in casual jobs, and in rural areas, poor

2. Different categories of poverty are:
   i. Always poor
   ii. Usually poor
   iii. Chronically poor
   iv. Churning poor
   v. Occasionally poor
   vi. Transient poor

3. It is true in case of overpopulated countries like India. Because of overpopulation, India is burdened with massive unemployment. In such a situation, growth of population would only compound the problem of unemployment. We all know that unemployment is just another name both poverty - higher level of unemployment implies higher level of poverty.

4. It is converted into Development when Poverty is reduced.

5. A poor man cannot afford expenditure on nutritious food and healthcare. It leads to sickness, and sickness leads to inefficiency.

6. MGNREGA (Mahatma Gandhi National Rural Employment Guarantee Act) Was enforced in the villages, in August 2005. Under this Act, all those who are willing to undertake unskilled manual work at the minimum wage are offered employment for a minimum period of 100 days. Those seeking employment are to report in those rural areas ready employment programme is being launched. This programme is becoming extremely popular in the rural areas. According to one estimate, nearly 5 crores households benefited from this programme in 2018- 19.

Multiple Choice Questions (MCQ's)

1. (c) 22%
2. (d) All of these
3. (b) Churning poor
4. (a) Rs. 816 and Rs. 1,000
5. (c) Pradhan Mantri Gramodaya Yojana
6. (a) Odisha
7. (a) November 2004
8. (b)   NSAP
9. (a) Swarna Jayanti Shahri Rozgar Yojana
10. (c)   Cons Mahatma Gandhi National Rural Employment Programme
11. (d)   (b) and d) Poor Health, Debt Trap and Gender Inequality
12. (b) Relative Poverty
13. (d) All of the above
14. (c) Lack of basic literacy and skills
15. (b) Sen Index
16. (d) National Social Assistance Programme
17. (a) Mahatma Gandhi National Rural Employment Guarantee Act
18. (c) Less than 2400
19. (b) The improper implementation of various schemes
20. (d) All of the above
21. (b) Adult Jail cost of living
22. (b) Tendulkar Committee
23. (d) All of the above
24. (a) Landless labourers
25. (b) Pradhan Mantri Jan Dhan Yojana

Your Notes :

CHAPTER 13

Current Challenges Facing Indian Economy Human Capital Formation In India

Chief concepts of this chapter –

- Human resource, human capital formation and human development

- Links between investment in human capital, economic growth and human development

- Need for government spending on education and health

- State of India's education attainment

Human Resource

Human resource refers to abilities (skill and expertise) of human beings to contribute to the process of value- addition in the economy.

Example: Farmer has the ability to grow Food and agricultural scientist has an ability to give us high yielding variety seeds(HYV). Likewise, or doctor has the ability to cure patients while a pharmacist has the ability to prepare medicines as prescribed by the doctor.

13.1 Human Capital Formation

It is the process of acquiring and increasing the number of people who* have the skills, education and experience which are critical for the economic and political development of a country.

In other words, human capital formation is the process of adding to the stock of human capital over time.

G.M. Meier defines human capital formation as, "human capital formation is the process of acquiring and increasing the number of persons who have the skiff education and experience which are essential for the economic and political development of a country".

Just as a country can turn physical resources like land into physical capital like factories, similarly it can also turn human resources like students into engineers and doctors. There by increasing their productivity and efficiency. So, human capital formation aims at converting human resources into human assets.

13.2 Human Capital and Human Development

Human capital and human development are related concepts, but certainly not identical. Human capital is a means to an end. Human development is an end itself.

Education as an Essential Element of Human Resource Development

It implies the process of teaching training and learning especially in schools or colleges, to improve knowledge and develop skills.

Growth of Education Sector in India

Following observations highlight the growth of education sector in India

- Expansion of general education
- Primary education
- Secondary education
- Higher education
- Vocationalisation of secondary education
- Technical, medical and agricultural education
- Rural education
- Adult and female education
- Total literacy campaign

Human development is the broader term than human capital. Human capital considers education and health as a means to increase labour productivity. Human development is based on the idea that education and health are integral to human well-being because when people have the ability to read and write and the ability to lead a long and healthy life, they will be able to make other choices they value.

In human capital view, any investment in education and health is unproductive, if it-does not enhance output of goods and services. In the human development perspective, human beings are ends in themselves. Therefore, basic education and basic health are important in themselves, irrespective of their contribution to labour productivity.

Deutsche Bank and World Bank Report on Indian Economy

- According to two independent reports one from Deutsche and other from World Bank have identified that India would grow faster due to Its strength in human capital formation.

- According to Deutsche Bank (a German Bank)'s report on Global Growth Centres, it has been identified that India will emerge as one among four major growth Centres in the world by 2020. This report also says that between 2005 to 2020, we expect a 40% rise in the average years of education in India, to just above 7 years.

- World's Bank report India and the Knowledge Economy-Leveraging Strengths and Opportunities states that India should make a transition to the knowledge economy and if it uses its knowledge as much as Ireland does, then the per capita income of India will increase from a little over US $1000 in 2002 to US $3000 in 2020.

- It further states that the Indian economy has all the key ingredients for making this transition such as a critical mass of skilled workers, a well-functioning democracy and a diversified science and technology infrastructure. Thus, two reports point out the fact that further human capital formation in India will move its economy to a higher growth.

13.3 Human Capital and Physical Capital

- **Human Capital** It refers to the stock of 'skill and expertise' of a nation at a point of time. It refers to the stock of skill, ability, expertise, education and knowledge in a nation at a point of time.

- **Human Capital Formation** It is the process of adding to the stock of human capital over time.

- **Physical Capital** It refers to all inputs which are required for further production such as machine, tools and implements, factory buildings, etc are called physical capital. The stock of produced means of production.

- **Financial Capital** It refers to the stocks/shares of the companies or these are simple financial claims against assets of the companies.

Difference Between Physical Capital and Human Capital

Basis	Physical Capital	Human Capital
Nature	It is tangible and can be easily sold in the market like any other commodity.	It is intangible, built in the body and mind of its owner. It is not sold in the market, only its services are sold.
Mobility	It is separable from its owner.	It is inseparable from its owner.
Ownership	It is completely mobile between countries except some artificial trade restrictions.	It is not perfectly mobile between countries as movement is restricted by nationality and culture.
Formation	It can be built even through imports.	It is to be done through conscious policy formulations.
Benefit	It creates only private benefit.	It creates both private and social benefits.

13.4 Sources of Human Capital Formation

- Expenditure on Education
- Expenditure on Health
- On-the-Job Training

- Study Programmes for Adults
- Migration
- Expenditure on Information

Investment in education is considered as one of the most important sources of human capital formation. There are several other sources as well. Investment in health, on-the-job training, migration and information are the other sources of human capital formation.

These sources are discussed below:

1. Expenditure on Education

The education expenditure is an important source of human capital formation as it is the most effective way on enhancing and enlarging a productive workforce in the country.

Nations and individuals invest in education with the objective

- increasing their future income.
- generating technical skills and creating manpower, well suited for improving labour productivity and thus, sustaining rapid economic development.
- tending to bring down birth rate which in turn, brings decline in population growth rate. It makes more resources available per person.
- education also results in social benefits since, it also spreads to others.

2. Expenditure on Health

Health is another important source of human capital formation. A sick labourer without access to medical facilities is compelled to abstain from work and there in a loss of productivity. The various forms of health expenditure are preventive medicine, curative medicine, social medicine, provision of clean drinking water, etc.

3. On-the-job Training

Expenditure regarding on-the-job training is a source of human capital formation as the return of such expenditure in the form of enhanced labour productivity is more than the cost of it.

Firms spend huge amounts on giving on-the-job training to their workers. It may be in different forms like a worker may be trained in the firm itself or under the supervision of a skilled worker or can be sent for off campus training.

The firms then insist that workers should work for at least some time in die company so that they can recover the benefits of the enhanced productivity owing to the training.

4. Migration

People sometimes migrate from one place to the other in search of better jobs that fetch them higher salaries than what they may get in their native places. It includes migration of people from rural areas to urban areas in India. Unemployment is the reason for the rural urban migration in India and technically qualified people migrate from one country to another in order to get high salaries.

5. Expenditure on Information

People spent to acquire information relating to the labour market and other markets like education, health, etc.

For example, people seek information regarding salaries and other facilities available in different labour markets, so that they can choose the right job. Expenditure incurred for acquiring information regarding labour markets and other markets like education and health have also becomes an important source of human capital formation.

13.5 Human Capital Formation and Economic Growth

- Higher Productivity of Physical Capital Human capital formation increases productivity of physical capital specialised engineers and skilled workers can certainly handle machines better than the other.
- Innovative Skills It facilitates the use and growth of innovative skills. Innovation is the lifeline of growth.
- Higher Rate of Participation and Equality By enhancing productive capacities of the labour force, human capital formation induces greater employment.

Thus, there is a cause and effect relationship between human capital formation and economic growth.

India recognised the importance of human capital in economic growth long ago. The Seventh Five Year Plan says, 'Human resources development has necessarily to be assigned a key role in any development strategy, particularly in a country with a large population'.

The following points show clearly the interdependence among the two

- Higher Productivity of Physical Capital Human capital increases productivity of physical capital as specialised and skilled workers can handle machines or techniques better than the unskilled works. This increased productivity and hence production in leads to economic growth.
- Innovative Skills Human capital facilitates innovation of new methods of production and this increase the rate of economic growth in the form of increase in GDP.
- Higher Rate of Participation and Equality Human capital formation leads to a higher employment rate. With increase in employment, the productivity rises. Also, increase in employment opportunities also increases the level of income and this helps in reducing inequalities of wealth.

Both, increase in employment rate and decrease in income inequalities are pointers of economic development.

- Brings Positive Outlook The process of human capital formation bring in a positive outlook to the society which is different from orthodox and traditional ways of thinking, and hence increases the rate of participation in the workforce causes increase in level of production.

13.6 Economic Growth and State of Human Capital Formation in India

Human Capital and Economic Growth

India recognised the importance of human capital in economic growth long ago. The Seventh Five Year Plan says, 'Human resources development has necessarily to be assigned a key role in any development strategy, particularly in a country with a large population'.

The following points show clearly the interdependence among the two

- Higher Productivity of Physical Capital Human capital increases productivity of physical capital as specialised and skilled workers can handle machines or techniques better than the unskilled works. This increased productivity and hence production in leads to economic growth.

- Innovative Skills Human capital facilitates innovation of new methods of production and this increase the rate of economic growth in the form of increase in GDP.

- Higher Rate of Participation and Equality Human capital formation leads to a higher employment rate. With increase in employment, the productivity rises. Also, increase in employment opportunities also increases the level of income and this helps in reducing inequalities of wealth.

Both, increase in employment rate and decrease in income inequalities are pointers of economic development.

- Brings Positive Outlook The process of human capital formation bring in a positive outlook to the society which is different from orthodox and traditional ways of thinking, and hence increases the rate of participation in the workforce causes increase in level of production.

13.7 Problems of Human Capital Formation in India

- Rising population
- Brain drain
- Deficient manpower planning
- Long-term process
- High Poverty Levels

The main problems of human capital formation in India are:

- Rising Population Rapidly rising population adversely affects the quality of human capital in underdeveloped and developing countries like India. It reduces per head availability of existing facilities like sanitation, employment, drainage, water system, housing, hospitals, education, food supply, nutrition, roads, electricity, etc.

- Brain Drain Migration of highly skilled labour termed as 'brain drain. This slow down the process of human capital formation in the domestic economy.

- Inefficient of Manpower Planning There is inefficient manpower planning in less developed countries where no efforts have been made either to raise the standard of education at different stages pr to maintain the demand and supply of technical labour force. It is a sad reflection on the wastage of human power and human skill.

- Long-term Process The process of human development is a long-term policy because skill formation takes time. The process which produces skilled manpower is thus, slow. This also lowers our competitiveness in the international market of human capital.

- High Poverty Levels A large proportion of the population lives below poverty line and do not have access to basic health and educational facilities. A large section of society cannot afford to get higher education or expensive medical treatment for major disease.

13.8 Human Development Index

The Human Development Index (HDI) is a composite statistic of life expectance education, and income indices rank countries into four tiers of human development.

It was created by economist Mahbub Ul Haq, followed by economist Amartya Sen in 1990, and published by the United Nations Development Programme. India has 136th position in the World Human Development Index

13.9 Education is an essential element of human resource development

Education is an essential element of human resource development. Education implies the process of teaching, training and learning, (especially in schools or colleges). It improves the knowledge and develops the skills.

Education is the under- current of economic and social change post op however, compared to other countries of the world, spread of education in India has not been so encouraging. Even today literacy rate in the country continues to be very low.

13.10 Importance and objectives of Education

Following points highlight the importance and objectives of education:

i. Education produces responsible citizens.

ii. It develops science and technology.

iii. It facilitates use of natural and human resources of all regions of the country.

iv. It expands mental horizon of the people will stop

v. It helps economic development through greater participation of the people in the process of growth and development.

vi. It promotes cultural standard of the citizens.

vii. It develops human personality.

13.11 Education is Still a Challenging Proposition

Education system of the country which along with the following facts makes education still challenging proposition in India.

Large Number of Illiterates

- Inadequate vocationalisation
- Gender bias
- Low rural access level
- Privatisation
- Low government expenditure on education

13.12 Right to Education (RTE)

In the year 2012, the Government of India has brought about an Act, called RTE. It promises education to all. It makes education a matter of right to all children in the age group of 6-14 years.

The concept of human capital formation, source of human capital and its growth is revealed in the chapter. It also deals with the relationship among human capital, economic growth and human development.

13.13 India as a Knowledge Economy

The Indian software industry has been showing an Impressive record over the past decade. Entrepreneurs, bureaucrats and politicians are now advancing views about how India can transform itself into a knowledge-based economy by using Information Technology (IT).

There have been some instances of villagers using e-mail which are cited as examples of such transformation. Likewise, e-governance is being projected as the way of the future.

The value of IT depends greatly on the existing level of economic development.

13.14 Growth in Government Expenditure on Education

Government expenditure on education can be expressed in two ways

- As a percentage of the total government expenditure.
- As a percentage of Gross Domestic Product (GDP).

The percentage of 'education expenditure of total government expenditure' indicates the importance of education in the scheme of expenses before the government. Expenditure on education out of our GDP shows how much we are committed towards the development of education in our country.

During 1952-2010, education expenditure as percentage of total government expenditure increased from. 7.92% to 11.1% and as percentage of GDP increased from 0.64% to 3.25%. During this period expenditure on education was not constant. There was irregular rise and fell.

13.15 Expenditure on Elementary Education in India

Elementary education takes a major share of total education expenditure and the share of the higher/tertiary education is the least. But expenditure per student on tertiary education is higher than that of elementary.

As we expand school education, we need more teachers who are trained in the higher educational institutions, therefore, expenditure on all levels of education should be increased. The per capita education expenditure is as high as Rs. 2005 in Himachal Pradesh to as low as Rs. 515 in Bihar.

This leads to differences in educational opportunities across states.

13.16 Free and Compulsory Education

The Education Commission (1964-66) had recommended that at least 6% of GDP to be spent on education so as to make a noticeable rate of growth in education.

In December 2002, the Government of India, through the 86th Amendment of the Constitution of India, made free and compulsory education a fundamental right of all children in the age group of 6-14 years. Government of India in year 1998 appointed. The Tapas Majumdar Committee, which estimated an expenditure of around 1.37 lakh crore over 10 years (1998-99 to 2006-07) to bring all Indian children in the age group of 6-14 years, under the purview of school education. Desired level of expenditure an education is 6% of GDP but the current level is little over 4% which is not inadequate. It is necessary to reach the level of 6% which is considered as must for coming years.

Recently, Government of India has started levying a 2% 'education cess' on all Union taxes. The revenues from education cess has been earmarked for spending on elementary education.

13.17 Educational Achievements in India

Generally, educational achievements in a country are indicated in terms of

- Adult literacy level

- Primary education completion rate

- Youth literacy rate These statistics for the years 1990 to 2010 are given in the following table

13.18 Future Prospects

India government considers education a key sector where considerable growth and development is required. Thus, it has set some future prospects for framing its policies.

"Education for All is Still a Distant Dream". Although, the education level in India has risen for both adults as well as for youth. Still the number of illiterates in India are as much as the population was at the time of Independence.

In 1950, when the Constitution of India was passed by the constituent assembly, it was noted in the directive principles of the constitution that the government should provide free and compulsory education for all children up to the age of 14 years within 10 years from the commencement of the constitution.

The following factors makes education still a distant dream

- Large number of illiterates

- Inadequate vocationalisation

- Gender bias

- Low rural access level

- Privatisation

- Low government expenditure on education

13.19 Gender Equity: Better than Before

The differences in literacy rates between males and females are narrowing, signifying a positive development in gender equity; still the need to promote education for women in India is imminent for various reasons, such as

- Improving economic independence.

- Social status of women.

- Healthcare of women and children.

Therefore, we cannot show the satisfaction about the upward movement in literacy rates as we have miles to go in achieving cent percent adult literacy.

In India, Mizoram, Kerala, Goa and Delhi are the states having high literacy rate, while Bihar, Uttar Pradesh, Rajasthan and Arunachal Pradesh are the educationally backward states. The educational backwardness is due to social and economic poverty of the people.

Higher Education : A Few Takers

The Indian education pyramid is steep, indicating lesser and lesser number of people reaching the higher education level.

As per NSSG (National Sample Survey Organisation) data, in the year 2007-08, the rate of unemployment for youth with education up to secondary level and above was 18.1% whereas, the rate of unemployment for youth with education up to primary level was only 11.6%.

Therefore, the government should increase allocation for higher education and also improve the standard of higher education institutes, so that students are imparted employable skills in such institutions

13.20 Conclusion

Education in India has failed to reach the masses and has also failed to break the vicious circle of illiteracy - illiteracy breeding poverty and poverty breeding illiteracy.

Key Statements

Human Resource: it refers to abilities (skill and expertise) of human beings to contribute to the process of value- addition in the economy

Human Capital Formation: How people become resource; Role of human capital in economic development.

Gender Bias: means that one gender is treated in a more or less favourable way, based on gender stereotypes rather than real differences.

Vocationalisation of Education: The UNESCO defined vocational education as a "comprehensive term embracing those aspects of the educational process involving, in addition to general education, the study of technologies and related sciences and the acquisition of practical skills, attitudes, understanding, and knowledge relating to occupations in the various sectors of economic and social life.

Illiteracy: Illiteracy is a state whereby one is unable to read and write. In its simplest form, it can be defined as lack of any or sufficient education.

Literacy: The ability to read and write. In 2018, UNESCO includes "printed and written materials" and "varying contexts" in its definition of literacy, e.g. "the ability to identify, understand, interpret, create, communicate and compute, using printed and written materials associated with varying contexts".

Migration: Movement of people to a new area or country in order to find work or better living conditions.

Exercise

Frequently asked Questions (FAQ's)

1. What are the possible sources of human capital formation?
2. What is Right to Education?
3. What are 'Start-ups' and 'Skill Formation'?
4. Why is 'Brain drain' a serious bottleneck/constraint in human capital formation and growth process in India?
5. How is 'Gender Bias' in India is a hindrance to the process of skill formation?

Multiple Choice Questions (MCQ's)

1. Human capital formation leads to:
   (a) Increase GDP growth
   (b) Increase in the stock of physical capital
   (c) Efficient utilisation of inputs
   (d) Both (a)and (c)

2. Human capital and human development are:
   (a) opposite concepts
   (b) Related concepts, but certainly not identical
   (c) Different concepts
   (d) Both mean the same

3. Which of the following is the problem of human capital formation in India?
   (a) Brain Drain
   (b) Low Academic Standards
   (c) Rising Population
   (d) All of the Above

4. The process of addition to the stock of human capital overtime is called:
   (a) Human Capital Augmentation
   (b) Human Capital Formation
   (c) Human Capital Addition
   (d) Human Capital Stock

5. Which of the following highlight the fact that human capital formation contributes to the process of growth and development?
   (a) Higher productivity or physical capital
   (b) Innovative skills
   (c) Both (a) and (b)
   (d) None of the above

6. The stock of skill and expertise of a nation at a point of time is known as:
   (a) Physical Capital
   (b) Human Capital
   (c) Social infrastructure
   (d) None of the above

7. The ability to read and write is known as:
   (a) Vocational Skill
   (b) Human Capital
   (c) Literacy
   (d) Human development

8. Which of the following organisations is engaged in designing text material up to the senior secondary level?
   (a) AICTE   (b) NCERT
   (c) ICMR   (d) UGC

9. The need for government intervention in education and health arises because:
   (a) these sectors need huge investments with a very high fixed expenditure
   (b) It is difficult to private investors to invest under price regulation framework
   (c) Both (a) and (b)
   (d) None of the above

10. The responsibility of direction and control of higher education is with:
    (a) Department of higher education
    (b) University Grants Commission
    (c) Government of India
    (d) None of the above

11. Which of the following is the important way of adding to the stock of human capital?
    (a) expenditure on education
    (b) Expenditure on health
    (c) On- the- job training
    (d) All of the above

12. Primary educational completion rate in 2017- 18 for female was :
    (a) 95%   (b) 96%
    (c) 97%   (d) 98%

13. Who is responsible for the implementation of rules and regulations for technical education in the country?
    (a) University Grants Commission
    (b) All India Council of Technical Education
    (c) National Council of Educational Research and
    (d) Indian Council for Medical Research

14. Overall literacy rate census 2011 in India is:
    (a) 56%   (b) 60%
    (c) 65%   (d) 74%

15. Education is still a challenging proposition in the country on account of which of the following:
    (*a*) Large number of illiterates
    (*b*) Inadequate vocationalisation of education
    (*c*) Gender Bias
    (*d*) All of the above

16. Female literacy in India is:
    (*a*) 66%   (*b*) 70%
    (*c*) 75%   (*d*) 85%

17. What refers to the produced means of production?
    (*a*) Human Capital
    (*b*) Human Development
    (*c*) Physical Capital
    (*d*) None of the above

18. Which cost is involved in Migration?
    (*a*) Transportation cost
    (*b*) Higher Living cost in different places
    (*c*) Both (*a*) and (*b*)
    (*d*) None of these

19. What is the desired level of public expenditure on education as per education Commission?
    (*a*) 6%
    (*b*) 7%
    (*c*) 8%
    (*d*) 10%

20. Education is important because:
    (*a*) Expand mental horizon
    (*b*) Develops human personality
    (*c*) Helps in economic development
    (*d*) All of the above

21. Which institution is the primary funding authority for universities in India?
    (*a*) NCERT   (*b*) AICTE
    (*c*) ICMR   (*d*) UGC

22. There is a growing trend towards __________ of education, which makes it expensive for poor people.
    (*a*) Socialisation   (*b*) Privatisation
    (*c*) Both (*a*) and (*b*)   (*d*) None of the above

23. __________ Capital is tangible and can be sold in the market.
    (*a*) Human   (*b*) Physical
    (*c*) Service   (*d*) None of the above

24. Institutions providing elementary education have increased:
    (*a*) Three times   (*b*) Two times
    (*c*) Four times   (*d*) Five times

25. Human development is __________ of human welfare.
    (*a*) A para metre   (*b*) An index
    (*c*) An attribute   (*d*) None of the above

🔑 Solutions

Frequently asked Questions (FAQ's)

1. Sources of human capital formation are:
   i. Expenditure on Education
   ii. Expenditure on Health
   iii. On- the- job training
   iv. Adult Education-Study programmes for adults
   v. Migration
   vi. Expenditure on information

2. 2009, the Government of India has passed an act, called RTE. It makes education a matter of right to children in the age group of six- 14 years

3. 'Start-ups' (new business ventures) helps utilisation of the idle entrepreneurial abilities of the people. It, thus, promotes skill formation.

   'Skill formation' (Through higher education and training) helps the establishment of 'Start-up's'.

4. Brain drain refers to migration of skilled manpower to developed countries of the world. They migrate for greener pastures (higher wages and better quality of life). Those who migrate include scientists, engineers, doctors and educationists. These are the people of high calibre. Migration of such people is a serious bottleneck in human capital formation in India. 'Loss of skill' causes a dent in the process and pace of growth.

5. 'Gender Bias' particularly in rural India does not favour female education as much has made education which leads to hindrance to the process of skill formation.

Multiple Choice Questions (MCQ's)

1. (d) Both (a) and (c)
2. (b) Related concepts, but certainly not identical
3. (d) All of the above
4. (b) Human Capital Formation
5. (c) Both (a) and (b)
6. (b) Human Capital
7. (b) Literacy
8. (b) NCERT
9. (b) Both (a) and (b)
10. (b) University Grants Commission
11. (d) All of the above
12. (b) Cons 96%
13. (b) C All India Council of Technical Education
14. (d) 74%
15. (d) All of the above
16. (a) 66%
17. (c) Physical Capital
18. (c) Both (a) and (b)
19. (a) 6%
20. (d) All of the above
21. (d) UGC
22. (b) Privatisation
23. (b) Physical
24. (d) Five times
25. (b) An index

Your Notes:

CHAPTER 14

Current Challenges Facing Indian Economy Rural Development

LEARNING OBJECTIVES

❖ Rural Development:Meaning and significance

❖ Lingering Challenges of Rural Development: Rural Credit and Agricultural Marketing

❖ Emerging Challenges of Rural Development: diversification of Productive Activities and Organic Farming

Chief concepts of this chapter

- Rural development and the major issues associated with it
- How crucial the development of rural areas is for India's overall development
- Critical role of credit and marketing systems in rural development
- Importance of diversification of productive activities to sustain livelihoods
- Significance of organic farming and sustainable development
- Rural development: key issues- credit and marketing- role of cooperatives; agricultural diversification.

Rural Development and Rural credit

Rural development is a comprehensive term which essentially focuses on action for the development of areas that are lagging behind in the overall development of the village economy. It is a process whereby the standard of living of rural people, especially poor people, rises continuously. It means an action- plan for the social and economic upliftment of the rural areas.

14.1 The key issues of action plan for rural development are:

- Development of infrastructure
- Human capital formation
- Development of productive resources
- Poverty alleviation
- Land reforms

14.2 The basic objectives of rural development are:

- Increasing the productivity of the agricultural sector, so that the income of the formers increase.
- Generating alternative means of livelihood in the rural areas, so that dependency on agriculture sector is reduced.
- Promoting education and health facilities in the rural areas, so that human development is also achieved.

14.3 Rural Credit

Rural credit means credit for the farming families. Credit is the life line of farming activity credit needs of the typical Indian farmer may broadly be classified as underShort Term Credit It needs relates basically to the purchase of inputs like seeds fertilisers etc short term borrowings generally stretches over a period of 6 to 12 months.

- Medium Term Credit Medium term loans are required for purchasing machinery constructing fences and digging wells. Such loans are generally stretch over a period of 12 months to 5 years.
- Long Term Credit Long term credit is meant for the purchase of additional land. The period of such loan ranges between 5 to 20 years.

14.4 Rural Credit

Credit is the lifeline of the farming activity. Rural credit means providing credit for the forming community. Farmers need credit because

- Most formers in India are small and marginal land holders who practice subsistence farming. They have no surplus for further production.

- The gestation period between sowing and harvesting is quite high. So, farmers have to borrow to fulfil their various needs during this period.

Borrowings of a farmer can be for the following purpose:

- Productive Borrowings These borrowings include loans to buy seeds, fertilisers and agricultural equipment's and implements.

- Un-productive Borrowings These borrowings include loans for social purposes such as marriage and festive occasions.

14.5 Types of Rural Credit

Credit needs of farmers may be classified as

- Long-term Credit These loans are required to acquire permanent assets like tractors, land, costly equipment's, tube-wells, etc. These loans are for a period of 5 to 20 years.

- Medium-term Credit These loans are required for purchasing machinery, constructing fences and digging wells. Such loans are generally stretch over a period of 12 months to 5 years.

- Short-term Credit These loans are required for buying seeds, tools, manure and fertilisers, etc. This credit is given to the needy borrowers by cooperatives, moneylenders and banks. These loans are for a period of 6 to 12 months.

14.6 Sources of Rural Credit

- Non-institutional sources

- Institutional sources
  - o   Co-operative credit societies
  - o   State Bank of India
  - o   Regional Rural Bank
  - o   National Bank for Agriculture and Rural Development (NABARD)

Credit in the rural sector is available from two sources:

1. **Non-institutional Sources of Rural Credit** The major non-institutional sources of rural credit are moneylenders, friends, relatives, landlords, shopkeepers and commission agents. Moneylenders provided about 93.6% of total financial requirement

rural areas in 1951-52 and presently it is 30%. The short-term credit needs of the formers are met from commission agents, friends and relatives which supply roughly 50% of total rural borrowings, Non-institutional sources of credit are not encouraged by government because of the following reasons

- They charge high rate of interest.

- They acquire land on failure to pay interest and loan.

- They manipulate accounts.

The **Poor Women's Bank Kudumbashree** is women-oriented community based poverty i reduction programme being implemented in Kerala. In 1995, a thrift and credit society was started as a small savings for poor women with an objective to encourage savings. The thrift and credit society mobilised Rs. 1 crore as thrift savings. These societies have been acclaimed as largest informal banks in Asia in terms of participation and savings mobilised.

2. **Institutional Sources of Rural Credit** In regard to rural credit, major change occurred after 1969, when India adopted social banking and multi-agency approach to adequately meet the needs of rural credit. Different institutions were formed to provide the rural credit.

The major institutional sources of rural credit are as follows:

(i) **National Bank for Agriculture and Rural Development (NABARD)** It was set up in 1982 as an apex body to coordinate the activities of all institutions involved in the rural financing system. It has an authorised share capital of Rs. 500 crore. The RBI has contributed half of the share capital while the other half has been contributed by Government of India.

The main functions of NABARD are

- To grant long-term loans to the State Government for subscribing to the share capital of cooperative societies.

- To take the responsibility of inspecting cooperative banks, Regional Rural Banks (RRBs) and primary cooperative societies.

- To promote research in agriculture and rural development.

- To serve as a refinancing agency for the institutions providing finance to rural and agricultural development.

- To help tenant farmers and small farmers to consolidate their land holdings.

The national agricultural credit funds have been transferred from RBI to NABARD to form a part of its national rural credit fund.

(ii) **Self Help Groups (SHGs)** Formal credit system has proven inadequate. It has also not been fully integrated into the overall rural, social and community development.

Due to the demand of some kind of collateral, vast proportion of poor rural households were automatically out of the credit networks. Self Help Groups emerged to fill this gap, created by formal credit system.

Self Help Groups (SHGs) promote thrift in small proportions by a minimum contribution from each member. By March end 2003, more than Rs. 7 lakh SHGs had reportedly been credit linked. Such credit provisions are generally referred to as micro-credit programmes. SHGs have helped in the empowerment of women. However, borrowings from SHGs are mainly confined to consumption purposes.

(iii) **Regional Rural Banks (RRBs)** As a supplement to commercial banks, the regional rural banks have also been opened. These have been set up under the Regional Rural Banks Act-of 1976. Their banking services are meant for small and marginal formers and artisans, etc. They cater exclusively to the needs of weaker section. Nearly 90% of the loan of RRBs were provided to the weaker section.

Kisan Credit Card Scheme

Kisan Credit Card scheme (KCCs) was introduced by the government in 1998-99. It facilitates access to credit from commercial banks and regional rural banks. Under the scheme, the eligible farmers are provided with a kisan card and passbook from the relevant bank. The farmers can make withdrawals and repayments of cash within the credit limit as – specified in the Kisan Credit Card (KCC).

(iv) **Commercial Banks:** They were inducted into the field of agricultural credit under the Banking Reforms Act, 1972. The share of commercial banks in the supply of agricultural credit has considerably improved. It was 46.9% during the year 2006-07.

Commercial banks disburse agricultural credit for the purchase of inputs, cattle, tractors, dairy farming, installation of tube-wells, etc.

(v) **Cooperative Credit Societies** The cooperative credit societies are actively engaged in addressing credit needs of the farmers, besides offering a host of related services. Notably these societies provide guidance in diverse agricultural operations with a view to raise crop productivity. Currently, cooperatives account for 16-17% of rural credit flow. The main function of cooperative credit society is to provide timely and increased flow of credit to the farmers.

14.7 Key Areas in Rural Development

Some of the areas which are challenging and need fresh initiatives for development in rural India are as follows:

- Development of the productive resources of each locality.

- Development of human resources including literacy (more specifically female literacy) education and skill development.

- Development of human resources like health, addressing both sanitation and public health.

- Honest implementation of land reforms.

- Infrastructure development like electricity, irrigation, credit, marketing, transport facilities including construction of village roads and feeder roads to nearby highways, facilities for agriculture research and extension and information dissemination.

- Special measures for alleviation of poverty and bringing about significant improvement in the living conditions of the weaker sections of the populations emphasising access to productive employment opportunities.

The share of agriculture sector's contribution to GDP was on a decline, the population dependent on this sector did not show any significant change. Further, after the initiation of reforms, the growth rate of agriculture sector decelerated to 2.3% per annum during the 1990s, which was lower than the earlier years.

14.8 Latest Status of Agricultural Credit

The following points reveal the latest status of agricultural credit

- The credit flow in this sector in 2011-12 is placed at Rs. 475000 crore.

- The agricultural debt waiver and debt relief scheme was announced in the union budget 2008-09.

- Farmers have been receiving crop loans up to a principal amount of Rs.3 lakh at an effective rate of 4% per annum.

- To provide adequate and timely credit support to the formers, the Kisan Credit Card (KCC) scheme was introduced in February 1999. About 10.78 crore KCCs had been issued upto October 2011.

- Government is implementing a revival package for short-term rural cooperative credit structure involving financial outlay of Rs. 13596 crore.

14.9 Rural Banking : A Critical Appraisal

After the nationalisation of commercial banks in 1969, the rapid expansion of the banking system in rural areas has been witnessed. Rural banking has raised the level of rural farm and non-farm output, income and employment especially after the green revolution.

14.10　Advantages of Rural Banking

- Raising farm and non-farm output by providing services and credit facilities to farmers.

- Generating credit for self-employment schemes in rural areas.

- Achieving food security which is clear from the abundant buffer stocks of grains.

14.11　Limitations of Rural Banking

- Small and marginal formers receive only a very small portion of the institutional credit.

- Rural banking is suffering from the problems of large amount of over dues and default rate.

- The sources of institutional finance are inadequate to meet the requirements of agricultural credit.

- There exist regional inequalities in the distribution of institutional credit.

It is suggestible that more and more regional rural banks should be set up to need the credit need of the rural and backward areas of India.

14.12 Agricultural Marketing, Diversification of Agricultural Activities and Organic Farming

Agriculture Marketing

It includes all those activities or processes which help a former getting maximum price for his produce among others, these processes include grading packaging and storage.It is the process that involves functions of assembling, storage, processing, packaging, transportation, grading and distribution of agricultural commodities throughout the country.

In other words, agricultural marketing covers the services involved in moving an agricultural product from the farm to the consumer.

Need of agriculture marketing originates due to the problems faced by farmers.

Different types of problems faced by the farmers are:

- Farmers while selling their produce to traders suffered from faulty weighing and manipulation of accounts.

- Due to lack of knowledge about the prices prevailing in the markets, farmers are often forced to sell their produce at low prices.

- Farmers did not have proper storage facilities to keep back their produce for selling later at better price.

Approximately 10% of goods produced in farms is wasted due to lack of storage.

Distress Sale- Lack of agricultural marketing infrastructure often forces the farmers to sell their produce at low prices for fear of spoilage or to pay off an imminent debt. This is termed as distress sale. Farmers tend to suffer highly on account of these sales, because they not only get a low price for their produce but are also cheated by use of false weights and are charged a high commission.

Measures by Government to Improve Agriculture Marketing

Four measures which were initiated to improve the agriculture marketing aspect are discussed below

1. Regulation of Markets The first measure to improve agriculture marketing aspect is regulation of markets to create orderly and transparent marketing conditions. Regulated markets have been established where sale and purchase of the produce is monitored by the Market Committee consisting of representatives of government, farmers and the traders.

   Market committee ensure that the formers get appropriate price of their produce. By and large, this policy benefited farmers as well as consumers. However, there is still need to develop about 27000 rural periodic markets as regulated market places to realize the full potential of rural markets.

2. Improvement in Physical Infrastructure It is the second measure to improve the agriculture marketing aspect. The current infrastructure facilities like; roads, railways, warehouses, godowns, cold storages and processing units etc are inadequate to meet the growing demand. Through this measure government ensures the improvement in physical infrastructure.

3. Cooperative Marketing It is the third measure taken by government in realising the fair prices for farmers products. As members of these societies, formers find themselves better bargainers in the market and get better prices of their produce through collective sale. The success of milk cooperatives in Gujarat and some other parts of the country are the brilliant examples of cooperative marketing.

Different problems faced by cooperative during the recent past are

- Inadequate coverage of former members.

- Lack of appropriate link between marketing and processing cooperatives.

- Inefficient financial management.

14.13 Supporting Policies

It is the fourth measure taken by government to improve agriculture marketing system. Different supportive policies applied in this regard are

- Minimum Support Price (MSP) It is an important step to improve agriculture market system. MSP is an assurance to the farmers that a minimum price will be fixed by the government to formers' produce, no purchasing can be done below this price, however farmers can sell their produce in open market above MSP. This policy assured a minimum income to the farmers.

- Maintenance of Buffer Stocks of Wheat and Rice Purchases from the farmers are kept by Food Corporation of India as buffer stocks.

- Distribution of Food grains and Sugars Through Stocks purchased by government at MSP are used primarily for Public Distribution System (PDS). Distribution of food grains and other necessary items like kerosene oil at subsidised price to the poor takes place through fair price shops.

- Emerging Alternative Marketing Channels In India, alternative marketing channels are emerging. Through these channels, farmers directly sell their products to the consumers. This system increases farmers' share in the prices paid by the consumers.

Important examples of such channels are

- Apni mandi (Punjab, Haryana and Rajasthan).

- Hadaspar mandi (Pune); Rythu Bazars (Vegetables and fruit market in Andhra Pradesh).

- Uzhavar sandies (Farmers' Markets in Tamil Nadu).

- Several national and international fast food chains and hotels are also entering into contracts with the farmers to supply them farm products (fresh vegetables and fruits) of the desired quality.

14.14 Diversification into Productive Activities

Diversification means a major proportion of the increasing labour force in the agricultural sector needs to find alternate employment opportunities in other non-farm sectors. Diversification is an emerging challenge in the context of rural development. It has two aspects

- Diversification of crop production

- Diversification of productive activity

14.15 Diversification of Crops

This implies a shift from single cropping system to multi-cropping system. In India, where subsistence farming is still dominant, it may also mean a shift from subsistence farming to commercial farming.

Significance of Diversification of Crops Diversification of crops is important because it will

- Minimise the risk occurring. due to failure of monsoon.

- Minimise the market risk arising due to price fluctuations.

14.16 Need of Diversification into Productive Activities

Agriculture sector is a seasonal based activity, most of agriculture employment activities are concentrated in Kharif season. But during Rabi season, in the areas where irrigation facilities are inadequate, it becomes difficult to find gainful employment.

So, there is a need to focus on allied activities, non-farm employment and other emerging alternatives of livelihood. Also, agriculture sector is already overcrowded, a major proportion of the increasing labour force needs to find alternate employment opportunities in other non-farm sectors.

14.17 Some non-farm activities are discussed below

1. Animal Husbandry

In India, the forming community uses the mixed crop-livestock forming system. Cattle, goats, fowl are the widely domesticated species. Livestock production provides increased stability in income, food security, transport, fuel and nutrition for the family without disrupting other food producing activities.

Today, livestock sector alone provides alternate livelihood options to over 70 million small and marginal farmers including landless labourers.

Poultry accounts for the largest share with 55% followed by others. India has about 304 million cattle, including 105 million buffaloes.

A significant number of women also find employment in the livestock sector.

Milk production in the country has increased by more thlkn five times between 1960-2009. This can be attributed mainly to the successful implementation of 'operation flood'.

Meat, eggs, wool and other by-products are also emerging as important productive sectors for diversification.

In numbers, our livestock population is quite impressive but its productivity is quite low as compared to other countries. It requires improved technology and promotion of good breeds of animals to enhance productivity. Improved veterinary care and credit facilities to small and marginal formers and landless labourers would enhance sustainable livelihood options through livestock production.

2. Operation Flood

It is a system whereby all the farmers can pool their milk produced according to different grading (based on quality) and the same Is processed and marketed to urban centres through cooperatives.

In this system farmers are assured of fair price and Income from the supply of the milk to urban markets. Gujarat state is held as a success story in the efficient implementation of milk cooperatives which has been emulated by many states.

3. Fisheries

The socio-economic status of fishermen is comparatively lower because of

- rampant underemployment
- low per capital earnings
- absence of mobility of labour to other sectors
- high rate of illiteracy
- indebtedness

4. Horticulture

Due to varying climate and soil conditions, India has adopted growing of diverse horticultural crops such as fruits, vegetables, tuber crops, flowers, medicinal and aromatic plants, spices and plantation crops. These crops play an important role in providing food, nutrition and employment.

The period between 1991-2003 is called 'golden revolution' because during this period, the planned investment in horticulture became highly productive and the sector emerged as a sustainable livelihood option.

India has emerged as a world leader in producing a variety of fruits, like mangoes, bananas, coconuts, cashew, nuts and a number of species and is the second largest producer of fruits and vegetables.

Economic conditions of many formers engaged in horticulture has improved and has become a means of improving livelihood for many unprivileged classes.

Flower harvesting, nursery maintance, hybrid seed production and tissue culture, propagation of fruits and flowers and food processing are highly profitable employment opportunities for rural women. It has been estimated that this sector provides employment to around 19% of the total labour force.

5. Cottage and Household Industry

This industry has been dominated by such activities as spinning, weaving, dyeing and bleaching.

14.18 Other Alternate Livelihood Options

The Information Technology (IT) has revolutionised many sectors in the Indian economy.

It plays a very significant role in achieving sustainable development and food security in the following ways

- It can act as a tool for releasing the creative potential and knowledge embedded in our people.

- Issues like weather forecast, crop treatment, fertilisers, pesticides storage conditions, etc can be well administered, if expert opinion is made available to the farmers.

- The quality and quantity of crops can be increased manifold, if the farmers are made aware of the latest equipment's, technologies and resources.

- It has ushered in a knowledge economy.

- It has potential of employment generation in rural areas.

14.19 Every Village A Knowledge Centre

MS Swaminathan Research Foundation, an institution located in Chennai, Tamil Nadu, with support from Sir Ratan Tata Trust, Mumbai, has established the Jamshedji Tata National Virtual Academy for Rural Prosperity. The academy envisaged to identify a million grass root knowledge workers who will b% enlisted as fellows of the academy.

The programme provides an info-kiosk (PC with internet and video conferencing facility, scanner, photocopier, etc) at a low cost and trains kiosk owner; the owner then provides different services and tries to earn a reasonable income. The Government of India has decided to join the alliance by providing financial support of Rs. 100 crore.

14.20 Diversification is an emerging challenge in the context of rural development. It has two aspects:

- Diversification of Crop Production It implies production of diverse variety of crops rather than one specialised crop. It means a shift from single-cropping system to multi-cropping system.

- Diversification of Production Activity/Employment It implies a shift from crop farming to other areas of production activity employment.

14.21 Sustainable Development and Organic Farming

Conventional agriculture uses chemical fertilisers and toxic pesticides, etc which enter the food supply, penetrate the water resources, harm the livestock, deplete the soil and devastate natural eco-system. Due to these problems, an eco-friendly technology is required.

Organic farming is a system of farming that relies upon the use of organic inputs for cultivation. Organic inputs basically include animal manures and composts.

Organic farming is such technology which restores, maintains and enhances the ecological balance. There is an increasing demand for organically grown food to enhance food safety throughout the world.

Benefits of organic farming are as follows:

- Discards the use of non-renewable resources

- Environment friendly

- Sustains soil fertility

- Healthier and tastier food

- In expensive technology for the small and marginal farmers

- Organic forming substitutes costlier agriculture inputs like HYV seeds, chemical fertilizers, pesticides, etc with locally produced organic inputs that are cheaper and thereby generate good returns on investment.

- Organic forming also generates income through exports.

- Organically grown food has more nutritional value than chemical forming, thus providing us with healthy foods. Produce pesticide free and produced in an environmentally sustainable way.

- Due to more labour requirement in organic farming, it is an attractive proposition for India.

Limitations of Organic Farming

- Yields from organic forming are less than modern agricultural forming in the initial years. Therefore, small and marginal formers may find it difficult to adapt to large scale production.

- Organic produce have shorter shelf life than sprayed produce.

- Choice in production of off-season crops in quite limited in organic forming.

14.22 Golden Revolution

The rapid growth in the production of diverse horticultural crops such as fruits, vegetables, toper crops and plantation crops is known as Golden Revolution.

14.23 Conclusion

Agriculture is the major source of livelihood in the rural sector. Mahatma Gandhi once said that "real progress of India did not mean only the industrial growth but also the development of villages because two-third of India's population depends on agriculture". One-third of rural Indians still live in poverty. This is the reason, why there is need to develop rural India.

Key Statements

Rural Development: It means an action- plan for the economic and social growth of the rural areas.

Agricultural marketing: It includes gathering the produce after harvesting, processing the produce, grading the produce according to its quality, packaging the produce according to buyers' preferences, storing the produce for future sale, and selling the produce when price is lucrative.

'Low Yield and High Cost for Unit of ': It is the principle constraint in switching over from conventional farming to organic farming.

Distress Sale: refers to a situation when the farmers are compelled to sell their produce immediately after the harvest, no matter how low the market price is. The compulsion to cell arises because:

i. the farmers need immediate cash to pay off their debts.

ii. they lack storage facilities or the cost of storage is very high.

Buffer Stocks: The stock of food grains, namely rice and wheat, procured by the Government through the Food Corporation of India (FCI) is known as the Buffer Stock. The purchased food grains are stored in granaries. The Food Corporation of India (FCI) purchases rice and wheat from the farmers in states which have surplus production.

- Buffer stock helps in resolving the food shortage issues faced during natural calamities like droughts, floods, earthquakes etc.

- Buffer stock is used to meet the food requirements of poorer strata of society, by selling the food grains at lower price when compared to market price. This is known as Issue Price.

TANWA: Tamil Nadu women in agriculture is a project launched in Tamil Nadu with a view to training women to diverse techniques of farming. This is expected to raise employment of women as well as their income through higher levels of productivity. Having acquired specialised skills through training, women are forming Farm Women's Groups. These groups function like SHGs and promote cottage in household production activity using their own pool of funds.

Exercise

Frequently asked Questions (FAQ's)

1. How does grading of output raise revenue of the farmer?
2. How does organic farming promote sustainable development?
3. How is 'Green Revolution' different from 'Golden Revolution'?
4. Why is agricultural diversification essential for sustainable livelihoods?
5. How does 'Information Technology'(IT), plays a significant role in achieving sustainable development and food security?

Multiple Choice Questions (MCQ's)

1. MSP means:
   - (a) Minimum support price to the farmers
   - (b) Maximum support price to the farmers
   - (c) Minimum price of the crop in the retail market
   - (d) Maximum price for the farm inputs

2. Why is the minimum support price fixed by the government?
   - (a) For government's own benefit
   - (b) To safeguard the interest of farmers' next line
   - (c) To safeguard the interest of consumers
   - (d) None of the above

3. Which of the following is an institutional source of rural credit?
   - (a) Co- operative credit
   - (b) Land Development Banks
   - (c) NABARD
   - (d) All of the above

4. Agriculture marketing does not comprise of:
   - (a) Transportation of the produce to the marketplace for sale
   - (b) Grading of the produce according to the quality
   - (c) Storage of the produce for sale in future
   - (d) Credit taken to meet agricultural expenditure

5. Distress sale by the farmers refer to:
   - (a) Sale of rotten Croft
   - (b) Sale of the crop through Commission agents
   - (c) Sale of the crop at MSP fixed by the government
   - (d) Sale of the crop at a very poor price

6. The government established the institutional sources of finance:
   - (a) To provide adequate credit to farmers at a cheaper interest rate
   - (b) To assist small farmers in raising agricultural productivity and maximising their income
   - (c) To earn profits
   - (d) All of the above

7. Name the state which is held as a success story in the efficient implementation of milk cooperatives.
   - (a) Maharashtra
   - (b) Jammu and Kashmir
   - (c) Gujarat
   - (d) Andhra Pradesh

8. Which of the following is a non-farm area of employment?
   - (a) Livestock farming (b) Horticulture
   - (c) Fisheries   (d) All of the above

9. Organic Farming is beneficial because:
   - (a) It generates income through international exports
   - (b) It makes use of chemical fertilisers and pesticides
   - (c) It is produced in an environmentally sustainable way
   - (d) Both (a) and (c)

10. The period between ____________is known as 'Golden Revolution Period'
    - (a) 1991-2001   (b) 1991-2003
    - (c) 1993-2001   (d) 1990- 2003

11. Which among the following is an initiative taken for the development of rural India?
    - (a) Human Capital Formation
    - (b) Land Reforms
    - (c) Poverty Alleviation
    - (d) All of these

12. What was the growth rate of agricultural output during 2007-12?
    - (a) 32% per annum (b) 6% per annum
    - (c) 1.5% per annum (d) 5% per annum

13. When was the National Bank for Agricultural and Rural Development set up?
    - (a) 1962   (b) 1972
    - (c) 1982   (d) 1992

14. White Revolution is associated with:
    - (*a*) Horticulture
    - (*b*) Fisheries
    - (*c*) Dairying
    - (*d*) Animal Husbandry

15. Which of the following is an institutional source of rural credit?
    - (*a*) Moneylenders
    - (*b*) Regional Rural Banks
    - (*c*) Traders
    - (*d*) Landlords

16. How much do the "inland sources" contribute to the total fish production in India?
    - (*a*) 64 percent
    - (*b*) 39 percent
    - (*c*) 50 percent
    - (*d*) 75 percent

17. Which status has been accorded to the retail chains and supermarkets for selling organic food?
    - (*a*) Economic Status
    - (*b*) Sustainable Status
    - (*c*) Nutritional Status
    - (*d*) Green Status

18. What is the name of the vegetable and fruit market in Andhra Pradesh?
    - (*a*) Apni Mandi
    - (*b*) Hadaspar Mandi
    - (*c*) Rythu Bazars
    - (*d*) Uzhavar Sandies

19. Which among the following is a process that involves the assembling, storage, processing, transportation, packaging, grading, and distribution of different agricultural commodities across the country?
    - (*a*) Agricultural Management
    - (*b*) Agricultural Banking
    - (*c*) Agricultural Diversification
    - (*d*) Agricultural Marketing

20. The duration of short- term credit is:
    - (*a*) 6 to 12 months
    - (*b*) 2 to 5 years
    - (*c*) 5 to 20 years
    - (*d*) 12 months to 5 years

21. Short term credit is required for:
    - (*a*) For Construction.
    - (*b*) Purchasing inputs like seeds, fertilisers, etc.
    - (*c*) For purchasing land or tractor.
    - (*d*) None of the above

22. Non- institutional source of rural credit includes:
    - (*a*) Money Lenders
    - (*b*) Commercial Banks
    - (*c*) Regional Rural Banks
    - (*d*) None of the above

23. Qualitative credit societies ensure:
    - (*a*) Rapid flow of credit to farmers
    - (*b*) Guidance in diverse agricultural operations
    - (*c*) Elimination of money lenders
    - (*d*) All of the above

24. The main function of NABARD is:
    - (*a*) Serves as an apex Funding Agency
    - (*b*) Coordinate the rural financing activities
    - (*c*) Monitor and evaluate the refunded projects
    - (*d*) All of the above

25. Which is an important source of occupation for women in rural areas?
    - (*a*) Fishing
    - (*b*) Agriculture
    - (*c*) Livestock farming
    - (*d*) Horticulture

🔑 Solutions________________________

Frequently asked Questions (FAQ's)

1. Grading of output refers to division of output in different categories on the basis of 'quality'. The farmers can charge higher prices for the high- graded of output. This increases his total revenue from the sale of his output.

2. organic farming focuses on 'soil health' rather than 'crop health'. fertility of soil is maintained over a long period of time. Accordingly, organic farming promotes sustainable development.

3. 'Green revolution' refers to a series of research, development, and technology transfer initiatives that increased agriculture production remarkably. On the other hand, 'Golden Revolution' refers to a series of research, development and technology transfer initiatives that increased production of horticulture crops (vegetables and fruits) and honey.

4. Agricultural diversification refers to the allocation of farms productive resources to diverse areas of crop output, so as to reduce market risk. Owing to changes in the relative price structure, if one crop fetches low revenue, the other may fetch high. Thus, diversification helps stabilisation of farm income by lowering the market risk.

5. Information technology plays a significant role in achieving sustainable development and food security. Global COVID crisis has enhanced the use of information technology in rural areas. Presently, Internet users in India are more in rural than in urban areas. This underscores the significance of information technology as an alternative source of employment for the educated youth in the rural areas. This would reduce their dependence upon crop farming as a conventional source of livelihood which is extremely overcrowded and highly uncertain.

Multiple Choice Questions (MCQ's)

1. (a) Minimum support price to the farmers
2. (b) To safeguard the interest of farmers
3. (d) All of the above
4. (d) Credit taken to meet agricultural expenditure
5. (d) Sale of the crop at a very poor price
6. (a) To provide adequate credit to farmers at a cheaper interest rate
7. (c) Gujarat
8. (d) All of the above
9. (d) Both (a) and (c)
10. (b) 1991-2003
11. (d) All of these
12. (a) 32% per annum
13. (c)1982
14. (c) Dairying
15. (b) Regional Rural Banks
16. (a) 64 percent
17. (d) Green Status
18. (c) Rythu Bazars
19. (d) Agricultural Marketing
20. (a) Cons 6 to 12 months
21. (b) Purchasing inputs like seeds, fertilisers, etc.
22. (a) Money Lenders
23. (d) All of the above
24. (d) All of the above
25. (c) Livestock farming

CHAPTER 15

Current Challenges Facing Indian Economy Employment

Chief concepts of this chapter

- Basic concepts relating to employment such as economic activity, worker, workforce and unemployment.

- Nature of participation of men and women in various economic activities in various sectors.

- Nature and extent of unemployment

- Initiated taken by the government in generating employment opportunities in various sectors and regions

Unemployment

According to Prof Pigou, "A man is unemployed only when he is both without a job or not employed and also desires to be employed".

In every section of society there will be a large number of unemployed persons. It is a situation, in which all those who, owing to lack of work are not working but either seek work through employment exchanges, intermediaries, friends or relatives or by making applications to prospective employers or express their willingness or availability for work under the prevailing condition of work and remunerations.

There are a variety of ways by which an unemployed person is identified. As per the view of some economists, unemployed person is one who is not able to get employment of even one hour in half a day.

One can get the data of unemployed persons through below stated sources

- Reports of Census of India

- NSSO's (National Sample Survey Organisations) reports of employment and unemployment situation

- Directorate General of Employment and Training Data of Registration with Employment Exchanges.

15.1 Types of Unemployment in India

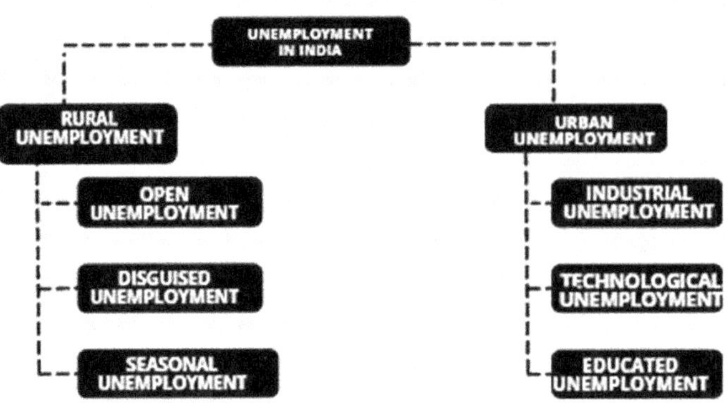

15.1.1 Rural Unemployment

Around 70% of India's population lives in village. Agriculture is the single largest source of their livelihood. Agriculture suffers from a number of problems like dependence upon rainfall, financial constraints, obsolete techniques, etc.

Rural unemployment can be of following three types

- Open Unemployment It refers to that situation wherein the worker is willing to work and has the necessary ability to work yet he does not get work and remains unemployed for full time. "

- Seasonal Unemployment It refers to a situation where a number of a persons are not able to find a job in a particular season. It occurs in case of agriculture, ice-cream factories, woollens factories, etc.

- Disguised Unemployment It exists when marginal physical productivity of labour is zero or sometimes it becomes negative. Important features of disguised unemployment are as under
  - o Marginal physical productivity of labour is zero.
  - o There is disguised unemployment among wage earners.
  - o Disguised unemployment is invisible.
  - o It is different from industrial unemployment.

15.1.2 Urban Unemployment

In urban areas, unemployed people are often registered with employment exchanges. Between 1961 and 2008, the number of unemployed registered in employment exchanges has increased more than eight-fold.

Urban unemployment is of three types:

- Industrial Unemployment It includes those illiterate persons who are willing to work in industries, mining, transport, trade and construction activities, etc.

- Problem of unemployment in industrial sector has become acute because of increasing migration of rural people to urban industrial areas in search of employment.

- Educated Unemployment In India the problem of unemployment among the educated people is also quite grave. It is a problem spread across all parts of the country, because the massive expansion of the education facilities have contributed to the growth of educated persons who are on the look out for white collar jobs.

- Technological Unemployment Technological upgradation is taking place in all spheres of activity.

- People who have not updated their skills in the latest technology become technologically unemployed.

15.1.3 Causes of Unemployment in India

1. Slow Economic Growth In Indian economy, the rate of economic growth is very slow. This slow growth rate fails to provide enough employment opportunities to the rising population. Supply of labour is much more than the available employment opportunities.

2. Rapid Growth of Population Constant increase in population has been a grave problem of India.

It is one of the main causes of unemployment. The number of unemployed has actually increased instead of decreasing during the plan period.

3. **Faulty Employment Planning** The Five Year Plans in India have not been designed for employment generation. A frontal attack to solve the problem of unemployment is missing. It was thought that economic growth will take care of unemployment problem.

4. **Excessive Use of Foreign Technology** Lack of scientific and technical cosearch at home, due to its high cost has resulted in excessive use of foreign technology which has led to technical unemployment in our country.

5. **Lack of Financial Resources** The expansion and diversification programme of agriculture and small scale industries have suffered because of lack of financial resources. This has been accompanied by increasing government control of economic activities.

6. **Increase in Labour Force** The population explosion stage of Indian economy has added young people to the labour force who are seeking employment.

15.1.4 Suggestions to Solve the Problem of Unemployment in India

- Increase in production
- Increase in productivity
- High rate capital formation
- Help to self-employed persons
- Technique of production
- Co-operative industries

15.2 Government Policy and Programmes to solve problems of Unemployment

Government seeks to solve the problem of unemployment through its poverty eradication programmes generating employment opportunities for poorer sections of the society. Rural employment Guarantee scheme is a significant recent attempt of the government, offering guaranteed employment to those in the rural areas who are below poverty line.

Some of the basic issues related to unemployment in India are emphasised in this chapter. It also addresses the growth rate of Indian economy and various employment generation, schemes. It also specifies the need of transformation of workers from in formal sector to formal sector.

15.3 Employment and Informalisation of Indian workforce

Work plays an important role in our lives as an individual or a group of members can earn their living after doing work. Being employed gives us a sense of self-worth and enables us to relate ourselves meaningfully with others. In this way, every working person can actively contribute towards national income.

Thus, there is need to know who a worker is and what is an employment.

A person is classed as a worker if:

- he has contract or agreement to do work.
- he gets reward or other benefits from doing a work.
- he works for himself or is self-employed.

So, it can be concluded that all those who are engaged in production activities, in whatever capacity high or low, are workers."

15.3.1 Types of Workers

Broadly, workers can be categorised into self-employed and hired workers. They are discussed below

- **Self-Employed** The workers who own and operate an enterprise to earn their livelihood are known as self-employed.

  For example, a farmer working on his own farm. This category accounts for more than 50% of the workforce.

- **Hired Workers** Those people who are hired by others and are paid wages or salaries as a reward for their services are called hired workers.

15.3.2 Hired workers can be of two types

- **Casual Workers** Those people, who are not hired by their employers on a regular/permanent basis and do not get social security benefits are said to be casual workers.

  For example, construction workers.

- **Regular Salaried Workers** When a worker is engaged by someone or by an enterprise and paid his or her wages on a regular basis, they are known as regular salaried employees or regular workers.

  For example, teachers, chartered accountants, etc.

15.3.3 Self-Employed and Hired Workers in India

1. According to Region (Rural and Urban)

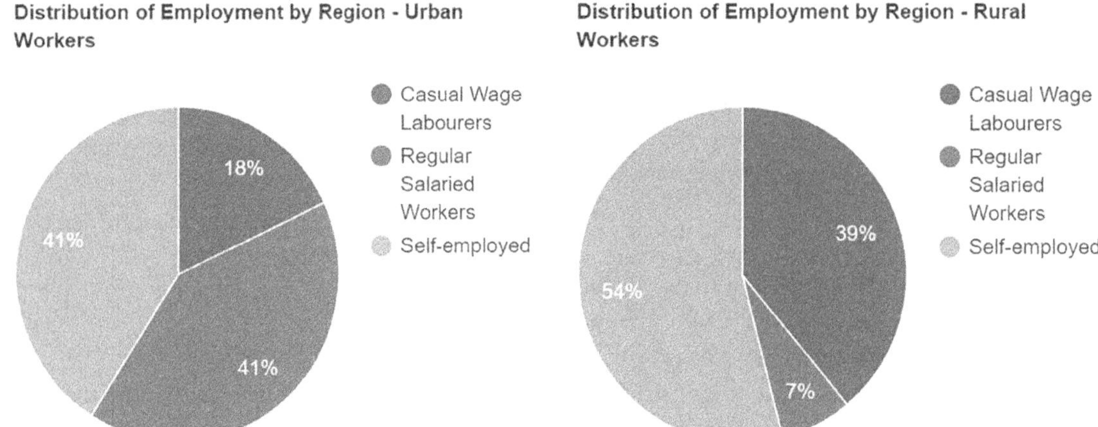

The above chart shows that the self-employed and casual wage labourers are found more in rural areas than in urban areas. It is -because in urban areas, people are skilled and work for jobs in offices and factories. But in rural areas, people work on their own farms.

2. According to Gender

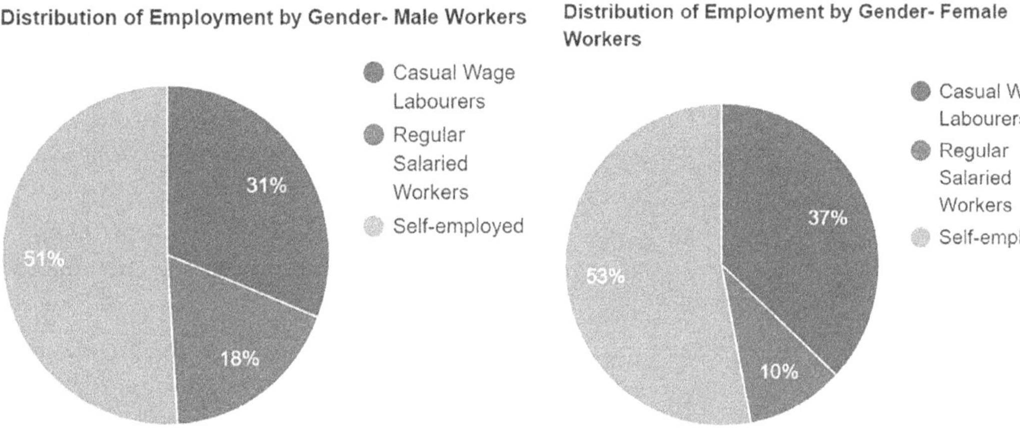

Distribution of Employment by Gender The above chart shows that self-employment and hired employment are equally important for male workers. But female workers give preference to self-employment than to hired employment. It is because women, both in rural and urban areas are less mobile and thus, prefer to engage themselves in self-employment.

So, it can be concluded that self-employment is a very important source of livelihood for people in India. Size of Workforce in India. India has a workforce of nearly 40 crore of people.

15.4 Employment

It is a relationship between two parties i.e., employer and the employee who are binded in a contract of doing something valuable or it is an act of employing or state of being employed.

The nature of employment in India is multifaceted. Some get employment throughout the year or some others get employed for only a few months in a year. Many workers do not get fair wages for their work but still while estimating the numbers of workers, all those who are engaged in productive activities are included as employed.

Terms associated with workers and employment are accumulated below

- Productive Activities Those activities which contribute to the gross national product are called productive activities.

- Workforce Persons who are engaged in productive activities are termed as workers and they constitute the workforce.

    Workforce is the total number of persons actually working.

- Workforce Participation Rate (Ratio) It is measured as the ratio between workforce and total population of a country.

$$\text{Participation Ratio} = \frac{\text{Total Workforce}}{\text{Total Population}} \times 100$$

- Labour Supply It refers to the amount of labour that the workers are willing to work, corresponding to a particular wage rate.

- Labour Force It refers to the number of workers actually working or who are able to work. It is not related to wage rate.

Rate of Unemployment

$$= \frac{\text{Number of Person Unemployed}}{\text{Size of Labour Force}} \times 100$$

15.4.1 Participation of People in Employment

It refers to participation of people induction activity. It is measured as a ratio of or force to total population of the country.

The data on rate of participation of people in employment are as follows

- Rate of participation for the urban areas is about 35%.

- Rate of participation for the rural areas is about 41%.

- In urban areas, rate of participation is about 54.3% for men and 13.8% for women.

- In rural areas, rate of participation is about 54.7% for men and 26.1 % for women.

- Overall rate of participation in the country is about 39.2%.

Worker-Population Ratio in India, 2009-2010 Worker-Population Ratio

Sex	Total	Rural	Urban
Men	54.6	54.7	54.3
Women	22.8	26.1	13.8
Total	39.2	40.8	35.0

The above data reveals the following

- Overall rate of participation in the country is not very high, implying not many people are engaged in production activity.

- Participation rate in rural areas is higher than in urban areas.

- Participation rate for women is higher in rural areas compared with urban areas.

15.4.2 Employment in Firms, Factories and Offices

In the course of economic development of a country, labour flows from agriculture and other related activities to industry and services. In this process, workers migrate from rural to urban areas.

Generally, we divide all productive activities into different industrial divisions, they are as follows

- Primary Sector It includes agriculture, forestry and logging, fishing, mining and quarrying.

- Secondary Sector It includes manufacturing, construction, electricity, gas and water supply.

- Tertiary Sector It includes trade, transport, storage and services.

Distribution of Workforce by Industry, 2009 – 2010

Industrial category	Place of residence		Sex		Total
	Rural	Urban	Male	Female	
Primary Sector	68.0	7.5	47.1	68.7	53.2
Secondary Sector	17.4	34.4	33.5	16.3	21.5
Tertiary Sector	14.6	58.1	19.4	15.0	25.3
Total	100	100	100	100	100

15.4.3 Growth and Changing Structure of Employment

During the period 1960-2000, Gross Domestic Product (GDP) of India grew positively and was higher than the employment growth. However, there was always fluctuation in the growth of GDP. During this period, employment grew at a stable rate of about 2%.

Trends in Employment Pattern (Sector-wise and Status- wise) 1972- 2010 (in %)

ITEM	1972-73	1983	1993-94	1999-2000	2009-2010
SECTOR					
Primary Sector	74.3	68.6	64	60.4	53.2
Secondary Sector	10.9	11.5	16	15.8	21.5
Tertiary Sector/Services	14.8	16.9	20	23.8	25.3
Total	100	97	100	100	100
STATUS					
Self - Employed	61.4	57.3	54.6	52.6	51
Regular Salaried Employees	15.4	13.8	13.6	14.6	15.6
Casual Wage Labourers	23.2	28.9	31.8	32.8	33.5
Total	100	100	100	100	100.1

In 1972-73, about 74% of workforce was engaged in primary sector and in 2009-10, this proportion has declined to 53%. Secondary and service sectors are showing promising future for the Indian workforce. The distribution of workforce in different status indicates that over the last four decades (1972-2010), people have moved from self-employment and regular salaried employment to casual wage work. Yet self-employment continues to be the major employment provider.

The movement of labour from regular workers to casual wage workers is known as 'The Process of Casualization'.

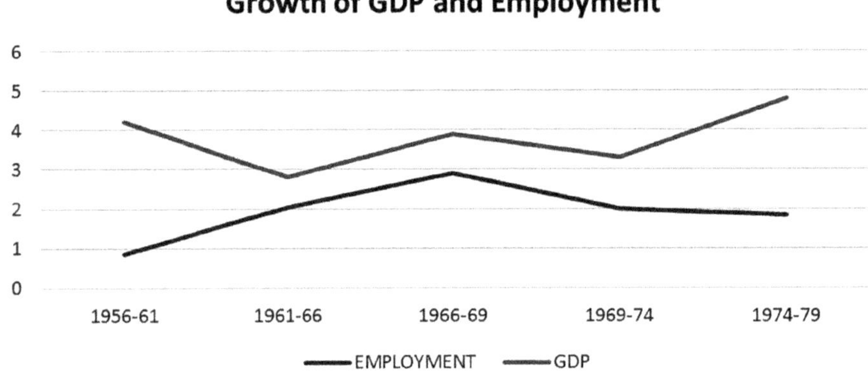

The chart given above points that in the late 1990s, employment growth started declining and reached the level of growth that India had in the early stages of planning. During these years, there is a widening gap between the growth of GDP and employment. This means that in the Indian economy, without generating employment, we have been able to produce more goods and services. This phenomenon is referred as Jobless Growth.

Distribution of workforce by industrial sectors shows substantial shift from farm work to non-farm work.

15.5 Informalisation of Indian Workforce

Development planning in India is always focused to provide decent livelihood to its people. It was thought that the industrialisation strategy would bring surplus workers from agriculture to industry with better standard of living as in developed countries. Over the years, the quality of employment has been deteriorating. A small section of Indian workforce is getting regular income. The government through its labour laws, enable them to protect rights in various ways. This section of workforce forms trade unions, bargains with employers for better wages and other social security measures.

Workforce can be classified into two categories

Formal Sectors All the public sector establishments and those private sector establishments which employ 10 hired workers or more are called formal sector establishments and those who work in such establishments are formal sector workers.

Informal Sectors All other enterprises and workers working

in those enterprises form the informal sector. Informal sector includes millions of farmers, agricultural labourers, owners of small enterprises and people working in those enterprises as also the self employed who do not have any hired workers.

Those who are working in the formal sector enjoy social security benefits. They earn more than those in the informal sector. Workers and enterprises in the informal sector do not get regular income; they do not have any protection or regulation from the government. Workers are dismissed without any compensation.

As the economy will grow, more and more workers would become formal sector workers. Owing to the efforts of the International Labour Organisation (ILO), the Indian government has initiated the modernisation of informal sector.

Informalisation in Ahmedabad is a prosperous city with its wealth based on the produce of more than 60 textile mills with a labour force of 150000 workers employed in them. These workers had, over the course of the century, acquired a certain degree of income security.

They had secure jobs with a living wage, they were covered by social security schemes protecting their health and old age. They had a strong trade union which not only represented them in disputes but also ran activities for the welfare of workers and their families. In the early 1980s, textile mills all over the country began to close down. In some places, such as Mumbai, the mills closed rapidly.

In Ahmedabad, the process of closure was long drawn out and spread over 10 years. Over this period, approximately over 80000 permanent workers and over 50000 non-permanent workers lost their jobs and were driven to the informal sector.

The city experienced an economic recession and public disturbances, especially communal riots. A whole class of workers was thrown back from the middle class into the infor mal sector, into poverty. There was widespread alcoholism.

15.6 Government and Employment Generation

In 2005, the government had passed an act in parliament known as the National Rural Employment Guarantee Act, 2005. It promises 100 days of guaranteed wage employment to all rural households who volunteer to do unskilled manual work. This scheme is one of the important measure adopted by government to generate employment for those who are in need of jobs in rural areas.

Since independence, the Union and State Government have played an important role in generating employment or creating opportunities for employment generation. Their efforts can be broadly categorised into two i.e., direct and indirect.

- Direct Employment: In this government employs people in various departments for administrative purposes. It also runs industries, hotels and transport companies and hence provides employment directly to workers.

- Indirect Employment: It can be understood as when output of goods and services from government enterprises increases, then private enterprises which receive now materials from government enterprises will also raise their output and hence increase the number of employment opportunities in the economy. This is the indirect generation of employment opportunities by the government initiatives in the economy.

15.7 Employment Generation Programmes

Many programmes that governments implement with the aim of alleviating poverty through employment generation are called employment generation programmes.

These programmes aim at providing not only employment but also services in areas such as primary health, primary education, rural drinking water, nutrition, assistance for people to buy income and employment generating assets, development of community assets by generating wage employment, construction of houses and sanitation, assistance for constructing houses, laying of rural roads, development of waste lands/degraded lands.

Key Statements

Worker: A worker is an individual who is in some employment to earn a living.

Self-employed and Hired workers: Self- employed workers are those who are engaged in their own business/profession. Hired workers are those who work for a wage/salary.

Casual and Regular workers: Casual workers are like daily-wagers, Not hired on regular basis. Regular workers are hired on regular basis, are on permanent roles of the employers.

Labour Supply: Is to amount of labour (hours of work) that the people are willing to supply/offer corresponding to a given wage rate. Labour supply changes in response to change in wage rate.

Labour Force: It refers to the number of people who are able to work and willing to work at the existing wage rate.

Workforce: It refers to a number of people actually in employment.

Jobless Growth: It refers to a situation when GDP grows faster than the opportunities of employment, resulting in unemployment.

Exercise

Frequently asked Questions (FAQ's)

1. Who is a casual wage labourer?
2. Why are less women found in regular salaried employment?
3. Why are regular salaried employees more in urban areas than in rural areas?
4. Are the following workers: a beggar, or thieve, a smuggler, a gambler? Why?
5. Urban unemployment is ha spill over of rural unemployment?

Multiple Choice Questions (MCQ's)

1. Find the odd one out:
   (a) A cashier in a shop
   (b) Public transport driver
   (c) Owner of Restaurant
   (d) Construction worker

2. What is the distribution of the workforce in rural and urban areas?
   (a) 60 : 40　　(b) 75 : 25
   (c) 50 : 50　　(d) 40 : 60

3. Out of these which of the following is a worker?
   (a) Beggar　　(b) Gambler
   (c) Cobbler　　(d) Smuggler

4. What percent of urban workers are casual labourers?
   (a) 54 percent　　(b) 41 percent
   (c) 39 percent　　(d) 18 percent

5. Which of the following statements is not true for a worker?
   (a) A worker contributes to the GDP.
   (b) Workers may temporarily abstain from work due to illness.
   (c) Self-employed are not workers.
   (d) Those who help the main workers are also workers.

6. Which of the following is not a feature of organised sector?
   (a) Job Security
   (b) Social security benefits
   (c) Irregular payment
   (d) Fixed working hours

7. What was the average rate of growth of employment during 1950-2010?
   (a) 1 percent　　(b) 2 percent
   (c) 5 percent　　(d) 10 percent

8. Which of the following is not an employment generation programme?
   (a) Rural Employment Generation Programme (REGP)
   (b) Prime Minister's Rozgar Yojana (PMRY)
   (c) National Food for Work Programme (NFWP)
   (d) Valmiki Ambedkar Awas Yojana

9. Which of the following is the correct definition of self-employed?
   (a) Not able to find jobs during some months of the year
   (b) Own and operate their own enterprises
   (c) Receive wages on a regular basis by the employer
   (d) Casually engaged in other individual's enterprises

10. What type of unemployment does urban areas suffer from?
    (a) Seasonal unemployment
    (b) Disguised unemployment
    (c) Open unemployment
    (d) None of the above

11. Workers enjoy job security in:
    (a) Private Sector
    (b) Agriculture Sector
    (c) Organised Sector
    (d) Unorganised Sector

12. Unemployed people is calculated as:
    (a) Labour Force – Workforce
    (b) Labour Force + Workforce
    (c) Workforce – Labour Force
    (d) None of the above

13. Increase in the level of output of the economy is achieved through:
    (a) greater employment opportunities in the economy
    (b) Employing better technology
    (c) Both (a) and (b)
    (d) None of the above

14. Less employment of females in comparisons to male is an indication of :
    (a) Economic backwardness
    (b) Social backwardness
    (c) Both (a) and (b)
    (d) None of the above

15. Data for formal employment is collected by:
    (a) Ministry of Labour
    (b) Ministry of Human Resources and Development
    (c) Ministry of Statistics and Programme Implementation
    (d) National Sample Survey Organisation

16. Which type of unemployment is predominant in agricultural sector?
    (a) Disguised unemployment
    (b) Structural unemployment
    (c) Industrial unemployment
    (d) Educated unemployment

17. Percentage of adult population participating in production activity is called:
    (a) Labour force   (b) Participation rate
    (c) Workforce   (d) Labour supply

18. What refers to the number of people actually working, and does not account for those who are willing to work?
    (a) Labour force
    (b) Workforce
    (c) Both (a) and (b)
    (d) None of these

19. The number of people who are able to work and willing to work at the existing wage rate is known as:
    (a) Participation rate
    (b) Labour force
    (c) Workforce
    (d) Labour supply

20. A regular salary worker is:
    (a) On permanent payroll of employer
    (b) Not entitled to Social Security benefits
    (c) Both (a) and (b)
    (d) Unskilled

21. The number of workers actually working or willing to work is called:
    (a) Workforce
    (b) Labour Force
    (c) Labour Supply
    (d) None of the above

22. The percentage of female workers is lower in urban areas because:
    (a) Female education in India is still a far cry
    (b) Females in urban areas does not prefer to take jobs
    (c) Job work for women is the governed by family decisions
    (d) Both (a) and (b)

23. When the number of persons willing to work (at the existing wage rate) increases or decreases it changes the size of:
    (a) Labour Force
    (b) Labour Supply
    (c) Workforce
    (d) All of the above

24. Increase in the level of output of the economy is achieved through:
    (a) greater employment opportunities in the economy
    (b) Employing better technology
    (c) Both (a) and (b)
    (d) None of the above

25. High rate of participation of women in rural areas compared with urban areas happen because:
    (a) Need to support the family for more owing to low family income in rural areas
    (b) Poverty compels women to avoid education and seek employment
    (c) High productivity requirements in the available jobs in rural areas
    (d) Both (a) and (b)

Solutions

Frequently asked Questions (FAQ's)

1. Casual wage labourers are the daily wagers. They are not hired by their employers on regular basis. Such labourers or casually engaged in some work and generally paid on daily basis. Example: Construction workers

2. Less women are found in regular salaried employment because of the following reasons:
   i. Female education in India is still a far cry, implying low eligibility or for salaried jobs.
   ii. Among most families in urban areas, job work for women is still governed by family decisions rather than the individual's own decision. Implying that even the availability opportunities are not actually availed.
   iii. Higher employment among women in rural areas is owing to widespread rural poverty. Female workers in rural areas are largely engaged in low paid and less productive jobs just to add to their family income. Example: working as labourers in fields for Landlords

3. Regular salaried employees are more in urban areas than in rural areas because of the following reasons:
   i. Due to various infrastructural facilities, more factories and enterprises are run in the urban areas. This raises the demand for workers on a regular basis. Abundance of social infrastructure including schools and hospitals itself generates the demand for workers in urban areas
   ii. In rural areas common non- farm job opportunities are limited. Accordingly, people generally are not inclined to acquire scale and training for known- farm occupations. They prefer to stay on family farms and fields as self-employed.

4. Beggars, thieves, smugglers or gamblers are not workers because they are not in any employment to earn a living and are not generating any kind of factor income.

5. Owing to the lack of opportunities of employment, people in the rural areas are compelled to migrate to the urban areas in search of livelihood. This compounds the problem of urban unemployment.

Multiple Choice Questions (MCQ's)

1. (a) M
1. (c) Owner of a Restaurant
2. (b) 75 : 25
3. (c) Cobbler
4. (d) 18 percent
5. (c) Self-employed are not workers.
6. (c) Irregular payment
7. (b) 2 percent
8. (d) Valmiki Ambedkar Awas Yojana
9. (b) Own and operate their own enterprises
10. (c) Open Unemployment
11. (c) Organised Sector
12. (a) Labour Force – Workforce
13. (c) Both (a) and (b)
14. (c) Both (a) and (b)
15. (a) Ministry of Labour
16. (a) Disguised unemployment
17. (b) Participation rate
18. (b) Work Force
19. (b) Labour Force
20. (a) On permanent payroll of employer
21. (b) Labour Force
22. (d) Both (a) and (b)
23. (b) Labour Supply
24. (c) Both (a) and (b)
25. (c) Both (a) and (b)

CHAPTER 16

Current Challenges Facing Indian Economy Infrastructure

Chief concepts of this chapter

- Role of Infrastructure in economic development
- Principle Challenges India faces in the field of economic and social infrastructure considering energy economic infrastructure and health as a critical component of social infrastructure
- Infrastructure: Meaning and types: Case studies; Energy and Health; Problems and Policies- A critical assessment.

16. Economic Infrastructure

It refers to all such elements of economic change which serve as a support system to the process of economic growth.

16.1 Social Infrastructure

It refers to the core elements of social change which serve as a support system for the process of social development of a country.

16.2 Infrastructure and Development

Following observations show how exactly infrastructure contributes to the process of growth and development.

- Infrastructure impacts productivity
- Infrastructure induces investment
- Infrastructure generates linkages in production
- Infrastructure enhances size of the market
- Enhance ability to work
- Induces Foreign Direct Investment (FDI)

16.3 The State of Infrastructure in India

(i) Energy is the most important component of economic infrastructure. Industrial production is not possible if energy is not available.

Energy is broadly classified as commercial and non-commercial energy.
- Components of Commercial Energy Coal, petroleum products natural gas, electricity.
- Components of Non-Commercial Energy Firewood, animal waste, agricultural waste.

(ii) Conventional Sources
- Coal
- Natural gas

(iii) Non-Conventional Sources
- Solar energy
- Wind energy
- Biomass energy including energy in the form of Gobar gas
- Geothermal energy
- Energy through tides and waves as well as temperature gradient over sea

(iv) Power/Electricity The most visible form of energy, which is often identified with progress in moderation civilization is power, commonly called electricity.

(v) Some Challenges in the Power Sector
- Inadequate generation of electricity

- Less capacity utilisation
- Losses of electricity boards

(vi) Health is a state of complete physical, mental and social well-being. It does not simply mean absence of disease; rather it means a sound physical and mental state of the individual.

16.4 Concept, Types and Importance of Infrastructure

Infrastructure is basic physical and organisational structure needed for the operation of a society or enterprise. It provides supporting services in the main areas of industrial and agricultural production, domestic and foreign trade and commerce. Infrastructural installations do not directly produce goods but help in promoting production activities in an economy. e.g., transport, communication, banking, power, etc.

These services include roads, railways, ports, airports, dams, power stations, oil and gas pipelines, telecommunication facilities, etc. They also include country's educational system including schools and colleges, health system including hospitals, sanitary system including clean drinking water facilities and the monetary system including banks, insurance and other financial institutions.

Types of Infrastructure

Infrastructure is broadly categorised as social and economic infrastructure. They are discussed below:

Social Infrastructure It refers to the core elements of social change which serve as a foundation for the process of social development of a country. It contributes to economic processes indirectly and from outside the system of production and distribution, e.g., educational institutions, hospitals, sanitary conditions and housing facilities, etc.

Economic infrastructure It refers to all such elements of economic change which serve as a foundation for the process of economic growth. These helps in the process of production directly. e.g., transportation, communication, energy/power, etc.

Difference between Social and Economic Infrastructure

Social Infrastructure	Economic Infrastructure
It help the economic system from outside. (i.e., indirectly).	It help the economic system from inside. (i.e., directly).
It improves the quality of human resources.	It improves the quality of economic resources.
Expenditure on it, will raise the stock of human capital overtime.	Expenditure on it, will raise the stock of physical capital overtime.
For example, health, education and housing	For example, energy, transport and communication.

16.4.1 Relevance of Infrastructure

Infrastructure is the support system which provides support to the efficient working of a modem industrial economy. Modem agriculture also largely depends on it for speedy and large scale transportation of seeds, pesticides, fertilisers, etc.

We use modern roadways, railways and shipping i facilities. In recent times, agriculture also depends on insurance and banking system.

Inadequate infrastructure can have multiple adverse effects on health. Improvements in water supply and – sanitation have a large impact by reducing morbidity (state of being unhealthy or diseased) from major waterborne diseases and reducing the severity of disease, when it occurs. Air pollution and safety hazards connected to transportation also effect morbidity particularly in densely populated areas.

16.4.2 Importance of Infrastructure in Development

Following points highlights how exactly infrastructure contributes to the process of growth and development:

- Impact on Productivity Infrastructure plays a major role in the raising productivity, with improved roadways, warehouses etc farmers can easily sell their products in different markets. Also, irrigation facilities has reduced dependence on monsoon for water needs, which not only increases productivity but also production level.

- Induces Investment Infrastructure induces investment. Low investment points to low level of production and backwardness of an economy. A well-developed infrastructure attracts foreign investors. Which gives investment avenues and profitable ventures.

- Generates Linkages in Production Better means of transport and communication, robust system of banking and finance generates better inter-industrial linkages. It is a situation when expansion of one industry facilitates the expansion of the other.

- Enhances Size of the Market Infrastructure enhances the size of the market as large scale of production can capture more market.

- Enhances Ability to Work Social infrastructure increases the quality of life of workers, thereby increasing their efficiency. Health care centres, educational institutions and other such facilities inherit skills which increases ability and efficiency to work.

- Facilities Outsourcing India is emerging to be a global destination for all kinds of outsourcing. For example, call centres, study centres, medical

- transcription and such other services, owing largely – to its sound system of social and economic infrastructure.

16.4.3 The State of Infrastructure in India

Traditionally, the government has been solely responsible for developing the country's infrastructure. But it was found that the government's investment in infrastructure was inadequate. Today, the private sector by itself and also in joint partnership with the public sector has started playing a very important role in infrastructure development. India invests only 5% of its GDP on infrastructure, which is for below than that of China and Indonesia.

Some infrastructure in India and other countries, 2008-10

Country	Investment in infrastructure as a % of GDP 2003	Access to safe drinking water (%)	Access to improved sanitation(%)	Mobile Users/ 1000 people 2010	Power generation (billion kwh)
China	20	98	55	642	3700
Hong Kong	4	100	100	1900	40
India	5	97	31	642	900
South Korea	7	99	100	703	452
Pakistan	2	96	45	592	95
Singapore	5	100	100	1440	42
Indonesia	14	92	52	920	155

16.4.4 Infrastructure State in Rural Area

Majority of India's population still lives in rural area.

Infrastructure state in rural India can be understood from the following points

- Despite of so much technological progress, women of rural India are still using biofuels to meet their daily energy requirement.

- Women go long distances to fetch water and other basic needs.

- The Census 2001 shows that in rural India, only 56% households have an electricity connection and 43% still use kerosene.

- About 90% of the rural households use biofuels for cooking.

- Tap water availability is limited to only 24% rural households.

- About 76% of the population drinks water from open resources such as wells, ponds, etc.

- Access to improved sanitation in rural areas was only 20%.

16.4.5 Future Prospects for Infrastructure in India

Some economists have projected that India will become the third biggest economy in the world, a few decades from now. For that to happen, India will have to boost its infrastructure investment.

In an economy as the income rises, requirement of infrastructure will change. For low income countries, basic infrastructure services like irrigation, transport and power are more important. On the contrary the developed economies require more service related to infrastructure. That is why, share of power and telecommunication infrastructure is greater in high income countries.

Thus, development of infrastructure and economic development go hand in hand. Obviously, if proper attention is not paid to infrastructure development, economic development will be severely affected.

In this chapter, we will focus only two kinds of infrastructure, those associated with energy and health. Other types of infrastructure are not included in our syllabus.

16.5 Energy

Energy is a critical aspect of development process of a nation. It is essential for industries, agriculture and related areas like production and transportation of fertilisers, pesticides and farm equipment. It is also required in house for cooking, household lighting and heating etc.

16.5.1 Sources of Energy

1. **Conventional Sources of Energy**

   There are two types of conventional sources of energy

   - Commercial Sources Coal, petroleum and electricity are commercial sources of energy as they bought and sold in the market. They account for over 40% of total energy sources consumed in India. Commercial sources of energy are generally exhaustible in nature.

- Non-commercial Sources Firewood, agricultural waste and dried dung non-commercial sources of energy. They are found in nature free of cost. Non-commercial sources are generally renewable in nature.

More than 60% of Indian households depend on the traditional sources of energy. In meeting their regular cooking and heating needs.

2. Non-conventional Sources of Energy

Solar energy, wind energy and tidal power are non-conventional sources. India has almost unlimited potential for producing all three types of energy if some appropriate cost effective technologies (that are already available) are used.

Note India is fifth largest producer of wind energy.

16.5.2 Difference between Conventional and Non-conventional Sources of Energy

Conventional Sources of Energy

These are the traditional sources of energy which are generally bought and sold in the market.

In India, conventional sources are being used in total disregard to the environment, i.e. These sources creates pollution.

Conventional Sources of Energy	Non-conventional Sources of Energy
These are the traditional sources of energy which are generally bought and sold in the market.	These are modern sources of energy.
In India, conventional sources are being used in total disregard to the environment. These sources create pollution.	These are being developed as sources of commercial energy with a view to checking environmental pollution.

16.5.3 Primary and Final Sources of Energy

Primary Sources They are those sources which are the gift of nature to the Earth. They do not require any transformation before their use. They are directly used as the inputs of production. e.g., coal, lignite, petroleum, gas, etc.

Final Sources They sources are used as a final product.

This involves transformation process, transforming inputs into final outputs like transformation of coal energy into electricity.

16.5.4 Consumption Pattern of Commercial Energy in India

At present, commercial energy consumption makes up about 74% of the total energy consumed in India. This includes coal with the largest share of 54%, followed by oil at 33%, natural gas at 9% and hydro energy at 3%. Non-commercial energy sources account for over 26% of the total energy consumption.

The critical feature of India's energy sector and its linkages to the economy, is the import dependence on crude and petroleum products, which is likely to grow rapidly to more than 100% of the need in the near future.

16.5.5 Sectoral Pattern of Energy Consumption in India

Earlier till 1953-54, transport sector was the largest consumer of commercial energy but it declined thereafter and industrial sector has been increasing. The share of oil and gas is highest among all commercial energy consumption.

16.5.6 Power/Electricity

The most visible form of energy, which is often identified with progress in modern civilisation, is power, commonly called electricity. It is a critical component of infrastructure that determines the economic development of a country. The growth rate of demand for power is generally higher than the GDP growth rate. Studies point that in order to have 8% per annum, power supply needs to grow around 1. annually.

In 2010-11, thermal sources accounted for almost 65% generation capacity in India. Hydel and wind power accounted for 32.5% while nuclear power accounted only 2.5%. India's energy policy encourages two energy sources; hydel and wind, as they do not rely on fossil fuel and hence, avoid carbon emissions and are renewable in nature. It has resulted in faster growth of electricity produced from there two sources.

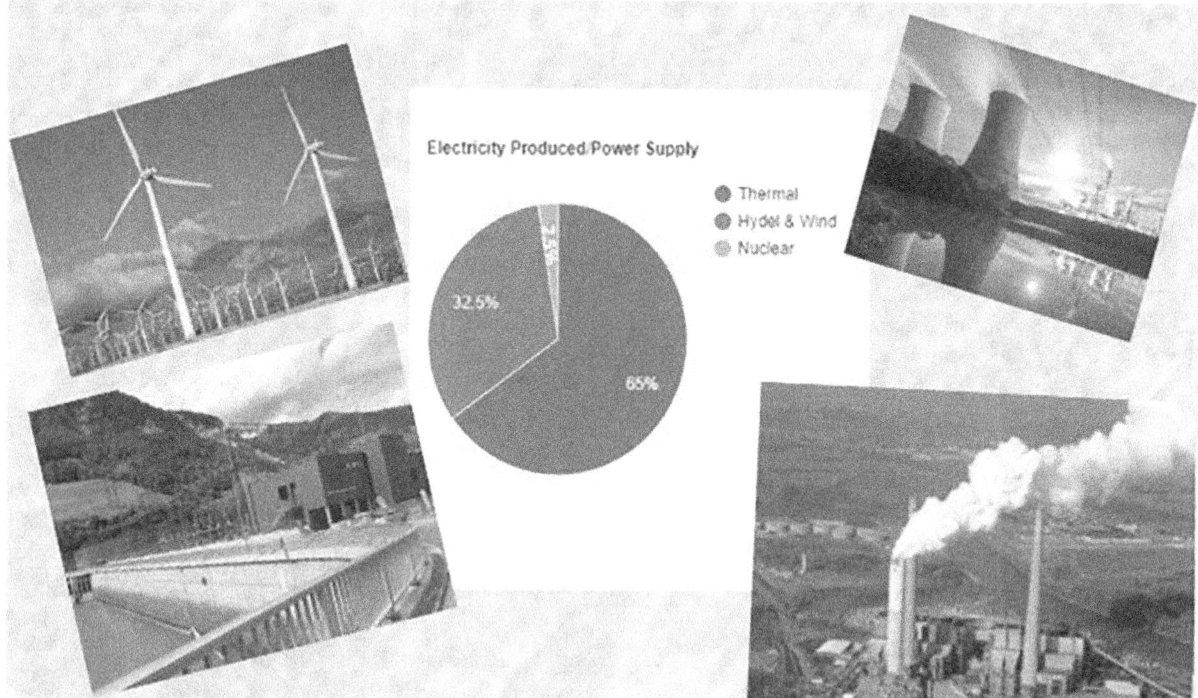

Atomic energy is an important source of electric power. At present, nuclear energy accounts for only 2.5% of total energy consumption, against a global average of 13% which is too low. Hence, some scholars suggest to generate more electricity through atomic sources.

16.5.7 Use of Solar Energy in Thane

There is a use of solar energy on large scale in Thane city. The use of solar energy, which was considered a somewhat far-fetched concept, has bought in real benefits and results in cost and energy saving, In this city, solar energy is being applied to heat water, power traffic signals and advertising hoardings, The experiment is led by Thane Municipal Corporation. It has made compulsory for all new buildings in the city to install solar water heating system.

16.5.8 Some Challenges in the Power Sector

Energy, in a developing country like India, is a basic put required to sustain economic growth and to provide basic amenities of life to the entire population of a country.

Energy generated at various power stations is not totally used by the consumers, some of it is consumed by the power station itself and some of it is wasted in transmission.

Some of the challenges that India's power sector faces today are

- India's installed capacity to generate electricity is , not sufficient to feed an annual economic growth of 9%. At present, India is able to and only 20,000 MW a year. Even the installed capacity is underutilised.

- State Electricity Boards (SEBs) which distribute electricity, incur losses which exceed ? 500 billion due to transmission and loss in distribution, wrong pricing of electricity and other inefficiencies.

- Private sector power generators are yet to play their role in a major way, same is the case with foreign investors.

- There is general public unrest due to high power tariffs and prolonged power cuts in different parts of the country.

- Thermal power plants which are the mainstay of India's power sector, are facing shortage of raw material and coal supplies.

Continued economic development and raising population is driving the demand for more energy than what India is currently producing. Instead of investing in already installed power sector, government has shifted interest into the private sector particularly for the distribution of electricity at much higher prices.

16.5.9 Power Distribution : The Case of Delhi

Since, independence power management in the capital has changed hands four times. The Delhi State Electricity Board (DSEB) was set up in 1951. This was succeeded by the Delhi Electric Supply Undertaking (DESU) in 1958. The Delhi Vidyut Board (DVB) came into existence as SEB in February 1997.

Now the distribution of electricity vests with two leading private sector companies—Reliance Energy Limited (BSES Rajdhani Power Limited and BSES Yamuna Power Limited) and Tata—Power Limited (TPDDL). They supply electricity to approximately 28 lakh customers in Delhi.

The tariff structure and other regulatory issues are monitored by the Delhi Electricity Regulatory Commission (DERC). Though it was expected that there will be greater improvement in power distribution and the consumers will benefit in a major way, experience shows unsatisfactory results.

16.6 Health

A Vital Public Good and a Basic Human Right All citizens can get better health facilities if public health services are decentralised. Success against diseases depends on education and efficient health infrastructure. Therefore, it is necessary to create awareness on health and provide efficient system. The role of telecom and IT in this regard is very important. The ultimate goal should be to help people move towards a better quality of life.

16.6.1 Development of Health Services After Independence

There has been a large scale improvement in health facilities. Following are the highlights

- Decline in death rate

- Reduction in infant mortality

- Rise in expectancy of life

- Control over deadly diseases

- Reduction in child mortality rate

16.6.2 Women's Health

Women in India suffer from a serious neglect not only in the area of education, but in the area of health care as well. More than 50% of women in India in the age group of 15-49 years suffer from nutritional deficiency.

16.6.3 Health as an Emerging Challenge

Points given below highlight the deficiencies of our social infrastructure in terms of health facilities.

- Unequal distribution of healthcare services

- Communicable diseases

- Poor management

- Privatisation

- Poor upkeep and maintenance

- Poor sanitation level

A person's ability to work depends largely on his health. Good health enhances the quality of life. Health is not only absence of disease but also the ability to realise one's potential. It is a yardstick of one's wellbeing.

Health is an important component of social infrastructure. It is the holistic process related to the overall growth and development of the nation. Scholars assess people's health by taking into account indicators like infant mortality and maternal mortality rate, life expectancy and nutrition levels, along with incidence of communicable and non-communicable diseases.

Development of health infrastructure ensures a country about healthy manpower for production of goods and services.

Health infrastructure includes hospitals, doctors, nurses and other para-medical professionals, beds, equipment required in hospitals and a well-developed pharmaceutical industry. Only the presence of infrastructure is not enough to have healthy people but it should be accessible to all the people easily.

State of Health Infrastructure in India

The government has the constitutional obligation to guide and regulate all health related issues such as medical education, adulteration of food, drugs and poisons, medical profession, vital statistics, mental, deficiency and lunacy. Central Council of Health and Family Welfare collects information and renders financial and technical assistance to State Governments, union territories and other bodies for implementation of important health programmes in the country.

16.6.4 State of health infrastructure in India can be understood from the following points

- At the village level, a variety of hospitals known as Primary Health Centres (PHCs) have been set.

- There are large number of hospitals run by voluntary agencies and the private sector, equipped with professionals and para medical professionals trained in medical, pharmacy and nursing colleges.

- Since independence, there has been a significant expansion in the physical provision of health services. Public Health Infrastructure in India, 1951-2000

Development of Health Service In India

S.No.	Health Infrastructure	1950-51	1999-2000
1.	Registered medical practitioners (Per 10,000 population)	1.7	5.5
2.	No. of Medical Colleges	.28	167
3.	Hospital beds of all types (Per 10,000 population)	3.2	9.3
4.	No. of Doctors (in '000)	61.8	535.2
5.	Hospitals and dispensaries	9,209	70,000
6.	No. of Nurses	16.550	5,65,696

16.6.5 Private Sector Health Infrastructure

In recent time, private health infrastructure has grown largely. Private sector health, infrastructure is explained below

About 70% of the hospitals running in India belong to private sector. Nearly 60% of dispensaries are run by the same private sector.

Private sector has also been contributing significantly to medical education and training, medical technologies and diagnostics, manufacture and sale of pharmaceuticals, hospital construction and medical services.

16.6.6 Health System in India

India's health infrastructure and healthcare is made up of a three tier system

1. Primary Healthcare

Primary healthcare system in India includes

- Education concerning prevailing health problems and methods of identifying, preventing and controlling them.

- Promotion of food supply and proper nutrition and adequate supply of water and basic sanitation.

- Maternal and child health care.

- Immunisation against major infectious diseases and injuries.

- Promotion of health and provision of essential drugs.

Auxiliary Nursing Midwife (ANM) is the first person who provides primary healthcare. Primary Health Centres (PHCs), Community Health Centres (CHCs) and sub centres.

2. Secondary Healthcare

When condition of a patient is not managed by PHCs, they are referred to secondary or tertiary hospitals. Health care institutes having better facilities for surgery, X-ray, ECG (Electro Cardio Graph) are called secondary healthcare institutes. They function both as primary health care provider and also provide better health care facilities. They are mostly located in district and headquarters in big towns.

3. Tertiary Healthcare

In tertiary sector, there are the hospitals which have advanced level equipment and medicines and undertake all the complicated health problems, which could not be managed by primary and secondary hospitals.

This sector also includes many premier institutes which not only impart quality medical education and conduct research but also provide specialised health care.

For example, All India Institute of Medical Sciences (AIIMSs), Post Graduate Institute (PGI), Chandigarh, Jawaharlal Institute of Postgraduate Medical Education and Research (JIPMER), Pondicherry, National Institute of Mental Health and Neurosciences (NIMHNSs), Bangalore and All India Institute of Hygiene and Public Health, Kolkata.

16.6.7 Indian Systems of Medicine ASM

It includes six systems, Ayurveda, Yoga, Unani, Siddha, Naturopathy and Homeopathy (AYUSNH). At present there are 3529 ISM hospitals 24943 dispensaries and as 6.5 lakhs registered practitioners in India.

16.6.8 Medical Tourism – A Great Opportunity

Now-a-days foreigners visit India for surgeries, liver transplants, dental and even cosmetic care etc, the reason is, our health services combine latest medical technologies with qualified professionals and is cheaper for foreigners as compared to costs of similar health care services in their own countries. In 2004-05, as many as 150000 foreigners visited India for medical treatment, this figure is likely to increase by 15% each year. Health infrastructure can be upgraded to attract more foreigners to India. ISM has huge potential and can solve a large part of our health care problems because they are effective, safe, and inexpensive.

16.6.9 Indicators of Health and Health Infrastructure : Critical Appraisal

Health status of the country can be assessed through indicators such as infant mortality and maternal mortality rates, life expectancy and nutrition levels, along with the incidence of communicable diseases.

Scholars argue that there is greater scope for the role of government in the health sector.

Indicators	India	China	USA	Sri Lanka
Infant mortality rate/1,000 live birth	50	16	6.5	14
Under- 5 mortality/1,000 live births	63	18	8	17
Birth by skilled attendants (% of total)	53	99	99	99
Fully immunised	72	99	99	99
Health Expenditure as % of GDP	4.2	4.3	15.2	4.1
Government health spending to total government spending (%)	4.4	10.3	18.7	7.9
how to pocket expenditure as a % of private expenditure on health	74.4	82.6	24.4	86.7

Source World Health Statistics 2011. www.worldbank.org

From the given table above, following facts can be concluded:

- India's expenditure on health sector is only 4.2% of total GDP. This is very low as compared to other countries, both developing and developed.

- India has about 17% of the world's population but it bears a frightening 20% of the global burden of diseases.

- Global Burden of Diseases (GBD) is an indicator used by experts to gauge the number of people dying prematurely due to a particular disease as well as the number of years spent by them in state of 'disability' Owing to the disease.

- Every year around five lakh children die due to water borne diseases. The danger of AIDS is also looming large.

- Malnutrition and inadequate supply of vaccines lead to the death of 2.2 million children every year.

- At present, less than 20% c the population utilises public health facilities.

- Only 38% of PHC's, have required number of doctors and only 30% of PHC's have stock of medicines.

16.6.10 Urban-rural and Poor-rich Divide with regards to healthcare

Differences in medical healthcare between urban – rural and poor-rich can be understood from the points given belowOnly one-fifth of total hospitals are located in rural areas. Rural India has about half the number of dispensaries. People in rural areas do not have sufficient medical infrastructure. This lead to difference in the health status of people. Out of 7 lakhs beds, roughly 11% are available in rural areas.

- There are only 0.36% hospital for every one lakh people in rural areas while urban areas have 3.6% hospitals for the same number of people.

- The PHCs located in rural areas do not offer even X-ray or blood testing facilities which, for a city dweller, constitutes basic healthcare. Even though 315 recognised medical colleges produce 30,000 medical graduates every year. Still there is shortage of doctors in rural areas. One-fifth of these doctors migrate from one country to -another for better job opportunities.

- The poorest 20% of Indians living in both urban and rural areas spend 12% of their income on healthcare while the rich spend only 2%.

- Percentage of people who have no access to proper care has risen from 15 in 1986 to 24 in 2003.

16.6.11 Women's Health

Women constitute about half the total population in India. They suffer many disadvantages as compared to men in the areas of education, participation in economic activities and health care. The child sex ratio has been detonated from 927 in 2001 to 914 in 2011.

There is growing incidence of female foeticide in the country. Close to 300000 girls under the age of 15 are not only married but have already borne children, at least once.

More than 50% of married women between the age group of 15 and 49 years suffer from anaemia caused by iron deficiency. It has contributed to 19% of maternal deaths. Abortions are major cause of maternal morbidity and mortality in India.

16.7 Conclusion

As India moves towards modernisation, the increase in demand for quality infrastructure copper keeping in view their environmental impact, will have to be addressed. The reform policies by providing various concessions and incentives, aim at attracting the private sector, in general, and foreign investors, in particular. While assessing the two infrastructure- energy and health, it is clear that there is scope for equal access to infrastructure for all.

Key Statements

Energy: an important component of economic infrastructure –

Forms and Sources :

i. Commercial and non- commercial sources of energy

ii. Conventional and non-conventional sources of energy

iii. Primary and final sources of energy

Health: An important component of social infrastructure.

Health as an emerging challenge because:

i. Unequal distribution of healthcare services

ii. Communicable diseases like AIDS, HIV are rising

iii. Poor management of healthcare services

iv. Increasing privatisation

v. Poor upkeep on maintenance

vi. Poor sanitation level

Primary Health centres PHCs: have been set up by the government at village level

Ujjwala Yojana: Is a scheme launched in 2016 by the ministry of petroleum and natural gas for providing LPG Connexions to the bpl women in India. It focuses on discarding the use of fossil fuels an firewood in the Indian kitchens which lead two serious health hazards including heart disease and lung cancer. It is estimated that the use of firewood an fossil fuels in the kitchen is like burning 400 cigarettes an hour.

Key benefits:

i. Empowerment of women (as gas connection is to be in the name of women only) and protection of their health.

ii. Generation of employment opportunities in the supply chain of cooking gas.

iii. Environmental- friendly as it targets (and replaces) three conventional fuels causing environment pollution, namely kerosene oil, coal and firewood.

Exercise

Frequently asked Questions (FAQ's)

1. What is a 'global burden of disease'?
2. What are the six systems of Indian medicine?
3. How can we increase the effectiveness of the healthcare programme?
4. What are the two categories into which infrastructure is divided. How are they both inter dependent?
5. How does infrastructure boost production?

Multiple Choice Questions (MCQ's)

1. Analyse the image given above and suggest the name of the 5th symbol as per Indian system of medicine(ISM):
   (a) Naturopathy
   (b) Unani
   (c) Ayurveda
   (d) Homeopathy

2. On the basis of the above Pie diagram answer the following question:
   Which of the following is a major source of electricity generation in India?
   (a) Hydro energy
   (b) Nuclear energy
   (c) Thermal energy
   (d) New and renewable energy

3. Which of the following statements is not correct with regards to infrastructure?
   (a) Infrastructure contributes to economic development.
   (b) Infrastructure provides support services.
   (c) All infrastructural facilities have a direct impact on the production of goods and services.
   (d) Inadequate infrastructure can have multiple adverse effects on health.

4. Which of the following facilities is included in social infrastructure?
   (a) Roads and highway
   (b) Housing
   (c) Internet
   (d) Electricity

5. What is morbidity?
   (a) Proneness to fall ill
   (b) High infant mortality rate
   (c) High maternal mortality rate
   (d) Low life expectancy

6. What percent of rural households use bio-fuels for cooking?
   (a) 50%
   (b) 75%
   (c) 80%
   (d) 90%

7. Which of the following countries invest almost 50 percent of its GDP in infrastructure?
   (a) India
   (b) China
   (c) Pakistan
   (d) Siri Lanka

8. Low-income countries do not invest in which of the given infrastructural services?
   (a) Transport
   (b) Irrigation
   (c) Power
   (d) Telecommunication

9. Which of the following is not a function of primary health care?
   (a) Spreading education concerning prevailing health problems
   (b) Promoting food supply and proper nutrition
   (c) Conducting research
   (d) Providing essential drugs

10. Which of the following systems is not included in the Indian System of Medicines:
    (a) Allopathy
    (b) Homeopathy
    (c) Naturopathy
    (d) Ayurveda

11. India's energy policy encourages the following two energy sources:
    (a) Hydel and Thermal Power
    (b) Wind and Thermal Power
    (c) Hydel and Wind
    (d) Thermal and Nuclear

12. Electricity generated from radioactive element is called:
    (a) Thermal power
    (b) Hydro- electric power
    (c) Atomic power
    (d) Tidal power

13. Which of the following is a part of a three- tier system of health infrastructure?
    (a) Primary healthcare
    (b) Secondary healthcare
    (c) Tertiary healthcare
    (d) All of the above

14. Which of the following is considered a social infrastructure?
    (a) Communication
    (b) Education
    (c) Transport
    (d) Energy

15. Health infrastructure in India is biased against:
    (*a*) The poor   (*b*) The rich
    (*c*) Women   (*d*) Both (*a*) and (*c*)

16. Which of the following is not a type of commercial energy?
    (*a*) Electricity   (*b*) Firewood
    (*c*) Coal   (*d*) Natural gas

17. Which of the following is considered as non-conventional energy?
    (*a*) Electricity   (*b*) Firewood
    (*c*) Solar energy   (*d*) Natural gas

18. Infrastructure facilitates:
    (*a*) Outsourcing
    (*b*) Industrial linkages
    (*c*) Investment
    (*d*) All of the above

19. Which sector accounts for highest consumption of energy in India?
    (*a*) Transport   (*b*) Household
    (*c*) Industry   (*d*) Agriculture

20. Global Burden of Disease (GBD) an indicator is used to assess:
    (*a*) deaths caused by communicable diseases
    (*b*) the quality of disease free life lived by the people
    (*c*) the quantity and quality of life lived by the people
    (*d*) deaths caused by non- communicable diseases

21. Infrastructure contributes to growth and development on account of which of the following:
    (*a*) It promotes productivity
    (*b*) It generates linkages in production
    (*c*) It reduces the size of the market
    (*d*) Both (*a*) and (*b*)

22. With respect to coal as a conventional source of energy, choose the correct statement:
    (*a*) India has been experiencing shortage of coal supply in recent years
    (*b*) India is deficient in coal production
    (*c*) The principle consumers of coal are thermal power stations, steel plants among others
    (*d*) Both (*a*) and (*c*)

23. With respect to electricity generation in India, choose the correct statement:
    (*a*) The government has restricted the entry of private sector in power generation sector in India
    (*b*) For generation of power, India is mainly dependent on thermal power plants
    (*c*) Private sector accounts for major share of power generation in India
    (*d*) Share of new and renewable sources of energy in power generation has been increasing leaps and bounds in recent years

24. Which of the following are the emerging challenges in power generation in India?
    (*a*) inadequate generation of electricity
    (*b*) Less capacity utilisation
    (*c*) Transmission and distribution losses
    (*d*) All of the above

25. Which of the following facts illustrate the development of health services after independence in India?
    (*a*) Decline in death rate
    (*b*) Rise in life expectancy
    (*c*) Control over deadly diseases
    (*d*) All of the above

🔑 Solutions

Frequently asked Questions (FAQ's)

1. Global burden of disease is an indicator used to assess:
   i. the number of premature deaths due to a particular disease
   ii. The duration of disability of the person suffering from the disease

2. The six systems of Indian medicine are:
   i. Ayurveda
   ii. Yoga
   iii. Unani
   iv. Siddha
   v. Naturopathy
   vi. Homoeopathy (AYUSH)

3. We can increase the effectiveness of healthcare programmes in the following manner:
   i. create awareness on health and hygiene and provide efficient system of support
   ii. Reduce the rural- urban and rich- poor divide
   iii. Women's Health should be given due priority
   iv. Indian systems of medicine should be more explored and used to support public health

4. Infrastructure is divided into two categories:
   i. **Economic infrastructure:** it refers to such elements of support system like power, transport and communication which serve as a driving force for production activity in the economy.
   ii. **Social infrastructure:** it refers to such elements of support system like schools, colleges and hospitals which serve as a driving force for social development of the country.

5. Infrastructure provides support services like roads, railways, ports, airports, telecommunication facilities, etc., in the areas of industrial and agricultural production.

Some of these facilities have a direct impact on production of goods and services while others give him direct support by building the social sector of the economy. Across all sectors of economy primary, secondary and tertiary sectors, high productivity is possible only when we have a good infrastructural facilities

Multiple Choice Questions (MCQ's)

1. (c) Ayurveda
2. (c) Thermal energy
3. (c) All infrastructural facilities have a direct impact on the production of goods and services.
4. (b) Housing
5. (a) Proneness to fall ill
6. (d) 90 %
7. (b) China
8. (d) Telecommunication
9. (c) Conducting research
10. (a) Allopathy
11. (c) Hydel and Wind
12. (c) Atomic Power
13. (d) All of the above
14. (b) Education
15. (d) Both (a) and (c)
16. (b) Firewood
17. (c) Solar energy
18. (d) All of the above
19. (c) Industry
20. (c) the quality of life lived by the people
21. (d) Both (a) and (b)
22. (d) Both (a) and (c)
23. (b) For generation of power, India is mainly dependent on thermal power plants
24. (d) All of the above
25. (d) All of the above

Your Notes :

CHAPTER 17

Current Challenges Facing Indian Economy Sustainable Economic Development

Chief concepts of this chapter –

- Degradation of environment and depletion of resources as emerging challenges in the context of sustainable development of the Indian economy.
- Sustainable Economic Development: Meaning, Effects of Economic Development on Resources and Environment, including global warming.

17. Concept of Environment

Environment may be defined as all those conditions and their effects which influence human life. It is the sum total of surrounding and the totality of the resources.Environment includes living elements or biotic elements (birds, plants and animals, forests, fisheries) as well as non- living elements or abiotic elements (air, water, soil, minerals and commerce oil and other natural resources) which make up our surrounding and impact our existence and the quality of our life.

According to the Environment Act 1986, "Environment includes water, air and land and the inter relationship which exists among and between water air land and human beings and other creatures, plants, micro-organisms and property".

17.1 Functions of Environment

Environment performs four vital junctions, which are as follows:

- Supply Resources include both renewable and non-renewable sources of energy. Resources which can be used without any fear of getting depleted are renewable sources of energy, e.g., trees, fishes, etc. Non-renewable sources are those which are getting depleted or exhausted. e.g., fossil fuel, etc.

- Assimilates Waste Production and consumption activity generates wastes. It is generally in form of garbage which is absorbed by the environment.

- Sustains Life Sun, soil, air, water are the essential ingredients of environment for the human life. Absence of these will lead to an end of life on the Earth.

- Aesthetic Services Environment provides aesthetic services like scenery, which includes rivers, ocean, mountains and deserts. Enjoying these surroundings adds to the quality of life.

17.2 Significance of Environment

- Environment offers resources for production.
- Environment sustains life.
- Environment Enhance quality of life.

17.3 Two Basic Problems Related to Environment

- Problem of pollution.
- Problem of excessive exploitation of natural resources.

Pollution It refers to those activities of production and consumption which challenge purity of air and water and serenity of the environment.

Pollution unfolds itself in three ways:

- Air Pollution of air implies pollution of an essential elements of life.
- Water Pollution Water is an equally important element of life and its pollution is equally serious. Polluted water is the principal cause of diseases like diarrhoea and hepatitis.
- Noise Pollution Excessive noise causes irritation and unnecessarily fatigues the body and the mind.

17.4 Causes of Environmental Degradation

- Population explosion
- Widespread poverty
- Increasing urbanisation
- Increasing use of insecticides, pesticides and chemical fertilisers
- Rapid industrialisation
- Multiplicity of transport vehicles
- Disregard to the civic norms

17.5 Environmental Crisis

The environment is performing its functions without any interruption as long as the demand of these functions is within its carrying capacity. This means that if the rate of extraction of resources will be above the rate of their regeneration, the environment will fail to perform its functions.

Resources are becoming extinct and wastes are generated beyond the absorptive capacity of the environment. All this has led to the environmental crisis, it refers to ecological crisis that occurs when the environment of a species or a population changes and destabilises its survival.

17.5.1 Consequence of Environmental Crisis

The points given below describe the consequences of environmental crisis

- Development has polluted and dried up rivers and other aquifers, which was deteriorated the quality of water.
- Intensive and extensive excavation of both renewable and non-renewable resources has exhausted some of the vital resources, compelling to spend a huge amount of money on technology and research to explore new resources.

- Decline in air and water quality have resulted in increased number of respiratory and water borne diseases i.e., expenditure of health care is also rising according to a data 70% of water of . India is polluted which cannot be used for drinking purpose.

17.6 Global Environmental Issues

The environmental issues which affect the whole world are called global environmental issues such as global warming and ozone depletion. These issues also contribute to increased financial commitments for the government.

These issues are discussed below:

1. **Global Warming**

   The gradual increase in the average temperature of Earth's lower atmosphere is called global warming.

   Causes/Effects

   It occurs due to greenhouse gases (carbon dioxide, methane and other gases which have the capacity to absorb heat) through burning of fossil fuels (coal and petroleum) and deforestation (increases the carbon dioxide level in atmosphere). Much of the recent observed and projected global warming is human induced.

   The atmospheric concentrations of carbon dioxide and methane have increased by 31% and 149% respectively above pre-industrial level since 1750.

   Different effects of global warming are described below:
   - During the past century, the atmospheric temperature has risen by 1.10° F (0.60° C).
   - Melting of polar ice resulting in increase in sea level (during the past century, sea level has risen by several inches) and the risk of coastal flooding has increased.
   - Disruption of drinking water supplies dependent of snow melts.
   - Extinction of species.
   - More frequent tropical storms.
   - Increased incidence of tropical diseases.

   Action Taken

   A United Nations Conference on Climate Change, held in Tokyo, Japan, in 1997, resulted in an international agreement to fight global warming which called for reductions in emissions of greenhouse gases by industrialised nations.

2. **Ozone Depletion**

   It refers to the phenomenon of reductions in the amount of ozone layer in the stratosphere.

Causes/Effects

It is caused by high levels of chlorine and bromine compounds in the stratosphere. Origin of these compounds are Chlorofluorocarbons (CFCs), used as cooling substances in air conditioners and refrigerators or as aerosol propellants and bromoflurocarbons. (halons) used in fire extinguishers.

Different effects of ozone depletion are described below:

- More ultraviolet radiation comes to Earth causing damage to living organisms, skin cancer in humans, low production of phytoplankton affecting aquatic organisms.

- Influences the growth of terrestrial plants.

Action Taken

Between 1979 to 1990, a reduction of 5% in ozone layer was detected. Since ozone layer prevents most harmful ultraviolet radiation from passing through the Earth's atmosphere, so reduction in ozone layer generated worldwide concern, leading to adoption of the Montreal Protocol banning the use of Chlorofluorocarbon (CFC) compounds as well as other ozone depleting chemicals such as carbon tetrachloride, trichloroethane (also known as methyl chloroform) and bromine compounds known as halons.

17.7 State of India's Environment

India has rich quality of natural resources in plenty of amount.

It is clear from the following points:

- India has rich quality of soil, hundreds of rivers and tributaries, lush green forests, plenty of mineral deposits beneath the land surface, vast stretch of the Indian Ocean, ranges of mountains, etc.

- The black soil of the Deccan Plateau is particularly suitable for cultivation of cotton. It has led to concentration of textile industries in this region.

- The Indo Gangetic plains spread from Arabian Sea to the Bay of Bengal are one of the most-fertile, intensively cultivated and densely populated regions in the world.

- India's forests though unevenly distributed, provide green cover for majority of its population and natural cover for its wildlife.

- Large deposits of iron-ore, coal and natural gas are found in the country. India alone accounts for nearly 20% of the world's total iron-ore reserves.

- Bauxite, copper, chromate, diamonds, gold, lead, lignite, manganese, zinc, uranium, etc are also available in different parts of the country.

17.8 Threat to India's Environment

Threat to India's environment is poverty, pollution, rapidly growing industrial sector. Air pollution, water contamination, soil erosion, deforestation and wildlife extinction are some of the most pressing environmental concerns of India. The developmental activities in India have resulted in pressure on its finite natural resources, besides creating impacts on human health and well-being.

Out of them the priority issues are

- Land degradation and solid waste management

- Biodiversity loss

- Air pollution with special reference to vehicular pollution in urban cities

- Management of fresh water

Some of these issues are discussed below:

17.9 Land Degradation in India

Land in India suffers from varying degrees and types of degradation stemming mainly from unstable use and inappropriate management practices.

The factors responsible for land degradation in India are

- Loss of vegetation occurring due to deforestation.

- Unsustainable fuel wood and fodder extraction.

- Shifting cultivation.

- Reduction into forest lands.

- Forest fires and overgrazing.

- Non-adoption of adequate soil conservation measures.

- Improper crop rotation.

- Indiscriminate use of Agro chemicals such as fertilisers and pesticides.

- Improper planning and management of irrigation system.

- Extraction of ground water in excess of the regain capacity.

- Open access resource.

- Poverty of the agriculture-dependent people.

17.9.1 Biodiversity Loss

India is the owner of 2.5% of world's geographical area. India holds 17% of human and 20% of livestock population on its land. In order to hold livestock and human in country, country needs 0.47 hectare of land to meet the basic needs but it has only 0.08 hectare of land which causes felling of forests and soil erosion. 5.3 billion tonnes of soil is eroded every year. As a result, quantity of nutrients lost due to erosion each year ranges from 5.8 to 8.4 million tonnes.

17.9.2 Chipko Movement or Appiko Movement :

Chipko Movement aimed at protecting forests in the Himalayas. In Karnataka, a similar movement took a different name, 'Chpiko', which means to hug.

On 8th September 1983, when the felling of trees was started in Salkani forest in Sirsi district, 160 men, women and children hugged the trees and forced the woodcutters to leave. They kept vigil in the forest over the next six weeks. Only after the forest officials assured the volunteers of the trees will be cut scientifically and in accordance with the working plan of the district, did they leave the trees, When commercial felling by contractors damaged a large number of natural forests, the idea of hugging the trees gave the people hope and confidence that they can protect the forests. On that particular incident, with the felling discontinued, the people saved 12000 trees. Within months, this movement spread to many adjoining districts.

17.9.3 Air Pollution

In India, air pollution is widespread in urban areas where vehicles are the major contributors and in a few other areas which have a high concentration of industries and thermal power plants.

Pollution from vehicles and industries are the major sources of air pollution.

- Vehicle Pollution Vehicle emissions are of particular concern since these are ground level sources and thus, have the maximum impact on the general pollution. The number of vehicles has increased from 3 lakh in 1957 to 67 crores in 2003.

  In 2003, personal transport vehicles (two wheeled and cars only) contributed about 80% of the total number of registered vehicles thus, contributing significantly to air pollution load.

- Industrial Pollution India is one of the ten most industrialised nations of the world. This status has brought with it unwanted and unanticipated consequences like unplanned urbanisation, pollution and the risk of accidents.

  The CPCB (Central Pollution Control Board) has identified seventeen categories of industries (large and medium scale) as significantly polluting.

17.9.4 Factors Contributing to Deforestation

- Growing industrial demand for wood and other forest products.

- Growing demand for wood owing to explosive rise in population.

- River valley projects.

The economic development we have achieved so far is on the cost of environmental degradation. The era of globalisation promises higher economic growth, but on the same side it had adverse consequences that had impacted environment.

In order to understand the sustainable path of development, the significance and contribution of environment to economic development should be understood. With this in mind, we would be able to achieve sustainable development in India.

17.9.5 Management of Fresh Water

Water is an equally important element of life and its pollution is equally serious. Water becomes polluted when chemicals and other waste materials are dumped into it. Polluted water is the principal cause of diseases like diarrhoea and hepatitis. Thus, the management of fresh water is essential to sustain life.

17.10 How to Save Environment?

The various measures adopted by Ministry of Environment and the central and state pollution control boards may not yield reward unless, we make ourselves conscious.

Following are required measures which should be taken to save the environment:

- Social Awareness There should be awareness among the people regarding the threats of the increasing pollution and how can each of us contribute to the check this menace.

- Population Control Biggest issue which should be controlled is increasing population to protect the environment.

- Enforcement of Environment Conservation Act The Environment act was passed in year 1986. It was passed to check the detoriated quality of the environment.

- Afforestation Campaign Extensive afforestation campaign should be launched to protect environment.

- Water Management There should be means which can harvest the rainwater in order to use it in the areas where there is scarcity of water, so that clean drinking water can be provided to the rural people.

- Management of Solid Waste Management of solid waste is very essential. It should be treated chemically. Rural garbage should be converted into compost.

17.11 Pollution Control Boards

To address two major environmental concerns in India; water, air and land pollution, the government set up the Central Pollution Control Board (CPCB) in 1974. This was followed by states establishing their own state level boards to address all the environmental concerns.

Different functions of pollution control boards are

- To investigate, collect and disseminate information relating to water, air and land pollution.

- To lay down standards for sewage/trade effluent and emissions.

- To provide technical assistance to governments in promoting cleanliness of streams and wells by prevention, control and abatement of water pollution.

- To improve the quality of air and to prevent, control or abate air pollution in the country.

- To carry out and sponsor investigation and research relating to problems of water and air pollution and for their prevention, control and abatement.

- To organise mass awareness programme for pollution control.

- To prepare manual, codes and guidelines relating to treatment and disposal of sewage and trade effluents.

- To assess the air quality through regulation of industries.

- State boards through their district officials, periodically inspect every industry under their jurisdiction to assess the adequacy of treatment measures provided to treat the effluent and gaseous emissions.

- State pollution boards also provide background air quality data needed for industrial siting and town planning.

  In nutshell, it can be said that pollution control boards collect, collate and disseminate technical and statistical data relating to water pollution. They monitor the quality of water in 125 rivers (including the tributaries), wells, lakes, ponds, tanks, drains and canals.

17.12 Sustainable Development

It is that process of economic development which aims at raising the quality of life of both and future generation.

17.12.1 Features of Sustainable Development

- Sustained rise in real per capita income and economic welfare

- Rational use of natural resources

- No reduction in the ability of future generations to meet their own needs

- No increase in pollution

17.12.2 Strategies for Sustainable Development

1. Use of Non-conventional Sources of Energy India heavily depends on thermal and hydro power plants to meet its power needs. Both of these have adverse environmental impacts. Thermal power plants emit large quantities of carbon dioxide, which is a greenhouse gas. If it is not used properly, it may cause land and water pollution.

2. LPG, Gobar Gas in Rural Areas Rural households in India generally use wood, dung cake (upla) or other biomass as fuel. This practice has several adverse implications like deforestation, reduction in green cover and air pollution.

   To rectify the situation, subsidised LPG is being provided. Besides it, gobar gas plants are being encouraged through easy loans and subsidy. LPG is the clean fuel. It does not create any household pollution and also wastage is minimised. For gobar gas plants, cattle dung is fed in the plant to function which produces gas and slurry is used as organic soil fertiliser.

3. CNG in Urban Areas In Delhi, the use of Compressed Natural Gas (CNG) as fuel in public transport system has significantly lowered air pollution and the air has become cleaner in the last few years.

4. Wind Power In areas, where speed of wind is usually high, windmills can provide electricity without any adverse impact on the environment. The turbines moves with wind and electricity gets generated. Its initial cost' remain high but it can be recovered easily.

5. Solar Power Through Photovoltaic Cells In India, solar energy is used in different forms for agriculture products, daily use products and even to warm ourselves in winters. Through photovoltaic cells, solar energy can be converted into electricity. This technology is extremely useful for remote areas and for places where supply of power lines is either not possible or proves very costly. This technique is also totally free from pollution.

6. Bio Composting In order to increase production, we have started using chemical fertilisers which are adversely affecting the waterbodies, ground water system, etc. But again, farmers in large numbers have started using organic fertilisers for production.

   In some parts, cattle are maintained only because their waste production is very useful in form of fertiliser. Earthworm can convert organic matter into compost faster than the normal composting process.

7. Mini-Hydel Plants Mountainous regions have streams everywhere. Most of such streams are perennial. Mini-hydel plants use the energy of such streams to move small turbines which generate electricity. Such power plants are more or less environment friendly.

8. **Traditional Knowledge and Practices** Traditionally, Indian people have been close to their environment. If we look back at our agriculture system, healthcare system, housing, transport, etc we find that all practices have been environment friendly. But in recent years, we have been moving away from these practices. This has caused large scale damage to our environment.

   During older times, we used Ayurveda, Unani, Tibetan and Folk systems for the treatments but now we are ignoring the traditional system and we are moving towards the western system. Not only these products were environment friendly but they are free from side effects too.

9. **Biopest Control** With the advent of Green Revolution, the country entered into the use of chemical pesticides to produce more which laid the adverse impacts on soil, water bodies, milk, meat and fishes. To meet this challenge, better methods of pest control should be brought. One step is pesticides based on plants like neem. Even many animals also help in controlling pests like snakes, peacocks, etc.

17.12.3 A Way to Sustainable Development

According to Herman Dalay, a leading environmental economist, the main needs of sustainable development are

- Limiting the human population to a level within the carrying capacity of the environment.

- Technological progress should be input efficient and not input consuming.

- Renewable resources should be extracted on a sustainable basis, i.e., rate of extraction should not exceed rate of regeneration.

- For non-renewable resources, rate of depletion should not exceed the rate of creation of renewable substitutes.

- Inefficiencies arising from pollution should be corrected.

17.13 Conclusion

Economic development, which aimed at increasing the production of goods and services to meet the needs of a rising population, puts greater pressure on the environment. The world is faced with increased demand for environmental resources but their supply is limited due to overuse and misuse.

Sustainable development does not mean a cheque on the existing pace of economic growth. It only means a judicious or optimum utilisation of resources in a manner such that the pace of growth is sustained without challenging the ability of the future generations to grow and prosper.

Key Statements

Renewable resources are those which can be replenished and are not likely to be exhausted or depleted on use. Example: Wood, Aquatic animals.

Non-Renewable resources are those which are likely to be exhausted or depleted on use. the rate at which these resources re- emerge is far short of the rate at which these resources are being exploited for use. Example Fossil fuels

Global Warming : It refers to a gradual, but consistent increase in global temperature.

Ozone Depletion : This refers to reduction in Ozone (a protective layer) in the stratosphere. This occurs owing to the excessive presence of chlorine and bromine compounds, like chlorofluorocarbons (CFCs)(used as cooling substances in air conditioners and refrigerators in aerosol propellants) and Bromo fluorocarbons (halons) used in fire extinguishers. As Ozone depletes, there is greater ultraviolet radiation reaching the earth which is a danger to living organisms. In the recent past, nearly 5% depletion of Ozone layer has been recorded which is an issue of global concern. The Montreal protocol has banned the use of CFC compound as well as other chemical compounds which lead to the depletion of Ozone, such as carbon tetrachloride, try chloroethene (also known as methyl chloroform), and bromine compounds known as halons.

Environment: it is defined as all those conditions that their effects which influence human life. It includes biotic components, such as, plants and animals, and abiotic components such as water and air.

Carrying Capacity of Environment: It refers to the state of balance between the rate at which natural resources are exploited and the rate at which these resources are regenerated.

Absorptive Capacity of Environment: It refers to the ability off the environment to absorb wastes occurring due to the production and consumption activities in the economy.

Environmental Crisis: It occurs when carrying capacity of the environment is challenged or exceeded through excessive exploitation of natural resources or when generation of ways exceeds the absorptive capacity of environment.

Causes of Environmental Crisis:

i. Population Explosion

ii. Widespread poverty

iii. Increasing urbanisation

iv. Increasing use of insecticides, pesticides and chemical fertilisers

v. Rapid industrialization

vi. Multiplicity of transport vehicles

vii. Disregard to the civic norms

Principle Concerns of Environmental Degradation In India:

i. Degradation of land

ii. Air pollution

iii. Water pollution and management of freshwater

iv. Loss of biodiversity

v. Solid waste management

Sustainable Development: is the process of growth which fulfils the needs of present generation generation without challenging the ability of the future generations to fulfil their needs. Implying that the resources are not fully exploited, but rationally utilised.

Strategies for Sustainable Development:

i. Reliance on non- conventional sources of energy

ii. LPG, Gobar gas in rural areas

iii. CNG in urban areas

iv. Wind power

v. Solar power through photovoltaic cells

vi. Mini- hydel plants

vii. Traditional knowledge and practises

viii. Bio-composting

ix. Bio -pest control

Chipko Movement: A drive to prevent deforestation: In India, two community- driven movements have taken place with the aim to protect forests to avoid deforestation. These are: Chipko Movement in the Himalayas and Appiko Movement in Karnataka. The words, Chipko and Appiko mean 'hugging'.

Chipko Movement was launched in Uttarakhand in 1973, while the Appiko Movement was launched in Karnataka in 1983 and was inspired by the Chipko Movement.

Exercise

Frequently asked Questions (FAQ's)

1. How does expanding production activity lead to over use of resources?

2. What is the main difference between economic development and sustainable development?

   Sustainable development refers to increase in real per capita income, along with equitable distribution both for the present and future generations.

3. How is sustainable development different from non- sustainable development?

4. How does migration from rural to urban areas lead to environmental degradation?

5. HYV technology caused a revolutionary change in agriculture productivity. But, at the same time, it silently contributed to the degradation of soil, implying environmental degradation. What is this paradox?

Multiple Choice Questions (MCQ's)

1. Which of the following options is correct when we only accomplished two out of the three pillars of sustainable development?
   (a) Economic + environmental stainability = Viable
   (b) Social + environmental sustainability = bearable
   (c) Social + economic sustainability = equitable
   (d) All of the above

2. In which year did the word sustainable development come into existence?
   (a) 1992   (b) 1978
   (c) 1980   (d) 1987

3. In video was the United nations Commission on sustainable development csd started by the UN General Assembly?
   (a) 1995   (b) 1994
   (c) 1993   (d) 1992

4. after mining, the huge holes left behind are used for ____________.
   (a) Wastewater storage
   (b) Waste and water storage
   (c) Waste disposal
   (d) Waste storage

5. Mercury and Lead a toxic elements that cause:
   (a) Noise pollution
   (b) Air pollution
   (c) Water pollution
   (d) Land contamination

6. What is the other word for landscaping?
   (a) Reduction
   (b) Restoration
   (c) Removing topsoil
   (d) Restructure

7. which of the following option is not incorporated as sustainable development parameters?
   (a) Gender disparity and diversity
   (b) Inter and intra- generational equity
   (c) Carrying capacity
   (d) None of the above

8. What is sustainable development?
   (a) The development that meets the needs of the present without compromising the ability of future generations to meet their own needs
   (b) To conserve natural resources and to develop alternate sources of power while reducing pollution and harm to the environment
   (c) It is the practise of developing land and construction projects in a manner that reduces their impact on the environment by allowing them to create energy efficient models of self- sufficiency
   (d) All of the above

9. Which of the following is/are not an objective(s) all sustainable development?
   (a) Continue to implement the family planning programme
   (b) Maintain a dynamic balance of land (not less than 123 million hectares) and implement an agricultural development strategy
   (c) Maintain a dynamic balance of water resources by reducing water consumption for every unit of gross development product growth and agricultural value added
   (d) To bring about a gradual and sometime catastrophic transformation of environment

10. Social, economical and ecological equity is the necessary condition for achieving:
    (a) Social development
    (b) Economical development
    (c) Sustainable development
    (d) Ecological development

11. The maximum number of individuals that can be supported by a given environment is called:
    (a) Biotic potential
    (b) Carrying capacity
    (c) Environmental resistance
    (d) Population size

12. Meeting 'the needs of the present without compromising the ability of future generations to meet their own need' is given by:
    (a) Brundtland
    (b) Mahatma Gandhi
    (c) Maathai
    (d) Sunder Lal Bahugana

13. This is not the effect of transportation:
    (a) Air emission
    (b) Material consumption
    (c) Solid waste generation
    (d) Acid mine drainage

14. Underground an Open Cast is the methods of:
    (a) Agriculture   (b) Mining
    (c) Housing   (d) Transportation

15. Electronic waste is the adverse effect of:
    (a) Industry   (b) Agriculture
    (c) Housing   (d) Mining

16. Sustainable development will not aim at:
    (a) Social economic development which optimise the economic and social benefits available in the present, without spoiling the likely potential for similar benefits in the future
    (b) Reasonable and equitable distributed level of economic wellbeing that can be perpetuated continually
    (c) Development that meets the needs of the present without compromising the ability of the future generation to meet their own needs
    (d) Maximising the present day benefits through increased resource consumption

17. Which of the following statements in relation to sustainable development is not true:
    (a) Sustainable development is defined as the development that meets the needs of the present without compromising the ability of our future generations to meet their own needs
    (b) Sustainability has the main objective of purely focusing on the natural environment
    (c) Sustainable development of various countries and the entire world is the only solution left with mankind to survive for a longer period on Earth
    (d) Sustainable development not only considers the protection of the environment but also the maintenance of economic viability as well as the social and ethical considerations

18. Which of the following is a component of environment?
    (a) Living elements only
    (b) Known- living elements only
    (c) Both (a) and (b)
    (d) None of the above

19. Which of the following is not considered as an element of environment?
    (a) Air   (b) Electricity
    (c) Land   (d) Weather

20. The term used for the property of environment to absorb degradation is:
    (a) Carrying capacity
    (b) Absorptive capacity
    (c) Ability to assimilate waste
    (d) Both (a) and (b)

21. Which of the following is a cause of environmental crisis?
    (a) Population Explosion
    (b) Increasing urbanisation
    (c) Rapid industrialization
    (d) All of the above

22. Ujjwala Yojana Is focused on promoting use of:
    (a) LPG   (b) CNG
    (c) Gobar gas   (d) Solar power

23. Mini- hydel plants are good for environment because:
    (a) They generate electricity only for local areas
    (b) They do not change the land use pattern
    (c) They rely on the perennial streams
    (d) Both (b) and (c)

24. Which of the following factors contribute to air pollution?
    (a) smoke emitted by industries
    (b) Poisonous gases emitted in the process of chemical treatment of the materials
    (c) Emission of gases by motor vehicles
    (d) All of the above

25. Which of the following is the strategy for sustainable development?
    (a) CNG in urban areas
    (b) Reliance on non- conventional sources of energy
    (c) Output- efficient technology
    (d) Both (a) and (b)

🔑 Solutions

Frequently asked Questions (FAQ's)

1. While expanding production activity, natural resources are excessively exploited to achieve higher rate of growth. Example, excessive exploitation of fossil fuels to cope with the growing need of energy

2. Economic development refers to long- term increase in real per capita income, along with equitable distribution for the present generation.

   Sustainable development refers to increase in real per capita income, along with equitable distribution both for the present and future generations.

3. Non- sustainable development is that process of growth which focuses on the pace of growth without accounting for environmental degradation.

   Sustainable development is that process of growth which focuses on the pace of growth but always accounts for the environmental degradation.

4. Migration from rural to urban areas leads to a stress on civic amenities, housing in particular. Often forests a invaded for the construction of houses. It implies deforestation and deforestation implies environmental degradation.

5. HYV technology induces environmental pollution as it is based on the extensive application of chemical fertilisers my insecticides and pesticides will stop this technology is crop-friendly, but not soil- friendly. It erodes fertility of the soil and pollutes groundwater. Organic farming is recommended as an alternative which is soil- friendly. But this technology is not cropped- friendly. Crop productivity is significantly reduced when we shift from HYV-based conventional farming to organic farming. Accordingly, there is a need to strike a balance between the two technologies.

Multiple Choice Questions (MCQ's)

1. (d) All of the above
2. (c) 1980
3. (d) 1992
4. (c) Waste disposal
5. (d) Land contamination
6. (b) Restoration
7. (d) None of the above
8. (d) All of the above
9. (d) To bring about a gradual and sometimes catastrophic transformation of environment
10. (c) Sustainable development
11. (b) Carrying capacity
12. (b) Brundtland
13. (d) Acid mine drainage
14. (b) Mining
15. (a) Industry
16. (d) Maximising the present day benefits through increased resource consumption
17. (b) Sustainability has the main objective of purely focusing on the natural environment
18. (c) Both (a) and (b)
19. (b) Electricity
20. (b) Absorptive capacity
21. (d) All of the above
22. (a) LPG
23. (d) Both (b) and (c)
24. (d) All of the above
25. (d) Both (a) and (b)

CHAPTER 18

Development Experience Of India: A Comparison With Neighbours

Chief concepts of this chapter

A comparison with neighbours

- India and Pakistan
- India and China
- Issues: economic growth, population, sectoral development and other Human Development indicators

18.1 Comparative Development Experiences Of India And Its Neighbours Introduction

India, Pakistan and China have many similarities in their development strategies. Every country has been trying to adopt various means to strengthen their domestic economies.

- They are forming various regional and global economic groups such as the EU (European Union), SAARC (The South Asian Association for Regional Cooperation), ASEAN (Association of Southeast Asian Nations), BRICS(Brazil, Russia, India, China and South Africa), GR and G-20, etc.

- They are also trying to understand the development policies and strategies pursued by their neighbouring countries to realise/analyse des strengths and weakness because, in the process of globalisation, they are facing competition not only from developed countries but also from other developing countries.

18.1.1 Development Path of India, Pakistan and China.

(i) All the three countries started their development path at the same time. India and Pakistan got independence in 1947 and people's Republic of China was established in 1949.

(ii) All the three countries had started planning their development strategies in similar ways. India announced its First Five Year Plan in 1951, Pakistan announced in 1956 and China in 1953.

(iii) India and Pakistan adopted similar strategies, such as creating a large public sector and raising public expenditure on social development.

(iv) Both India and Pakistan had adopted 'mixed economy' model but China had adopted 'Command Economy' model of economic growth.

(v) Till 1980s, all the three countries had similar growth rates and per capita incomes.

(vi) Economic Reforms were implemented in China in 1978, in Pakistan in 1988 and in India in 1991.

18.1.2 Development Strategy:

A. China

(i) After the establishment of People's Republic of China under one party rule, all the critical sectors of the economy, enterprises and lands owned and operated by individuals, were brought under government control.

(ii) A Programme named 'The Great leap Forward (GLF) campaign was initiated in 1958, which aimed at industrialising the country on a massive scale. Under this programme, people were encouraged to set up industries in their backyards.

(iii) 1965, Mao Tse Tung introduced the 'Great Proletarian Cultural Revolution (1966-1976)', under which students and professionals were sent to work and learn from the countryside (rural areas).

(iv) In rural areas, commune system was started, under which people collectively cultivated lands.

(v) Reforms were introduced in China in phases.

(vi) In the initial phase, reforms were initiated in agriculture, foreign trade and investment sectors. In the later phase, reforms were initiated in the industrial sector.

(vii) The reforms process also involved dual pricing. This means fixing the prices in two ways; farmers and industrial units were required to buy and sell fixed quantities of raw materials and products on the basis of prices fixed by the government and rest were purchases and sold at market prices.

(viii) In order to attract foreign investors, special Economic Zones (SEZ) were set up. SEZ is a geographical region that has economic laws different from a country's typical economic laws. Usually, the goal is to increase foreign investment.

B. Pakistan

(i) Pakistan followed the mixed economy model with co-existence of public and private sectors.

(ii) Pakistan Introduced tariff protection for manufacturing of consumer goods, together with direct import controls on competing imports.

(iii) The introduction of Green Revolution and increase in public investment in infrastructure in select areas, led to a rise in the production of food grains.

(iv) In 1970s, Capital goods industries were nationalised.

(v) In 1988, structural reforms were implemented. Major thrust areas were denationalisation and encouragement to private sector.

(vi) Pakistan also received financial support from western nations and remittances from emigrants to the Middle countries. This helped the country in stimulating economic growth.

C. India

After Independence, India has adopted mixed economy as economic developmental strategy. Both public and private sector co-exist side by side. In order to achieve rapid economic growth, planned development economy was introduced.

18.1.3 Economic Development Strategy after Independence:

(i) Both public and private sectors were allotted to carry business activities. Public sector was allotted activities like coal, mining, steel, power, roads etc. Private sector was allotted to establish industries subject to control and regulations in the form of law.

(ii) Public sector was given major push by the Government. Maximum revenues in this sector was invested which increased from Rs. 81.1 crore in First Five-Year Plan (1951-56) to Rs 34,206 crores in Ninth Five-Year Plan (1992-97)

(iii) Public sector was given importance in order to eliminate poverty, unemployment etc.

(iv) Public sector contributed to the industrialisation of the economy. It also helped Indian economy to achieve a considerable degree of self-sufficiency.

18.2 Comparative Study – India, Pakistan and China:

A. Demographic Indicators

a. The population of Pakistan is very small and accounts for roughly about one-tenth of China and India.

b. Though China is the largest nation geographically among the three, its density is the lowest.

c. Population growth is highest in Pakistan followed by India and China. One child norm which was introduced in China in the late 1970s is the major reason for low population growth. But this measure led to a decline in the sex ratio, that is the proportion of females per 1000 males.

d. The sex ratio is low and biased against females in all the three countries. There is strong son-preference prevailing in all these countries.

e. The Fertility rate is low in China and very high in Pakistan.

f. Urbanisation is high in both China and Pakistan- with India having 28 percent of its people living in Urban areas.

B. Gross Domestic Product (GDP) and Sectors :

a. China has the second largest GDP (PPP) os 10.1 trillion (approx in 2013 whereas India's GDP (PPP) and Pakistan GDP (PPP) are 4.2 trillion (approx.) and $0.47 trillion (approx.) respectively.

b. On this path of Development China's average growth rate is about 9.5% while India's and Pakistan's average growth rate is about 5.8% and 4.1% respectively.

c. In China, in the year 2011. with 37 percent of its workforce engaged in agriculture, its contribution to GDP is 9 percent (approx.). While in India and Pakistan the contribution of agricultural sector in GDP is about 19% and 21% respectively. In India about 56% are engaged in agricultural sector, while in Pakistan this figure is about 45%.

d. In China, manufacturing contributes the highest to GDP at 47 percent whereas in India and Pakistan, it is the service sector which contributes the highest (more than 50 percent of GDP)

e. Though China has followed the classical development pattern of gradual shift from agriculture to manufacturing and then to services, India and Pakistan's shift has been directly from agriculture to service sector.

f. In the 1980s, India, China and Pakistan employed 17, 12 and 27 percent of its workforce in the service sector respectively. In 2011, It reached the level of 25, 33 and 35 percent respectively (approx.).

g. China's growth is mainly contributed by the manufacturing sector whereas in both India and Pakistan, the service sector is emerging as a major player of development.

D. Human Development Indicators:

The human development index is one of the most important indicators to study the human development of a country.

This index was introduced by the United Nations Development Programme (UNDP). The first Human development report was prepared under the guidance of Mehbub -ul-Haq and published in 1990. It is a Composite Index of such indicators as life expectancy, infant mortality rate, maternal mortality rate, per capita income (PPP), poverty, sanitation, drinking water, etc. which is used to measure the performance of a country in social and economic development.

a. In most areas of human development, China has performed better than India and Pakistan. This is true for many indicators-per Capita GDP or proportion of population below poverty line, health indicators such as mortality rates, access to sanitation, literacy, life expectancy or malnourishment etc.

b. Pakistan is ahead of India in reducing proportion of people below the poverty line and also its performance in transferring labour force from agricultural sector to industrial sector and access to water is better than India.

c. Contrary to it, India is ahead of Pakistan is education sector and providing health services.

d. India and Pakistan are ahead of China in providing improved water sources.

18.3 Conclusion

A. India-India performed moderately as is clear from

a. A majority of its people still depend on agriculture.

b. Infrastructure is lacking in many parts of the country.

c. It is yet to raise the level of living of more than 22% of its population that lives below the poverty line.

B. Pakistan-Pakistan has performed poorly. The reasons for the slowdown of growth and re-emergence of poverty in Pakistan's economy are:

(i) Political instability.

(ii) Volatile performance of agriculture sector.

(iii)Over dependence on remittances.

(iv)Growing dependence on foreign loans on the one hand and increasing difficulty in paying back the loans on the other.

C. China-China has performed comparatively the best as is clear from:

a. Success in raising the level of growth along with alleviation of poverty.

b. It used the market mechanism to create additional social and economic opportunities without political commitment.

c. By retaining collective ownership of land and allowing individuals to cultivate lands, China has ensured social security in rural areas.

d. Public intervention in providing social infrastructure has brought about positive results in human development indicators in China.

Key Statements

SAARC (The South Asian Association for Regional Cooperation): The South Asian Association for Regional Cooperation (SAARC) is the regional intergovernmental and geopolitical union of states in South Asia.

Its member states are Afghanistan, Bangladesh, Bhutan, India, Maldives, Nepal, Pakistan and Sri Lanka.SAARC was founded in Dhaka on 8 December 1985. Its secretariat is based in Kathmandu, Nepal. The organization promotes development of economic and Regional integration. It launched the South Asian Free Trade Area in 2006. SAARC maintains permanent diplomatic relations at the United Nations as an observer and has developed links with multilateral entities, including the European Union.

ASEAN (Association of Southeast Asian Nations): is a political and economic union of 10 member states in Southeast Asia, which promotes intergovernmental cooperation and facilitates economic, political, security, military, educational, and social cultural integration between its members and other countries in Asia. ASEAN›s primary objective was to accelerate economic growth and through that social progress and cultural development. A secondary objective was to promote regional peace and stability based on the rule of law and the principle of United Nations charter.

BRICS (Brazil, Russia, India, China and South Africa): The BRICS members are known for their significant influence on regional affairs. Since 2009, the governments of the BRICS states have met annually at formal summits. India hosted the most recent 13th BRICKS summit on 9 September 2021 virtually. The BRICS Forum, an independent international organization encouraging commercial, political, and cultural cooperation among the BRICS nations, was formed in 2011.

Commune System: people collectively cultivated lands. In 1958, there were 26,000 communes covering almost all the farm population.

Great Proletarian Cultural Revolution: (1966- 76) under which students and professionals were sent to work and learn from the countryside.

Nationalization: is the process of taking privately-controlled companies, industries, or assets and putting them under the control of the government.

Urbanisation: is the development of cities and the concentration of populations away from rural lifestyles.

Economic Reforms: what introduced in 1978 in China, in 1988 in Pakistan and in 1991 in India.

Exercise

Frequently asked Questions (FAQ's)

1. Explain the Great Leap Forward campaign of China as initiated in 1958.

2. What is the important implication of 'one child norm' in China?

3. Give reasons for the slow growth and re-emergence of poverty in Pakistan.

4. Why are developing countries keen to understand the developmental processes pursued by their neighbours?

5. How has China managed to have an edge over India with their reforms ?

Multiple Choice Questions (MCQ's)

1. In terms of the sectoral contribution to GDP, the economy of China is relying more on:
   (a) Primary sector
   (b) Secondary sector
   (c) Tertiary sector
   (d) None of the above

2. Under _______________, people collectively cultivated lands. (Fill In the blank with correct alternative)
   (a) GLF
   (b) Five year plan
   (c) Commune system
   (d) None of the above

3. The five year plan in Pakistan is now known as ____________.
   (a) Planning development
   (b) People's plan
   (c) Medium term development plan
   (d) None of the above

4. _____ Started their development programme at the same time. (Fill In the blank with correct alternative)
   (a) China and Pakistan
   (b) Pakistan, China and India
   (c) India and Pakistan
   (d) China and India

5. The understanding of the economy of neighbouring country is essential because __________. (Fill in the blank with correct alternative)
   (a) it allows countries to better comprehend their own strengths and weaknesses
   (b) It helps countries to identify their competitors
   (c) For overall human development
   (d) All of the above

6. The Great Leap Forward (GLF) campaign in China focused on:
   (a) Widespread industrialization
   (b) New agricultural strategy
   (c) Privatisation
   (d) Economic reforms

7. In terms of the sectoral contribution to GDP, economies of India and Pakistan are now relying more on:
   (*a*) Primary sector (*b*) Secondary sector
   (*c*) Tertiary sector (*d*) None of the above

8. Which of the following countries resorted to one child policy?
   (*a*) India (*b*) China
   (*c*) Pakistan (*d*) None of the above

9. Growth rate of population is highest in which of the following countries?
   (*a*) India (*b*) China
   (*c*) Pakistan (*d*) None of the above

10. In the initial phase of reforms in China, reforms were introduced under ________. (Fill in the blank with correct alternative)
    (*a*) Agriculture (*b*) Foreign trade
    (*c*) investment sector (*d*) All of the above

11. In the later phase of reforms in China, reforms were introduced under:
    (*a*) Private sector firms
    (*b*) Trade policy
    (*c*) Investment sector
    (*d*) Banking sector

12. The introduction of __________ in Pakistan led to a rise in the production of food grains. (Fill In the blank with correct alternative)
    (*a*) Five year plan (*b*) Green revolution
    (*c*) Mixed economy (*d*) Communes

13. ________ is the largest nation and occupies the largest area among India, Pakistan and China. (Fill In the blank with correct alternative)
    (*a*) China (*b*) India
    (*c*) Pakistan (*d*) None of the above

14. The fertility rate is very low in ________ and very high in ________. (Fill in the blanks with correct alternative)
    (*a*) India, China (*b*) China, Pakistan
    (*c*) Pakistan, China (*d*) India, Pakistan

15. Read the following statement given below and choose the correct alternative:
    Statement 1: Urbanisation is very high in China
    Statement 2: China has the second largest GDP in the world
    (*a*) Both are correct
    (*b*) Both are incorrect
    (*c*) Statement one is correct and statement too is incorrect
    (*d*) Statement one is incorrect and statement two is correct

16. Reforms were introduced in China, because:
    (*a*) The new leadership wasn't happy with the slow pace of growth and lack of modernisation.
    (*b*) Maoist vision had failed
    (*c*) Both (*a*) and (*b*)
    (*d*) None of the above

17. "The poverty re-emerged in Pakistan" what are the possible reasons for this ?
    (*a*) Agricultural growth was not based on institutionalised process of technical change
    (*b*) Foreign exchange requirements of Pakistan
    (*c*) Non- developmental activities
    (*d*) All of the above

18. Which of the following countries are not able to save women from maternal mortality?
    (*a*) India (*b*) Pakistan
    (*c*) Both (*a*) and (*b*) (*d*) China

19. Under which of the following indicators, China is moving ahead of India and Pakistan ? (Choose the correct alternative)
    (*a*) GDP indicator
    (*b*) Health indicators
    (*c*) Poverty indicator
    (*d*) All of the above

20. Which of the following countries has the lowest density of population ?
    (*a*) India (*b*) China
    (*c*) Pakistan (*d*) None of the above

21. After independence, both India and Pakistan relied upon:
    (*a*) 'Mixed economy' as the strategy of growth
    (*b*) 'Capitalism' as the strategy of growth
    (*c*) 'Socialism' as a strategy of growth
    (*d*) 'Free economy' as a strategy of growth

22. HDI has limited usefulness because:
    (*a*) It gives more emphasis on literacy as compared to other indicators
    (*b*) It does not include sufficient indicators for health
    (*c*) it does not account for liberty indicators
    (*d*) it accounts for human rights

23. Liberty indicator relates to:
    (*a*) Political freedom
    (*b*) Freedom to gain education
    (*c*) Freedom to access health services
    (*d*) Both (*a*) and (*c*)

24. To analyse a comparative performance of the economies of India, China and Pakistan, which of the following is the correct ?
    (a) China achieved a breakthrough in GDP growth in early 1980s
    (b) With new economic policy NEP in place, India experienced a rebound in its GDP growth
    (c) Economic reforms in Pakistan were almost similar to that in India
    (d) All of the above

25. Which economy worsened after the introduction of economic reforms ?
    (a) India
    (b) Pakistan
    (c) China
    (d) Both (a) and (b)

 ## Solutions

Frequently asked Questions (FAQ's)

1. Communist China or the People's Republic of China, as it is formally known, came into being in 1949. There is only one party, i.e., the Communist Party of China that holds the power there. All the sectors of economy including various enterprises and all land owned by individuals was brought under governmental control. A programme called 'The Great Leap Forward' was launched in 1958. Its aim was to industrialise the country on a large scale and in as short a time as possible. For this, people were encouraged to set up industries in their backyards. In villages, village Communes or cooperatives were set up. Communes means collective cultivation of land. Around 26000 communes covered almost all the farm population in 1958.

   The Great Leap Forward programme faced many problems. These were:

   1. In the earlier phase, a severe drought occurred in China and it killed some 3 crore people.

   2. Soviet Russia was a comrade to communist China, but they had border dispute. As a result, Russia withdrew its professionals who had been helping China in its industrialisation bid.

2. One-child norm introduced in China in the late 1970s is the major reason for low population growth. It is stated that this measure led to a decline in the sex ratio, that is, the proportion of females per 1000 males.

3. Reforms were initiated in Pakistan in 1988.

   1. Pre-Reform Period : Failure
      (a) The proportion of poor in 1960s was more than 40 per cent.
      (b) The economy started to stagnate, suffering from the drop in remittances from the Middle East.
      (c) A growth rate of over 5% in the 1980s could not be sustained and the budget deficit increased steadily.
      (d) At times foreign exchange reserves were as low as 2 weeks of imports.

   2. Post-Reform Period (after 1988): Failure

   The reform process led to worsening of all the economic indicators.
      (a) The growth rate of GDP and its sectoral constituents have fallen in the 1990s.
      (b) The proportion of poor declined to 25 per cent in 1980s and started rising again in 1990s. The reasons for the slow-down of growth and re-emergence of poverty in Pakistan's economy are:
         (i) Agricultural growth and food supply situation were based not on an institutionalised process of technical change but on good harvest. When there was a

good harvest, the economy was in a good condition; when it was not, the economic indicators showed stagnation or negative trends.

(ii) Fall in foreign exchange earnings coming from remittances from Pakistani workers in the Middle East and the exports of highly volatile agricultural products.

(iii) There was also growing dependence on foreign loans on the one hand and increasing difficulty in paying back the loans on the other.

4. With the unfolding of the globalisation process, developing countries are keen to understand the developmental processes pursued by their neighbours as they face competition from developed nations as also amongst themselves.

5. The Chinese reform process began more comprehensively during the 80s, when India was in the mid-stream of slow growth process.

Rural poverty in China declined by 85% during the period 1978 to 1989. In India, it declined only by 50% during this period, Global exposure of the economy has been far more wider in China than in India. China's export-driven manufacturing has recorded on exponential growth, while India continues to be only a marginal player in the international markets.

Multiple Choice Questions (MCQ's)

1. (b) Secondary sector
2. (c) Commune system
3. (c) Medium term development plan
4. (b) Pakistan, China and India
5. (d) All of the above
6. (a) Widespread industrialization
7. (c) Tertiary sector
8. (b) China
9. (c) Pakistan
9. (d) All of the above
11. (a) Private sector firms
12. (b) Green revolution
13. (a) China
14. (b) China, Pakistan
15. (a) Both are correct
16. (c) Both (a) and (b)
17. (d) All of the above
18. (c) Both (a) and (b)
19. (d) All of the above
20. (b) China
21. (a) 'Mixed economy' as the strategy of growth
22. (c) it does not account for liberty indicators
23. (a) Political freedom
24. (d) All of the above
25. (b) Pakistan